BETWEEN OUR WORLDS:

THE LODESTONE BRIDGE

Extraterrestrial Cultural Exchanges

Francesca Thoman

Library of Congress Cataloguing-in-Publication data:
Thoman, Francesca

Between Our Worlds: The Lodestone Bridge, Extraterrestrial Cultural Exchanges

ISBN: 9798218391430 (Paperback)
ISBN: 9798218391447 (eBook)

1. OCC025000 Body/Mind/Spirit UFOs and
   Extraterrestrials
2. PSY035000 Hypnotism
3. BIO000000 General Biography

Empowered Whole Being Press
www.EmpoweredWholeBeingPress.com

TABLE OF CONTENTS

PREFACE

I wrote this book to tell the story of my several experiences with extraterrestrial beings, and to present a meaningful opportunity for people to engage with other beings from our galaxy through The Lodestone Bridge. Originally, what began as a search into my mind and memories on a winter day late in 1988 became an astonishing discovery of memories I hardly imagined I possessed. This led to my traveling along unexpected paths, including discovering an ability to work as a channel, which has led to wondrous and meaningful interactions with the extraterrestrial members and representatives from our galaxy.

My desire to understand myself led me on through images of darkness and light, into astonishment and wonder, and finally into an unexpected joy: the rediscovery of a life-long friendship. This revealed another mystery: the search for the nature of some of the beings that appear responsible for the UFO phenomenon.

I will not say the answers I present here are the only answers, but I know that any experiences as rich as these can best be approached with an open mind. I believe that my UFO experiences provide a point of view that is not based on fear. Several accounts published have described the fear and the horror of the abduction experience, the fear of the unknown, and the horror of the strange, although this has been changing.

For me, there was little fear of the beings in these experiences, or horror at what they were. I felt a little anxious or nervous about them or was startled by their strange, almost miraculous technology from time to time. But I did not fear them. I believe that is because I believe I have known them my entire life.

Fear of the unknown may be appropriate. But to me, as perhaps to others, the "space people" are a challenge, but they are not wholly the unknown.

Introduction

This book began as a search that became an inquiry into the nature of my perceptions and the nature of reality. The material in the first five chapters was gathered through hypnosis with the assistance of Dr. Stephen Field, then a practicing psychologist in Menlo Park, California. I had worked with him doing past-life regression ten years previously, with positive results.

In the hypnosis sessions, these memories revealed themselves easily. But all of them challenged my conceptions of reality. I wasn't prepared for the utter disregard some of these experiences seemed to have for my "common sense" concepts of time, matter, mind, and the limits of the human conceptions of self.

As I developed spiritually and with other skills such as reading the Akashic Records and channeling, I became more and more aware of the ET members of The Lodestone Bridge and was able to work with a representative of the Galactic Federation and the Galactic Center Council towards creating the Citizen Ambassadors.

I feel that these experiences are "real," but I cannot wholly prove that they are "factual." This concerns me, because much of the present scientific paradigm says, in part, that only "factual" things are "really real." It demands that I have the burden of proof.

But any proof will be impossible to present if my experiences are dismissed as hallucinations, inventions, or deceptions because and only because of their nature. To assume they are hallucinations beforehand is not scientific inquiry, but scientific dogmatism.

This kind of dogmatic attitude colors our perception of reality, remaining invisible to us. Believers in the benign nature of the UFO experience could find confirmation for their own experiences in these accounts; other readers will easily assume there are deeper, hidden meanings contained in these memories since they are only images from my "subconscious" or, worse yet, emplaced into my mind by those extraterrestrial beings.

Some may expect to find intentional fraud here, where none exists, simply because "there must be a logical, rational, reasonable explanation" even if this means making wild assumptions about the intentions, honesty, integrity, or sanity of the one telling the story whose parameters fall outside the debunkers' expectations. But I feel that these attitudes are limited points of view and that the phenomenon of "UFO abductions" demands that we break these limits of perceptual expectations to understand it.

These phenomena offer us an opportunity to grow and expand mentally, emotionally, psychically, and spiritually. We have a chance to increase who and what we are through positive engagements.

In sharing these stories, I have done my best to be honest. The emotional effect of re-living and releasing my earlier memories was profound, and the positive effect of the work with the beings in The Lodestone Bridge is dear and precious to me. But I cannot expect you to do more than weigh what I present here against your own experiences and better judgment, accepting or rejecting them as best fits your worldview.

MY JOURNEY BEGINS:

Preparing for ET Communication

CHAPTER ONE

Introducing The Hypnotic Regressions

The first part of this material was recorded during the spring, summer, and early fall of 1989, through several hypnosis sessions with psychologist Dr. Stephen Field, Ed.D. Dr. Field had much experience discovering buried traumas by examining the primary causes of painful, lingering emotions.

Encouraging me through the use of verbal imagery into the relaxed yet extremely alert state of mind known as the hypnotic trance, Dr. Field would instruct me to "go where I need to go" to release the source of my distress. I would remain conscious, yet detached, my mind temporarily disengaged from the usual concepts of time or the usual limits of recollection.

I'd done some work with the doctor with past-life memories that had been affecting my life in the present. Once relived and released, these memories of being attacked and harmed no longer caused me trouble: they had slipped back into the past. When I became aware of something else in my life I couldn't puzzle out on my own I asked for his help again.

I need to mention something important before I share these UFO experiences. For much of my life, I could not see well without my glasses. Because I was born two months early and put in an incubator with too much oxygen, I had 20/1000 uncorrected vision. (I could barely make out the large "E" on the standard eye chart.) I wore "coke bottle" glasses to correct this when my poor vision was discovered when I was 3 ½.

I couldn't see anything more than about five or six inches from my nose clearly and could be confident of seeing things for only about two feet further. I mention this here because, when I recalled the UFO experiences, I was often frustrated at not being able to see. It is not proof of their validity, but it is suggestive. My eyes have now been corrected by cataract surgery to 20/30, so I can read books without glasses.

For several years, my two brothers, my sister, and I lived in Flint, Michigan. Both my parents worked when I was growing up, even back then in the 50s. My father, a Unitarian minister, was at the church most of the time. My mother took care of us as best she could; our father met us for lunch and later for dinner, which she cooked.

The neighborhood was not a friendly one, particularly to a family of foreigners: my father was born in Holland and my mother was raised in Argentina, though her family was an American mixture of Scottish and French. This was also during the time of the big "Red Scare" of the middle 50s when anyone might be labeled a Communist, and so considered dangerous.

We were not communists, but our differences brought out fear and hostility and made us very unpopular. Many times I got attacked and pummeled by the other children when I was walking home from school. Though some of this seemed unavoidable, rather than let myself be beaten and reviled more than I had to be, I stayed to myself as much as I could manage.

Despite this, my clearest childhood memories were mostly happy ones, if a little solitary. I remember numerous small beauties of flowers and trees in the summer and fall, the smell of burning maple leaves; icicles, frost patterns on the windows, and hand-made "vanilla snow" under the brilliant skies of winter. I remember how frozen buds looked in the spring; I remember the thunder, and rain, and the way a perfect blueberry tasted, sun-warmed and plucked for free from a bush on the edge of a neighbor's yard.

I remember walking to the nearby park, coming in through the cathedral entrance of flaming maples in the fall, and watching the way ants moved on the bark of the tree branches I sat on, or listening to the sounds of barking dogs and the wind in the trees. I remember the way my mother's sweet peas smelled, warmed into glory on the gray flank of our house.

For many years I remembered very little else of my life before age five when I went to kindergarten. I had always thought this lapse of memory was due to my late start resulting from my poor eyesight. Getting glasses at three and a half was like starting practically from scratch. I had to fundamentally re-learn my whole world, and make sense of it in a way I had never been able to before. So it always seemed logical to me that these earlier years remained a blur and a blank, until, supposedly, my mind caught up with me.

When I saw the memories as they were revealed with the "light-trance" methods Dr. Field used of my experiences with extraterrestrials that occurred when I was 6, 7, and 8, it was like opening a hidden door. I did not lose conscious awareness in the trance, but I perceived these beings clearly in the hypnotic state: they were familiar. I did not recognize them at first, but they said they'd been with me at my birth.

I called these other beings the "space people." Following our wonder and curiosity, Dr, Field and I pursued the remembered moments of light and friendship that my experiences with these beings soon became, taping each session as we worked.

CHAPTER TWO

First Physical Experience:
Lake Michigan, July {1959}

Every summer from the time I was six until I was eight and the family moved to CA, we and others from my father's Unitarian Church in Flint, MI, spent two weeks in a group camp called Lake Geneva on the Wisconsin side of Lake Michigan.

For me, that place was a heaven made of trees and the sounds of birds everywhere; the wonderful lake and the sounds of water, and little pamphlets with drawings of tree leaves so we could identify them. I learned to swim one year and how to dive the next. I still remember the smell of the kerosene lamps and the peace of the night with the summer rain.

Our parents were there at the camp to work and teach. The four kids were mostly left alone, though there were numerous classes, kid-centered activities, a lovely craft center, a movie house, and storytelling arranged for our amusement. We could even have whatever we wanted for breakfast: scrambled eggs, hot oatmeal, or even sausages!

This was an incredible luxury for a child who had to get off to school by herself in the mornings. At home, my mother was already at work teaching by the time we woke up, and my father slept very poorly because of a meningitis infection that had damaged his hypothalamus and made his legs jerk him awake in second-stage sleep. So he was still in bed in the mornings, and essentially unavailable. A home, the best we had was some kind of sugar cereal and cold milk we kids threw together somehow for ourselves.

So these visits to the camp by the lake were such a treat! And it was there, at the Summer Camp when I was six, that I had my first physical contact with UFOs and the beings on them. (Note:

The material in these accounts has been presented from the recorded sessions, edited as little as possible to help in the presentation.)

One night I was asleep in the little tent/cabin we'd been assigned: a wooden platform with a canvas tent framed over it, fully enclosed. My sister and two brothers, my Mom and my Dad were all asleep, lying on cots with blankets on them.

Someone woke me up, calling my name.

I didn't feel afraid. It was almost like I was dreaming, but I knew I wasn't: I felt the night air, felt my breathing. There was a light, coming in from the back of the tent, a light like moonlight. I didn't know whether the moon was up or not: it had been raining earlier, intermittently through the night. I could still smell the kerosene from the lamps, and the air was warm.

I heard the wind rustle the trees outside and saw a white light through a flap in the back of the tent. It seemed as though the light was trying to get into the tent! Except that I also knew there were people there, too: little people, trying to get inside. People I knew.

It was very strange, but I felt quite relaxed. I was wearing my pajamas, and my sister was next to me, asleep. Someone called my name again, and said, "It's time to come out now." So, I went. I got off the cot; somehow I knew it was all right. I didn't even put on my glasses, because I was so much not afraid.

It wasn't as though something was controlling me, exactly, but I wanted to go to where the voice was. And there were these strange people outside, waiting for me. It was so peculiar: somehow, they took me out through the back of the tent! The front of the tent faced an asphalt path, common with all the other tents, with stairs from each tent platform leading down to the path. But these strange people took me out through the back of the tent. We just went right through it!

I was startled by this, but they told me, "Don't worry, it's all right, we don't mean to hurt you."

I wasn't sure what was going to happen. But I stopped being anxious: it was all right to go with them. I asked them, "What about my parents and my family?"

They replied, "Don't worry: we're not taking them this time."

Dr. Field asked me what made it all right for me to go with them. In the trance, I replied that I'd known them before I was born. It seemed strange to my six-year-old self to remember something from before my birth, but I realized that they had somehow been in the back of my mind a lot as I was growing up. Dr. Field asked whether or not this was the first time I'd experienced them in this lifetime. I said it wasn't, though this was the first time they'd brought my body along with them, too.

I described them to Dr. Field: to my child-self, their heads were shaped like balloons, being round on top and coming down to a point for the chin, and they were white, as far as I could tell in the dark. They had large dark eyes and wore dark gray clothes. As I came out to look at them, I felt them reassure me again that everything was all right.

They didn't look frightening: in fact, they looked almost friendly. They were strange, though, with their whitish skin, smooth like clay, without any hair on it. They had small mouths and not much of a nose. They must have been close enough for me to see them fairly well with my poor vision, even in the strange lights and shadows behind the tent. Their fingers were very long, and they were a little taller than I was, about three feet four inches.

One of them got in front of me, and one behind, and I just went with them. We went about twenty feet from the tent, I guess; this was a little difficult because of the slope and the trees behind the tent. They didn't touch me. But as I went with them, I wondered about my family and felt suddenly unhappy to go away. They were taking me away from my family!

They said, "It's all right, don't worry, it'll be fine, we won't take you away for long."

Okay, I thought, I don't know what this is all about. I didn't know what else to do, so I kept going with them.

And then all of a sudden I was floating up into the air! They weren't with me: I was by myself, but I was up in the air! I could see the lake, and was surprised: the lake looked almost bright in the starlight. The trees were all black shapes, but I was surprised at being able to see the lake. [The Summer Camp, though isolated enough, was not the only place where people were living: we could see the houses and other boat docks when we went swimming.]

As I looked, I also saw a building with a rounded top back from the lake edge that looked like an observatory, which was part of the Summer Camp's grounds. My mother had told me about it once when she had rowed us out into the lake for a bit, because her father had been an astronomer, and she used the round-topped building to explain what an astronomical observatory looked like. The lake was beautiful in the starlight. I couldn't see whether or not the moon was up or covered with clouds, because I saw the clouds, but everything else was dark around me, though the sky did have stars.

And I was being pulled, as though on a string! It was like getting vacuumed, a feeling of being sucked upwards. I was standing straight up, so I wasn't worried about falling, exactly, but I was getting pulled up, faster than an elevator, though it was different from an elevator because an elevator pushes you upwards: this pulled.

I didn't think to look up at what was pulling me until the last moment. When I did look up, I saw something as dark as a cloud above me, though there seemed to be some lights on it. It was very big. I was anxious that I would hit it, but I didn't: instead, it was like flipping around, somehow, turning inside out in a strange way, like going through an impossible twist and then in through a strange door. There was a moment of nothing and then I was suddenly standing in a strange place, so bright it seemed made out of light itself.

The walls around me were white, but their brightness was not glaring. I was holding a railing that was about chest high. The top edge of the railing was smooth, about as wide as my hand was long, with rounded edges, apparently made out of metal. The place around me was very large. I felt disoriented, though not afraid because everything was so bright here. But I hung onto the railing for a moment, feeling how cool and smooth it was.

I suddenly knew that I was inside a ship of some kind, a starship. Outside the summer night had been rather warm, but it felt quite cool and pleasant here.

In the area beyond the platform that the railing edged, there seemed to be various shapes, hanging in the white air. I guessed they were other ships: the shapes were very large. Some were round [i.e., saucer-shaped], some triangular, but they all seemed to be hanging by themselves in the air beyond the railing. I truly wished I had brought my glasses. I had to stare into the light in front of me, trying to figure out what it was.

After a moment I felt someone come up next to me, from behind me on my left, another of those people who'd been down there at the tent with me.

Figure 1

She was smiling. I didn't think to be afraid: somehow, she seemed so kind! Up close like this in the light, she looked unusual, but not too strange. She was wearing a dull silvery uniform that reflected the light a bit, but I hardly noticed. I was looking at her large, deer-like eyes and her smile, a very soft, little smile. Her mouth didn't look strange on her. It would have, on a human person. But she was put together correctly for herself, and did not look "alien" or "wrong," only unusual and interesting.

I asked, "What about my family?"

She replied, "Don't worry, they'll be all right, they're still asleep."

"Why am I here?"

"Well, we have something to show you; we need to do something."

It was very strange: she didn't move her mouth when she spoke. It was just like I knew what she was saying, without her saying anything aloud. To my six-year-old mind, this seemed a neat invention, to have one's thoughts understood directly!

I was a little anxious about the situation, not knowing where I was going or what was going to happen. But I could hardly be afraid of her. Since she was only as big as I was, she certainly didn't look as though she could hurt anyone.

As I came closer to her I could see the color of her skin. It was white, not stark white, but very much a "natural" color, like white clay, or a shell, with subtle touches of other colors in it. It was living skin, not a mask, or some kind of paint. She didn't seem to have any ears. Her hands and head were bare, but her uniform covered the rest, up to her remarkably thin neck.

She didn't seem to have any elbows. It wasn't as though she was made out of rubber, but I couldn't quite make out how she bent her arms: I don't remember her arms having an elbow point at all. Her fingers were very long. She never seemed to blink her large eyes, which I found fascinating. But she kept looking at me out of those huge eyes and telling me not to be afraid.

[Even though I know I am describing the kind of being many people have seen, I am including these details because they recount my fresh impressions as a child from the memories we pulled into my consciousness through the hypnotic trance process.]

It wasn't hard for me to relax; she was smiling and seemed very nice. And so when she began to lead me I followed her on, though I felt pretty ridiculous, trailing after this being in this strange white place, dressed in my pajamas!

There was a kind of ambient hum in the air. I guessed that it was from the ship. Strangely, the hum seemed familiar. The ceiling above the corridor seemed relatively high, though it was hard for me to tell. The light was a fascinating brilliance that didn't seem to come from any one place but shone throughout the air with a kind of pervasive clarity. I could see no dark corners, nothing dark at all… until she brought me to a doorway.

There was no door in it, but the area beyond the rectangular frame was completely black! It looked like a night sky without any stars: a room without walls or floor or any edges at all. I stopped, disconcerted, and saw her standing at the edge of the blackness. Beyond her some distance away was another white rectangle, another doorway, maybe. But I could see absolutely nothing of the "room" in between!

She stood on the threshold of the one door, and then she was suddenly standing where the other light was, at the other doorway! She just went blip! Straight across, and suddenly she was there on the other side!

Figure 2

She turned around to face me, and said encouragingly, "Come on, it's safe, you can try it."

But I stood there for a little while, and asked dubiously, "But what is this?"

"Don't worry about it," she replied. "Just go. Just follow me." So I stepped into the darkness…

And found I was not afraid of it at all. Because being in the dark felt like being wrapped up in a warm blanket; the dark felt soft and safe. It felt like being hugged by my mother. And I sensed someone, or something, there in the darkness, or maybe it was just the comfort of the darkness itself. I felt supported and happy: the darkness felt rich and full, like velvet and music. But I could see nothing at all, neither stars, nor walls, nor floor, just the warm, soft dark.

[Many years later, when I was in grammar school, my class went on a field trip to the San Francisco Exploratorium to see a new exhibit, the Tactile Dome. Inside the Dome was a maze, kept dark. Many different surfaces were used inside the dome, to give your hands many different tactile experiences. I found it interesting until I found a small, rounded space that had been lined with sheepskins.

[When I found that little cubby hole I thought to myself, "That's my place," and immediately curled myself up in it. Because we were allowed to go in and out three times I missed a whole go-round through the dome... but I didn't want to be anywhere else. It felt familiar, so very safe and familiar.]

And then I was suddenly at the other door. "That felt good!" I exclaimed. "That was fun!"

The small white being next to me replied, "Yes, I had hoped you would enjoy it. Please, follow me, there's something we have to do."

We went next through a corridor, the pale walls interrupted now and then with tall, narrow boxes that seemed made out of glass. I supposed at the time that one could fit a person into them, but I saw no one else in the boxes or around us. As far as I could tell, the glass shone and glinted colors like soap bubbles. I was getting frustrated at not having my glasses, and not being able to see. I wanted to look at these boxes, and hung back a bit, trying to puzzle them out. But the friendly being hurried me along, pulling me with her urgency.

We had not gone far along the corridor when she took me into another room. Inside there was stuff hanging on the walls that looked like white jackets on clothes hooks. She turned to me and said, "I'm afraid this is something we have to do, it's time to do this. So, please, take off your clothes. There's this garment here for you to wear. It will be all right: we won't hurt you."

Then she left. I had no idea what else to do, so I took off my pajamas and put on the jacket-like thing with the short sleeves that she had shown me. I couldn't guess what it was made out of: it crackled, but it was also soft. I didn't think it was paper, but it was lightweight. It was something like the paper gowns I'd gotten in the hospital when I was five because of an ear infection. This garment was short, only coming down as far as my knees and elbows, but it opened in the front instead of the back. It was not uncomfortable.

For a moment I just stood there, wondering what to do. Then all of a sudden I saw her at the door again. Man, the doors in this place were the strangest things! They appeared suddenly from the wall itself: there was no such thing as the opening or closing of any kind of mechanism. Doors were simply available, whenever someone seemed to need them.

"Well," she said, "I hope you won't be afraid, now, because this is very important."

"What's going to happen?" I asked.

She did not answer directly, merely saying, "Just come with me."

So I followed her back into the corridor.

Waiting in the corridor were two of the strangest little men I'd ever seen: they were shorter than she was, and their faces were black, absolutely charcoal black! They wore gray and white uniforms, with lots of pockets in them. The white trim on the pockets picked up subtle aspects of colors of the light, so they looked like mother-of-pearl.

But their faces were so odd! They had huge mouths, rather like frogs' mouths, except that they had black teeth, set against the dark skin of their mouths, which I could see when they smiled. Their teeth were shaped almost exactly like the erasers one finds on new pencils and staggered in their flat jaws. They had wide, flat noses, very much like a human nose; their heads were flat on top, too. Their eyes were also black, though they were shiny, and reflected the light. Their eyes were six-sided, and they seemed to have lumps in them! The visible structure of the eye was not smooth at all.

Figure 3

I giggled when I saw them: they seemed so funny! I felt that they were pleased that I wasn't afraid of them. They even seemed happy to see me! They were people: I could tell they were people. But I kept laughing because they looked so wonderfully strange with their lumpy eyes and lumpy teeth. I'd never seen anything so humorous and I laughed again.

One of them got on one side of me, and the other on the other side, encouraging me enthusiastically, "Let's go!"

"Um," I said, still cautious, and not intending to be ironic, "as long as it's going to be okay!"

"Don't worry, don't worry, it'll be okay," the one on the right replied, still seeming cheerful because of my laughter. The one on my right seemed friendlier; the one on the left acted as though he was in a hurry. I went on with them, but because I was so fascinated with them and with the taller, pale being that was still walking in front of us, I didn't notice much of the surrounding corridor, until we arrived at another room.

This room seemed a little darker inside than the rest. There were lights on the walls, rectangular banks or bars of lights with rounded corners, and other lights that were too small for me to see well. In front of us was a tall, narrow table, and I became a little frightened, seeing it, because it looked so much like an examination table.

Beyond the table was another, even darker place than the area right around us: an L-shaped room, it seemed, that was directly opposite the door we'd come in; the ceiling was lower there than

17

in the other rooms I'd seen. There were other people there. Some of them were tall, and looked human; others were short, but they all were very intent, each of them working on something.

This appeared to be in a control room of some kind, where they could work with computer-like consoles. [I didn't know what a computer was, then, in 1959; computers that small didn't come to public notice until about the middle 70s. But my visual memory of the consoles they were working on looked much like computers do now.] There were panels of light in this room, shaped like opaque windows, and colored "moldings" mid-way up the walls next to me.

Even as I examined the room, I could hear them talking, or thinking, quietly to each other, and I heard one of them say, "We'll see what we can do." They were talking about a great many other things I couldn't understand, about "time/space vectors," or other things I couldn't grasp.

The two little black beings helped me up on the table, somehow, even though it was almost as tall as they were, and I complained nervously, "What's going to happen, what's going to happen? I'm scared, I can't see!"

But the little guys reassured me: "It will be all right, it will be all right." I almost wanted to cry, lying there, although I didn't: instead, I tried to see what was going on.

Perhaps perceiving my attention or my worry, one of the other beings, the pale ones, came up to me as I lay on the table, and said firmly, "Don't worry, it'll be all right, we don't want to hurt you. But we want to try and do this and see if it works." So I waited, bewildered.

As my eyes adjusted to the dimmer light in the L-shaped room that was over on my right, I could see a very tall being there, taller than my father (who was 5'8"), dressed in white, standing with others who looked similar to the ones with the large eyes. The very tall being had come in through a door at the bottom of the L-shaped room when my attention was elsewhere. I suddenly thought of the two little black beings, and looked for them: they were at my shoulders, one on each side of the table.

I was a little unsure of the tall being: he was so tall and so thin, and he wore a helmet, so I couldn't see his head or face. The front of the helmet was large and pale gold, shaped like a large, open eye, a circle pinched at opposite sides. It reflected the lights in the room around us like a mirror. The being was dressed in white, and I could see where the cuffs of his sleeves were. His hands were white, too, and each hand had only three long, rounded fingers, and a thumb. It seemed as though he was wearing gloves, but he was too far away for me to tell.

Figure 4

I knew that he was someone important: he was wearing a square jewel, the only color he had on, a bright golden yellow, almost the color of citrine. It was centered in the middle of his narrow chest and seemed very large. I saw how the others in the L-shaped room were careful of how they moved around him, as though giving him some kind of special respect.

[When I was thirteen and went shopping for clothes at a rummage sale with my mother (a necessity for a minister's family!), I once discovered a piece of costume jewelry, a large, clunky bracelet with a square, golden "jewel" centered in it. I grabbed it with great delight and bought it, half-jokingly calling it my "Inter-communicatory Whatsit," insisting that I could use it somehow to "talk with the space people." My mention of the "space people" had been completely spontaneous. I do not ever remember my parents mentioning them to me, or even the idea of life on the other worlds.]

I was sure this being could see through his visor, even though it seemed that he couldn't have opened it. After my initial shock, he seemed very gentle. He felt gentle, somehow.

But I was not in a very forgiving mood. "I can't see you!" I complained again. "I can't see you: I can't see what's going on. I'm getting scared! I don't know what you're going to do to me. You haven't told me what you're going to do to me!"

The tall being turned to look at me, the shiny gold of the visor still showing nothing of his face. I kept on complaining. "I can't see, I can't see! I wish I had my glasses. I have bad eyes, I can't see! I don't have my glasses!"

As though he did not want to frighten me, the tall being moved towards me very slowly with great care, coming up beside me at my head, on my right. [I do not remember specifically, but the little black beings must have moved away.] The top of the table came up to about the middle of his body. I ceased complaining, and he reached out with his long, long fingers.

I was startled, and almost closed my eyes, but I watched his hand as he brought it to touch me. There were no nails on the fingers, nor any hair, just the white hands, white fingers. He put his hand up to my face, putting two fingers on my forehead, gently, so very gently, and the other on my right eyelid.

I flinched, but he moved quietly and soothingly, touching me so very softly that I could not be afraid. With exquisite care he used the one finger to barely lift the eyelid, bending his shiny, visored head down to look at me more closely.

His fingers felt like the softest leather, smooth and delicate and warm. I think I will always remember how that hand felt, touching my face. It made me feel better, to feel the warmth of his hands, because then I knew for sure he was a real person and wasn't a ghost. He wasn't cold or weird, or even very frightening then, because his hands were so soft, and he moved so gently. I don't remember any smell.

"Don't worry," he told me calmly, his inaudible, mental voice seeming a little stern, "you can see what you need to see."

And then he turned away, and I began blinking and crying suddenly, though I didn't know why. But my eyes were watering, and I could feel the tears running down into my ears. Blinking again, I looked down towards my feet and saw the tall being standing in the smaller, darker room with the others.

The tall being stood there looking at me, and somehow I knew that he and the others were talking about me, even though I could not figure out what they were saying, as their mental talk didn't include me directly. But they seemed sad, and I became anxious: why would they be sad? What was going to happen, what were they going to do?

The tall being turned away from me for a moment, and then when he turned back, his hands were surrounded by a close nimbus of brilliant, pure red light! I became quite anxious at the sight of it, so upset that I nearly broke free of the hypnotic trance in the session. Dr. Field had to speak to me quite sharply to have me remember what happened next.

I remembered the tall being coming close to me again, at my feet. He pulled at the little garment I was wearing… and then reached inside my body with his red and glowing hands! I could not see what he was doing, because he had folded the paper-like garment up and out of his way. The white garment hid what his hands were doing. I felt no pain, but I was sure he was reaching right inside my body. I could feel his hands, brushing against my skin.

I'd been trying not to fight him because I had felt he was very gentle, but I was very worried at what he was doing, and I couldn't move, I just couldn't move. Something had paralyzed me. I was breathing hard and fast and felt very tense. I felt the other minds around me, too, but they weren't afraid: they only seemed to be sad as they watched him work, touching deep inside of me; they were disappointed because of something that couldn't be.

I suddenly understood that this had something to do with my having a baby, and I was confused: I was too young to have a baby, what did they mean? I felt anxious: there must be something wrong with me! They were certainly trying very hard to do something, but they couldn't, and it made them very sad.

They said something like: "Well, we were afraid this might happen. The physical is not what we'd hoped. And we won't… there won't be a child, she won't have a child."

When the tall being dressed in white withdrew his hands from my body, they were still glowing with that strange nimbus of clear light, only now the light was green. As he turned away, I felt everyone's disappointment, and I asked the little black being on my right, "What happened? Did I do something wrong?"

The other reassured me. "No, you didn't do anything wrong, don't worry."

As he "spoke" with me I noticed a difference in the quality of his telepathic communication compared to the telepathy of that of the others, the pale beings with the large eyes. All of these smaller beings seemed to communicate clearly. But the short black being's thoughts were more conversational. It was as though he was simply talking to me.

The others, including the tall being, communicated well enough but it always seemed as though they were preoccupied with something else when they spoke with me. And yet, when they did speak, I never felt as though they were not paying attention to me, or to whomever they were communicating.

The tall being dressed in white seemed to have a very refined telepathy, restrained and reserved yet very clear. His thoughts in particular seemed to come from inside of me, somehow: he did not seem to have as distinct a mental "voice" in my head as the others did. But the little black guys seemed to give me their whole minds: when they talked with me, they truly talked with me, and it made their thoughts seem unusually perceptible.

The black being on my right said, "I know, they're very sad for you because we all took a gamble, and it didn't work out as well as we'd hoped."

Responding to questions from Dr. Field, I made the situation clear: apparently, I was an experiment. They had been trying to wrap the mind of one of their kind, the mind of a "space person" around my mind before I was born. This other mind would remain with me while I was growing up so that it could share in my experiences.

As I spoke in the trance I received an image of an egg, a human zygote I supposed, wrapped in golden light; the baby (I!) was to grow from that egg.

I do want to make it clear that my parents' bodies were the source of the zygote, not these other beings. However, even as a child, I had an instinctual notion that we are not our bodies. It seemed as though I'd always felt that my mind had created my body, and not the other way around. So the notion of another mind mingling with mine before I was even born seemed unusual, but hardly impossible.

In the trance, knew I'd arranged things with them so that this experiment with them could be attempted. I'd had other lives where I knew them, and that I would work with them in future lives as well. Altogether, this particular lifetime of mine just seemed a propitious time to try to work out a deeper connection, experimenting with this unique conjunction of minds.

I felt a great liking and warmth for them as I spoke to Dr. Field. I explained that our previous experiences together in my other lives had been positive and beneficial ones. I had the impression that any child I might have could be a good liaison for them, as I was, so there are at least a few others on this planet right now that are experiencing this kind of link.

But as I was talking with the little black person at my head to my right, the tall one dressed in white had gone. Standing at my feet where he had been was another of the pale beings, dressed in light blue. She seemed more aloof than any of the others. It seemed that some of them didn't talk very much. Or perhaps she saw no need to talk with me since I was already talking with the black one.

This second being was holding something in her hand, an instrument that looked something like a bent crochet hook, thicker at the base, then flattening out and narrowing to a point, a small, spiky thing hung on the instrument's point that was about the size of a small green pea.

Figure 5

Seeing this, I became a little worried. But she did not give me any chance to object (not that I was sure I could resist: the table seemed to keep me immobile). With a quick movement that I couldn't catch somehow, the being dressed in blue put the instrument up one of my nostrils and left the tiny spiked globe up high in my nose!

There was no pain, though I was startled: it had felt very strange. I could hear quite clearly a most peculiar crunching sound when she put the little thing in my head, a gritty sound like nothing I'd ever heard before.

When Dr. Field asked me what the spiky thing was, I replied that the black being described it as a tracer or a "tagline." Its purpose was apparently to keep me connected to them in some way. This way they would not have to "rummage high and low" looking for me, and they could find me when they needed me.

I asked the black alien, "Will it be okay?"

"It's okay, it's okay," he replied. "I'm sorry that you feel frightened."

"Well, I'm not sure if I was frightened, but it wasn't very comfortable!"

He laughed. "Well, sometimes we have to do things that aren't very comfortable."

Then all at once, everything changed: I began to hear a humming sound. The black being on my right said something that meant both, "Well, we'll have to go now," and "You'll have to go now." Somehow, I was down from the table, even though no one touched me. I don't know whether or not the table had moved, but suddenly I was down, standing on the floor again. The humming sound sounded as though it came from the air itself! A distinctive, pervasive sound, yet I wasn't sure that the sound was audible.

Everything in front of me had changed. Where the dark, L-shaped "control area" had been before, there was nothing but pale blue light. Even though I remembered the room as it had been, now there was nothing but blue light. The table I'd been lying on was the same, and the wall that had been on my right was the same, but the other little room had disappeared, and it seemed that everyone who'd been there before was gone, too.

I had the feeling that there were still others here, though, even though I didn't see anyone. I looked around and saw no one. Except for this incredible blue light in front of me it seemed as though everyone had just left for a minute. I looked down at the floor; it looked gray and soft.

"What's happening?" I called into the silence, disconcerted. "What… is there anybody going to come to get me? I've got to go back to my family! I'm scared! I gotta go back down to the Camp: you've got to let me go!"

The humming stopped abruptly, and I felt as though I was floating, sitting down, in a comfortable reclining position in the air. I was suddenly not afraid at all. I saw nothing but the pale blue light, getting steadily paler and whiter.

Moving forward, I hardly knew whether I was walking or not. Then the humming sound returned, slowly, and the light paled until it was completely white. Hardly aware of my body except to know that I felt very comfortable, I felt a deep, sure sense that everything was all right, that all was well. It was like the experience I'd had when I'd gone through the "black corridor," only many times deeper and stronger: all was well.

This white brilliance all around me didn't hurt my eyes. I felt held up, too, as though supported by some invisible, and completely trustworthy, force or beings. I was also distinctly aware of the point directly between my eyebrows, where the "tracer" had been placed. There was no pain.

Out of my calm certainty, I suddenly heard the words, "It's all right, and everything will be all right." It meant that nothing would harm me, not only then, but during my whole life. I knew then that, whatever happened, I would be protected. I still saw no one, but I had the impression that there were many around me, many minds: many voices in one voice.

He or she or they said, "Whatever happens in your life, you need never be afraid, because we take nothing without giving." The voice added humorously, "What we have given you is our constant protection. What you have given us is your constant attention." This meant that they could monitor me all the time, whenever they needed or wanted to.

In other words, because I had let myself get connected with them, through the tracer and the intermingling of minds with the other beings, they were returning my favor by making certain I would be all right, that I would never really be hurt, or at least not badly. I did not escape my childhood devoid of cuts and bruises, or my later life emotionally unscathed. But they meant that, despite outward appearances, the core of me, of my deep sense of being, would never be in real danger. I could count on this.

This profound feeling was strangely "matter of fact:" It simply was, existing with the same utter completeness as the sky, or a flower, or a bird. It just *was*. And I knew that what the voice said was true. And yet, "truth" was not part of it because it could not be untrue. It was like asking how true the sky was! It was not a question of "True," or "Not true:" what they told me was just what was: there was no doubt, no question.

The voice in the light was not loud. It made no thunderous sounds like an apotheosis of trumpets: it simply said, "It will all be all right."

I replied, "Good."

I understood things differently, too: because of the "tracer," because of the work I'd done with them here, everything made sense now. Nothing was strange, and I saw nothing to be frightened of anymore. Because now I knew, with a kind of certainty I could never explain, that they were not here to hurt anybody, but they were here to help people.

This help would be like healing, but healing done in the background of our world. It would be as though they were working behind the scenes in a play. If those unseen people didn't do what they needed to do, then the play could not continue. These beings were working with light, making small, hidden changes that would accumulate and accelerate into large effects, like tapping on a specific rock which would eventually bring the whole mountainside down.

I also knew that they were protecting the other human beings who were working with them. They had come here to Earth because of the light, that same strong, supportive light that I had felt: it had asked them to come. The light knew that they could help, so it asked them to do what they could.

After these long moments of knowing, I felt sleepy, and I wanted to go back. My return seemed odd: on the way into the ship, various beings were all around me, especially the pale ones with the big heads. But this time, it seemed that I was being moved along simply by the light. I had the impression of people next to me, but I did not see anyone.

However that was, I was taken back to the ship's "airlock," back to the way I'd come in. I must have exchanged my clothes, at some point: I certainly did not return wearing the gray jacket the first being had told me to put on. I looked around, trying to say goodbye to the "space people." I saw the one who was there when I'd first come in, the one who led me through the dark corridor.

I asked her for her name, but I could not pronounce it; the closest I could come was "Mohas," (accented on the second syllable, with a long "o" and the "a" as in "father), but that was only a fragment of it. But Mohas said, "Goodbye, we'll see you again. Thank you for helping."

"Will my family be all right?" I asked.

"Well…" She paused, seeming a little sad. "We'll have to tell you about that later, but right now everything's all right." And I believed her: I had no doubt.

I was still so moved and swept up into my experience with the light that I wanted my family to have it, too: I wanted them to be protected and safe, too.

And this time, I looked up as I left the ship and "fell" back to the ground, and saw the ship clearly, hanging in the night sky above me. It was very large, and black, except for the little square of light that I had been pulled in and out from. Gentle golden light streamed straight down out of this "airlock," shining perfectly straight down, not diverging at all, and I was floating down back to the ground in it.

I don't remember much after touching the ground again. It seemed that I lost consciousness for a moment, but I returned to our tent somehow and got into bed as usual. And I remembered nothing of the experience, not even dreams.

CHAPTER THREE

Thoyantir, My Main Et Contact

Dr. Field and I did not receive the following material in temporal sequence as it is arranged in this book, and we examined the first "abduction" experience at least once before thinking to take it down on tape for later reference in the middle of April 1989.

In this first experience, describing that another mind was "intertwined" with mine was not frightening: indeed, I was fascinated with the idea. This being, whose mind was linked with mine, is named "Thoyantir." In his language, the name translates roughly as, "Artful [or graceful], go lightly." The name is accented on the third syllable, "Tho-yan-TIR," with each syllable distinct.

This notion of being "melded" with a "space person" felt right. It was the most personally satisfying explanation for the fact that, in every hypnotic session dealing with the space people, I had a strong sensation of being "at home" with them, of feeling at peace. Could this be because I was experiencing Thoyantir's memories to some degree, and so felt his mind calming mine?

I rarely experienced that kind of welcoming peace when I was growing up, except when I was alone, or when my mother had some extra time with me; the other members of my family were difficult for me. It wasn't as though I had no happy times with my family. But I'd always felt slightly askew, and often they considered me very odd in my views and expectations.

The experiences uncovered in the hypnotic sessions explained many of my reactions and some of my dreams. I'd had dreams of space beings, especially in my adolescence: dreams of helping them, somehow, and half-conscious memories of strange faces at the window.

But by the time I was fourteen, I had the clear and complete conviction that the "space people" existed and that they had a kind of "mental access" to me. I must profoundly stress here that this "access" was never an invasive, coercive, or controlling influence. Rather, it was a sense of their presence, as though they were only in the next room, or on the other end of a phone.

Sometimes I got such a distinct sense of the presence of another being that it was almost like seeing someone, though I never saw any of them in my normal consciousness. They were present, though, and these beings always felt benign. There was no sense of threat or fear: there was no intention of harm. It was as though he or she or they were simply watching, seeing through my eyes, gentle and calm. They never meant to interfere and never tried to hurt me.

My experience of welcoming them, of not fearing them, appears to be rare. So many other physical contactees have told of the terror and horror that they have felt during their experiences and after. But that was not my experience. How could I fear what I already knew, especially when they treated me better than my species had, sometimes?

My next "abduction" experience was when I was seven, again at the Summer Camp. It seemed a likely enough place, for it was remote enough in the summer of 1960. But though this next experience was even stranger than the first, it was also quite beautiful.

CHAPTER FOUR

Second Physical Experience:
Late June /Early July (1960)

When we began the hypnotic session that examined the "abduction" incident that occurred when I was seven, I started describing the memory from the middle:

There was a "space person" next to me, on my left, and I knew there were others behind me. We were in some kind of room or corridor. The being next to me was crouching down on the floor, gesturing to something in front of me, encouraging me to look at a little, narrow doorway, with golden light coming through it. The light was so bright and strong that it seemed nearly solid. But I somehow knew I could go through the light and the door. The beings around me were smiling and seemed very, very happy.

These beings seemed to be of an entirely different race than any of the others I'd seen before. They did look something like the people with the "balloon heads," but they were taller and more slender, and their eyes were very different. The head shape was similar, but their skins were not white at all. They had instead more the mottled silver-green-brown of the mineral mica, a kind of muted shining.

[I believe it was in this year that I conceived an inexplicable liking for the mineral. My older brother was a rock hound, so I knew what mica was. I remember liking mica, especially the flat, layered kind used for heat-resistant windows.]

I didn't touch any of them, so I did not know whether or not their skins had a texture like mica, but it looked almost as though their skins would feel like a turtle's shell, or something made of horn, though their arms moved easily enough. Although there were several there, the one who stood near me was paying particular attention to me. I couldn't tell if it was a "he" or a "she." I guessed it was male. As I made this decision, I got the mental impression that he told me that "it didn't matter" whether "he" was male or female.

Wanting to study his face, I looked at this one closely. He seemed to have more jaw than the previous, pale beings I'd seen before; his jaw was more human in shape, coming more to a square than a point. But his eyes were very strange indeed! They were very large, blue and white at the same time: the blue and white were mingled somehow: looking at his eyes from some directions than from others I could see the blue more than white. It was like mother-of-pearl, but the eyes did not reflect light as much as the shell would

Figure 6

The being near me was smiling very broadly, showing his "teeth." They were not discrete, separate teeth like our own, seeming more like a solid curve of bone or tooth-like material. And his smile was much broader than a human being's, bigger than any other smile I'd seen, except for the little black beings' frog-like grins. (Seeing this one's smile made me think of the black ones, but I didn't see any of them this time.)

As I described this "space person" in trance, I realized that I'd gotten to this place with him earlier, because I had been woken up by thunder. I liked thunder, now that I was older, though I had been frightened of it the year before. But this night, it had been thundering and raining, then it had cleared, but there was mist in the air. I thought there was a moon, maybe a half-moon; there was wind in the trees.

I must have been half-asleep when they took me out, though I thought it was peculiar that, rather than going out of the back of the tent as I had the time before, I decided, why not go out the front? So out I went, dressed only in my pajamas. I felt very sleepy, so sleepy that although I knew I was walking, and I felt the ground, it seemed as though everything was muffled and cottony. I don't remember feeling the dampness from the rain.

[It is this, plus a few other impressions, which make me wonder if this was a physical experience. It seems that there are fewer of those than are generally supposed, with most abductions being accomplished in an altered state of consciousness of one kind or another, in what is sometimes called an etheric state.]

And then suddenly I was somewhere else, not at all sure how I arrived, except that there were three people near me now, the strange people with skins like mica. Their arms were very thin and long, and their fingers also, and they all seemed to be smiling. I was not afraid of them; in fact, I liked looking at them because they seemed so interesting.

I asked, "Where are the other guys?"

One of them replied, "Well, they told us to take you this time because we had something special to show you."

"Well, okay," I returned, "but what about the other guys? Are they okay?"

"Oh, yeah, but they're somewhere else on the planet right now, and we wanted to show you this. We're not… we won't be here for very long, but they said that you'd be a good subject." In other words, someone who would let herself be studied agreeably.

They took me down to the dock on the lake, though I did not remember very clearly how. Out in the water was a little craft, an underwater thing that immediately brought to my mind the Walt Disney movie version made in 1954 of Jules Vern's novel, "20,000 Leagues Under the Sea," which I had seen recently. It was a little ship that glowed with areas or windows of light, just like the shining "eyes" of Captain Nemo's underwater monster submarine.

I suddenly became a little unsure, because I thought of Nemo's submarine, and I wasn't at all happy about going down under the lake! I worried, "Are you guys going to take me under the water?"

They replied, "No, don't worry, it's all right. You don't have to go on the ship if you don't want to. We can do this another way, but we'd like you to see it. If you like, the ship will stand on the water, and you don't have to go under the water."

I replied fervently, "That's good because I don't know how to swim too well yet!" I swam well enough to play near the shore, but I didn't want to get trapped under the lake.

They reassured me again, insisting, "It's all right."

I did not remember exactly how they got me inside the ship; I thought that they suddenly covered my eyes somehow, or perhaps they simply told me to close them, but I suddenly realized I was inside the "submarine."

It was a rather small ship: where I was standing I had to crouch down a bit and felt cramped. As I got my bearings, one of them said, "Well, we're going now, down to the bottom of the lake."

This annoyed me, and I objected, "But you said the ship was going to stay above the water!"

They seemed slightly perplexed for some reason, and replied, "Well, the ship is going to stay but we'll take you down there; it's perfectly safe." [This is another factor that makes me believe this was an out-of-body experience, however physical some of the details seemed.]

I grumbled, "I don't know if I like this, you know. Are you guys lying to me?"

"Well, we didn't want to frighten you."

I grumbled even louder, "Well, if you lie to me you'll frighten me!"

"Okay," they answered, "we understand. We won't lie to you. We didn't mean to hurt you."

Content enough with their apology, I felt suddenly sleepy again and I sat down on the floor. They didn't seem to have any chairs: they simply stood a lot. Their legs were pretty short for their body length and they had large feet. But as with so many of the aliens I encountered, their shapes seemed right for them, and I was not afraid.

I fell asleep. When I woke up, one of them was quite close to me, looking at me very intently. Startled, I flinched back, and he said, "I didn't mean to startle you." It seemed that he'd been concerned for me.

"Well," I said, "what do you want me to do?

"Well, come on, I wanted to show you this."

He seemed to preface nearly every statement with the word, "Well," as though to make sure I was paying attention and would accept his thoughts because he, like all the rest, appeared to be telepathic. The quality of his mental touch seemed hesitant at times, having neither the robust liveliness of the black beings nor the peculiarly distant, loving quality that colored the thoughts of the paler beings' minds.

My permission granted, he showed me an elevator-like thing, a "box" in the ship, which moved. This took us to another door that opened up onto a large area, not part of the submarine at all. I went out of this second door and saw that the new place in front of me had lots of light, with very tall ceilings: a wide, open corridor.

One of the mica-skinned beings was telling me that, as far as I could understand with my seven-year-old mind we were now in the future! The place we had come to would be under the lake in the future, but it wasn't under the lake "now", in 1960, so if anyone searched for it, they wouldn't be able to find it. But, by going to this place in the lake now, we could get there in the future.

I got confused. But I didn't care about his explanation one way or the other: this place seemed too pleasant to worry about details. Plants were growing there, and I heard lots and lots of sounds of water: it seemed these beings liked plants and waterfalls and light. The air here was rather high in humidity. Not hot and muggy, nor even foggy: one could feel the cool water in the air, like a heavy mist, but the air was transparent. I could see things well enough, though I wasn't wearing my glasses.

We walked further; on the walls were very tall rectangles, almost like windows, which provided the light. I couldn't see anything at all beyond the openings. But the light was very odd. When you turn on a lamp, you can see where the light comes from: the source appears brighter than the area it illuminates. But these "lights" seemed to light everything as evenly as sunlight would, although they didn't look particularly bright at all! It was as though these peculiar rectangles made the air itself bright, somehow: the light was a clear blue-white.

I followed the "mica-skinned" being down the corridor, still feeling sleepy. I suddenly became alert when I saw a tall being almost behind us, moving down another part of the corridor. I couldn't quite make his shape out and craned my neck to look. He was very large, and dressed all in white; he seemed quite preoccupied. He looked a bit like a bear; he had large, bulky arms, short legs, and a long tail. It looked like a dinosaur's tail! His hands were big, like a monkey's hands but unexpectedly large for the size of his body.

I only caught a glimpse as I tried to look behind myself while I was following the first beings. Whatever this larger being was, it seemed in a hurry and was going away from us into another area. Curious, I asked the one I was following, "Who was that?" But no one answered me, so I asked again.

One of them replied in my mind, "Don't worry, he's just visiting!"

I thought at the time that this answer didn't help, but shrugged it off: there wasn't much that made sense here. So we went on. From the tall corridor with the windows we entered a tube and I saw the lake water, all around the tube! It must have been daytime, "here," in the future, because I could see the water, and there were fish!

"This is strange!" I exclaimed.

The beings leading me answered, "Well, where we are it isn't night."

I started feeling frustrated and a little angry: all these strange changes, and peculiar things going on! So I complained, "How can it be daytime here when it's night?!"

They replied, "Don't worry about it."

I was getting heartily sick and tired of being told, "Don't worry about it," especially when I was trying to find out something! But this absurd situation seemed to be what was going on, so I decided I might as well keep on following them. Why not?

The tube we'd gone through was pretty short because the next thing I remember was standing in an area with very high ceilings. I thought it was funny, to have ceilings that high. But they took me to a room, or, rather, took me by it, a large, tall room. Somehow the wall between us in the corridor and the tall-ceilinged room we saw next to us was made out of crystal, or something. Although I knew there was a wall, I could see through it.

I felt confused and didn't quite know how that worked out. I knew that even though I could see into the room I knew we couldn't go into it. But there didn't seem to be any glass or any other kind of solid barrier. It was most perplexing! It was strange at the time: why would you have a wall that you couldn't go in if you could see through it into the room?

They led me on, off to the left side, and said, "Here, will you put this on?"

They gave me a gray thing to wear that I took some time to puzzle out; it seemed to be a bit like a jacket, but it had peculiar parts or pieces added to it somehow. When I put it on, I found it fit rather like a poncho. It stuck out from my shoulders a bit. It felt a lot like plastic, but it squished, as though it was made of two layers of plastic with water in between them. "What's this for?" I demanded.

They replied, "Well, um, don't worry about it!"

While recounting this in the hypnotic session, I laughed aloud: yet another "Don't worry about it!" At that point, I decided that what I was experiencing had to be some silly kind of dream, because every time I asked them about anything, they kept saying the same thing.

I certainly thought it was awfully silly. I put the gray jacket-like thing on and found it had a hood. One of them reached up and pulled the hood over my head, and said, "Well, we want you to go in through that door."

I practically snorted my indignation: really, this was too much! "Well, how come?" I demanded testily.

They seemed puzzled. They replied, "Well, we need to go in through the door."

I stubbornly refused. "Well, you've got to tell me why."

"Well, ah…" They seemed very confused indeed! "You've got to."

"That's no reason!"

Trying again, one asked, "Well, um, could you go through the door?"

They seemed impervious! "Well, if all you're going to do is stand here and not tell me anything, then all right, I guess I'll do it, but I think it's kind of strange."

The entry in question was a round door; one of them opened it somehow, though I didn't know how. I went in and found myself in a gray place. One of them told me to shut my eyes, but not before I was able to see the gray inside.

Then, with my eyes closed, I could hear something humming. It seemed just like a cat's purr. It wasn't a nasty hum or an angry hum: it was just kind of a vibration. I didn't know how to describe it. I keep thinking, "This has got to be the strangest dream I've ever had."

And then, in this gray place with my eyes shut, it started to "rain." I felt the water falling on me even though I was wearing the jacket. I started laughing at this, and it seemed that the more I laughed, the more I laughed, until I suddenly stopped because I didn't think that you could laugh in a dream for too long without waking yourself up.

The gray place finished sprinkling, and all of a sudden I was in a different place again. It felt huge, here. I felt that there was a ceiling, but it was so very high, and the walls were so far back and away, that the place was just immense.

One of the beings that had been leading me came up to me; he seemed to be the one who had been talking to me the most. I asked him what his name was, and he said it was something like "Agantha," but I wasn't sure I understood him well enough.

I looked around in this huge area, and asked him, "What is this place?"

"Well, it's part of what we wanted to show you, but first you've got to go through here."

"I'm tired of being told to do this and do that and you not telling me why!"

"Well, you'll just have to wait."

By now, I was getting angry and annoyed: they were ordering me around so much here! But I went with him. He led me to another door, just to the right and on the same curved wall of the door I had just entered through. We came to another area where there were a large number of different beings, all of them busy working on something. I saw another "mica-like" being like the one that had been talking with me. When he came up to us I saw the door of golden light that I had described at the beginning of the hypnotic session.

"Gee, this is so strange!" I exclaimed.

"Well, yes, it is strange," the being next to me answered.

For once, he agreed with me! "But I have to go through that, huh?" I asked, pointing to the door.

"Well, yeah, if you want to see what we wanted to show you."

"What is it?"

"Well, you have to see it."

I was resisting them, more out of stubborn annoyance than because I was afraid: they never seemed to give me a straight answer for anything. So I asked, "Why do I have to see it?"

"Well, it's important."

I sighed. Okay, I thought. Best to get on with it, whatever it was. But I did ask doubtfully, "Will it hurt?"

"No."

"You're sure it'll be okay?"

"Yes."

I got the distinct impression of laughter from them: they thought I was being peculiar. I agreed with them on the peculiar part, but of course, I thought they were the ones who were being strange. Resigning myself once again, I went on through the door with the golden light.

I felt an unsettling spatial effect: was the door getting bigger, or was I getting smaller? I couldn't tell. In any event, I entered a place where there was nothing but light, nothing but a haze of soft, golden light. It was like being in someone's mind, somehow. There was a voice, in this place, and it seemed to come from the bright air. The mind said clearly into my mind: "Choose."

I didn't understand this a bit. "What?"

"Look around you," the voice replied.

I sputtered indignantly, "There's nothing but gold around here! All I see is gold light around here." And it was true: I couldn't see anything of the room in front of me. I told Dr. Field that the space in front of me was either completely round, or had no edges at all.

When Dr. Field asked me if there was any significance to the room being "without edges," I replied that it had something to do with making choices, because there were no edges in chooising. Was this a metaphor for an open-ended universe?

The placeless voice speaking with me was unperturbed by my complaints. "Well, you have to look a little further."

So, I began walking. But when I took a step forward, everything suddenly changed! It was like stepping into another place entirely, being sucked up or pulled into some other reality, into a slice of another world! Frightened, I stepped back, and squeaked, "What happened?"

"It's all right," the placeless voice reassured me."Just choose."

"How can I know what I'm choosing unless I'm seeing it so I know what I'm choosing? I mean, does stepping into something that changes mean that I'm choosing it?"

The voice repeated the command, with a strange, benign lack of emotion: "Just choose."

I knew somehow that what I did here mattered: my choice would be noticed and, perhaps, assessed. All right: I have to see it through, I thought. So I stepped forward again, cautiously. If I went carefully, I discovered, it was as though I was only half-committing myself, like stepping only halfway through an open door. But these "doors" were powerful. They seemed to be ways to enter other places, literally.

I thought suddenly: Doors, into other universes? Wait a minute, I know what to do! I closed my eyes and began to feel my way through the maze of choices. With each step, I noticed what emotions this new area evoked and then I stepped back, or forward, as my feelings dictated. I kept my eyes closed because it was too unsettling and difficult to watch the changes with my poor vision. Seeing some of the places hidden by the golden mist might be too fascinating: I was afraid of getting into something I could not get out of again.

Stepping one way felt nice, and I continued that way. Stepping in another direction was disquieting, so I avoided it. I kept my eyes tightly closed, but I held my hands out, just to make sure I wasn't going to bump into anything or to save myself if I did. The floor seemed level enough, but I didn't like working blind like this! The voice kept reassuring me. "It's all right, it's safe," meaning that I wasn't going to trip and fall. I ignored the voice and kept going. This way felt strange, and this way…

This way felt like something I recognized. It was something that I knew, that I had known before, and known very well. I still had my eyes closed, and couldn't see what I was going towards yet. I never did find out what those other places were, that made me feel those strange or frightening or interesting feelings, because I never saw them.

I felt the golden light around me all the time, however, because it was as though it permeated my body. I even saw the color through my closed eyelids. It was like walking through a crystal's facets: a very pleasant experience.

Throughout all this, I had heard no physical sound, except for more of the humming I had heard earlier. I had no idea what the humming meant. It was less a sound than a constancy of vibration, a soft white noise to go along with the soft, edgeless golden air. But at least the floor still kept its volume at a constant level.

With my eyes shut, I kept on playing "Hot and Cold," going on towards the sense of the familiar, towards something I felt I had already known before. Finally, I stood on the edge of the invisible entryway, opening my eyes and looking in.

I was convinced I was seeing another planet. It was as though I were standing on the ground of another world, looking out over a wide field. The view through the "door" seemed to catch a crystalline moment in time. The colors were remarkably brilliant and pure, even though I couldn't understand some of the shapes I was seeing, as they were too far away from me.

Even though I didn't fully understand what I was looking at, I knew somehow that everything was beautiful there, and that everything was happy there, if it wanted to be. I also knew that this wasn't any Heaven or any paradise. This was an actual, physical place. It was something one could even reach with a starship, given sufficient time and the proper circumstances. So I was not being granted any preview of death or dying. I was looking at another planet, a place of strange and alien beauty.

Then, abruptly, I had a picture in my hands, given to me somehow: it looked like a picture painted on glass. There was no frame, just the smoothed, beveled edges of the glass. It was a rectangular shape with the corners cut off, like the shape of an emerald, about eight inches by five. It was solid in my hands, heavy and cool, and there was a face on it.

A voice from somewhere said, "That's Thoyantir."

"Who's that?" I asked.

"Well, you know him now, and you'll know him again."

The being in the glass had beautiful eyes. They were large and round, red-gold, a kind of bright rust color. Like a lemur's eyes, I guessed later when I saw a picture of a lemur in a book. [Lemurs, like mica, are something else I loved the moment I saw them, "without reason," and still do.] The fur on his face seemed gray, or perhaps his skin was dark with an overlay of white fur, a frosting of white on black: certainly a striking combination.

In the picture, Thoyantir seemed to have a very unusual nose. It wasn't anything like an animal's nose or a human's nose, or any other kind of nose I'd ever seen. And he had things coming out and down from his upper jaw that looked a bit like the teeth of a saber-toothed tiger. These tooth-like projections didn't come down to a point, as a saber-tooth's or tiger's would. It was more as though they came down first in a straight line, and then angled back in a broad triangular shape, with a sharp, rippled inner edge.

Figure 7

The voice (although by now it was beginning to feel like more than one voice communicating with me at the same time) said, "Look again upon the world."

I'd been studying the picture very intently. "Is this my world?" I asked when I looked up again.

"Yes, it is, and yes, it isn't," the voice replied.

"What do you mean? Is it Earth?"

"It could be Earth. In this case, it is not. Yes, Earth might be like this. But this is Thoyantir's planet."

"How… how is it that I know him, that I know this place? I don't understand it!"

"Well, we've told you before that all time is simultaneous; you know him now because you will know him, and you will know him because you have known him." Hearing this paradox from

43

the voice in the light, I was not perplexed at all: at the time, it made perfect sense. (This seems to be one of the benefits, or disadvantages, of telepathy: you understand what is being said at the time, but not necessarily later.)

I looked into the view of the planet again. The sky was a clear turquoise blue. It was not the cobalt blue of Earth's sky, but greener, though the clouds were white. But it was clear that the place I was looking into was real. I could hear the wind. In the distance, there were tall things that looked like trees. They had long, thin trunks, but instead of branches, they seemed to have only puffs or bunches of green, with a bare trunk and a lump of green at a certain level, and other bunches at higher levels.

In front of me, just below the level of the "door," there were some white things, about the size of lawn chairs, or small rowboats, but floating on the air, and not on water. They were solid shapes, as far as I could tell with my marginal vision, flattened cylinders with rounded edges, and a pure, featureless white. I did not know what these things were.

"Interesting that you've chosen this," the voice remarked, still seeming to be the voice of many voices. It was as though there were many people around me, though I saw nothing else except the golden light and the living scene I was marveling at through the round "window." The voice continued, "But you still have further to go."

The way the voice spoke to me I could understand that I meant that I could and should go further. I felt encouragement, literally from everywhere around me, though I heard no audible voices, and saw no one.

"But how do I go on?" I wondered.

The answer seemed obvious a moment later: I should stand back a step, and close my eyes again, so I could feel my way through the light, as I had before. The voices told me that I didn't have to close my eyes at all, but I insisted, "Well, I'm afraid I'll get confused if I don't."

I was afraid that if I went too far in the wrong direction I'd suddenly see something so big and real that I'd be taken up into it, and I wouldn't know how to leave such a place, or how to get back out. I was sure that if I had chosen any of those invisible doorways, it would mean truly going to that place the door led me to. I would travel there instantly, and I had no idea of how I could return.

[If this was an out-of-body experience, I apparently should not have worried; according to beliefs about the process of out-of-body encounters, as long as the silver cord joining my etheric body to my physical one was not cut, I would always find my way back. But at the time it happened I was convinced this was a physical experience.]

So I went on, my eyes shut firmly. When I felt as though I was coming to some other world, I opened my eyes to see something strange and wonderful. There in front of me was a space station, or a star station, a huge construct hung in space within an incredible number of stars.

It was as though I was standing on the skin of the space station itself, or was looking through some kind of window, right on the edge of a huge, straight arm or rim of metal extending out into a huge arch of stars.

It was so beautiful: the starlight was silvery, and the arm of the station gleamed with a radiant, translucent kind of sheen. And somehow, as weird as it seemed, I seemed to smell the fragrance of beautiful flowers around me. Was this my mind trying to fathom the exquisite beauty of the place? Or by looking through the "window" in the room with the golden light was I "inside" the station, and smelling the ship's atmosphere?

Whatever the case, I was quite astonished at how exquisite the starlight looked. It was as bright as moonlight, though there was no moon. It all felt so grand and wide. At the same time, I felt so safe, as though I were perfectly protected. I felt as though I could just dive into the stars, just jump off the edge I was standing on, and swim out into space, like an otter dancing in shining water, swimming everywhere.

But somehow I didn't think it was time for that, not then. So I stepped back again, and asked, "What do I do now?"

The voices replied, "You can choose [again], or you can see what we want to show you."

I answered, "Well, I don't know where I'm going anyway, so I think I'll… what do you want to show me, anyway?"

They didn't reply in words, but all of a sudden I was in another place. I was standing on a balcony of sorts, looking down into another huge room, full of people. Space people? I couldn't tell for sure, they were too far away. But they were walking, or standing together in groups, moving about, and doing things I couldn't see. There was one particular "person" sitting at a horseshoe-shaped table just below me.

I was standing perhaps twenty feet above the area below. The railing came up to my chin. I don't remember much sound, though I got the distinct impression of much bustle and activity down below. But suddenly I was conscious of someone else beside me, and I looked to my left to see him.

He was very tall, twice my height at least. Close to seven feet, I would guess now. He had gray fur all over his body, and long, slender legs. In trance, I realized (with my present-day memories) that he looked a lot like a sifaka, or an indri, the largest lemurs known on Earth, though at the time I didn't know what to compare him to. He looked nothing like an ape or monkey, having instead a kind of lean elegance apes have never possessed.

But it was fascinating because although he looked very strange, and not human, his body seemed to make "sense." He had very large, round eyes of reddish-brown, and his face came out in a kind of a muzzle. The muzzle was short, so it looked something like a cat's face, instead of a dog's or a bear's, although neither the muzzle nor the nose had an especially feline shape.

His arms were quite long: noticeably longer from the shoulder to the elbow than from the elbow to the hand. The distance from his knee to his hip was also longer than it is with people, and from knee to foot much shorter. He had a thumb, which he showed me. His hand had three fingers springing from a flat palm, and the thumb fit underneath the hand, as though it came out of the wrist. His palm and finger-pads were black, though the rest of him was covered with gray, white-frosted fur.

His body was very narrow. He didn't seem to have shoulders or hips, and his chest jutted out rather like a bird's chest. I couldn't tell whether or not he had a tail. Somehow I had the impression he did, but I didn't remember it clearly. But I remembered his teeth, hanging down like the teeth of a saber-toothed tiger, and still, they were different. [See Figure 7, above.]

He was looking at me, and smiling. It was not a human grin, but somehow I still knew his face was smiling. I asked, "Who are you?"

It was Thoyantir, of course, though he did not give his name then. He laughed gently, and replied, "Well, I'm you."

I snorted. "That's silly. I'm me!"

He replied, "Well, but this is why."

I didn't understand what he meant then, and yet I did understand it: This was the being with whom I had been lovingly, deeply linked. Closer than friends, we were more like parts of the same self because our mental link was complete. The paired entity we had become was finally whole, with a joining of minds that created something greater than our separate selves. I felt perfectly safe with him, perfectly at home. Again, I must stress that there was no sense of coercion or fear. Our link was a link of friendship and mutual respect.

He then added that it was "because we [he and I] are who we are" that he was able to show me the things he was showing me now, in this amazing experience in an apparent future under the waters of the summer lake.

But it had been a long night for me, and I said, "I'm sleepy."

Thoyantir replied, "Don't worry, it won't be much longer, but I wanted to show you the Council. I wanted to show you this place because it's special to me."

"Okay," I said, "but am I going to get back to the tent?"

Still smiling, he reassured me, "Yeah: don't worry about it."

I didn't seem to mind that famous phrase from him as much as from the others!

"Look now, something is happening," he directed me, and I looked down again.

The table shaped like a wide, flat horseshoe that I'd seen before now had more people sitting there, each with his or her own mat or desk blotter in front. Some of them looked like human beings, and some of them looked very strange. Seven or eight beings were sitting on the outer edge of the horseshoe shape, looking into the center of the curve.

But I didn't have time to study the people around the table, because suddenly in front of them, a strange, spinning globe of light appeared, spinning in the air between the arms of the horseshoe. It looked a bit like a three-dimensional representation of an atom, a central core with things whirling in orbit around it.

I couldn't see the central core very well, even though I knew it was there, because the things whizzing around the "edge" were too bright. Their movement gave the impression that the whole ball was spinning, parts of it rippling with changing patterns of light. The shape was very bright, and there was not much color to it. But somehow I knew it was a picture of Earth!

The watchers sitting at the table seemed very pleased. And then I heard the voice I had heard in the room of golden light again, which seemed somehow to come from the air, from no particular place at all. It said, "The work has been well done. The work has been very well done." Everyone seemed very, very happy, with a feeling of rich satisfaction. They had been able to do what they had wanted to do. They had wanted to do something beautiful and benevolent, and they had done it right.

But by now I was very sleepy: I could hardly keep my eyes open. I said, "I want to go back. Can I go back? I'm so sleepy."

Thoyantir's reply was very strange: "I'll let some of you go back," he said, "and some of you will always stay here."

The rudimentary logic of my seven-year-old mind must have been taxed by this, because I replied, "Well, I guess that's okay, as long as my Mom and Dad can find me," making it clear that I had not understood what he'd said! "But I'm so sleepy right now," I went on, "I don't want to see anymore, 'cause my eyes are tired."

So the tall being with the gray fur picked me up in both arms. It wasn't very comfortable, because his chest was not flat at all, and jutted against my side. But feeling me squirm, he shifted me so that he held me in his left arm, and this was easier. I closed my eyes gratefully, and almost fell asleep right then. He began to say something, though I didn't know quite what. It sounded as though it were another language, strange and beautiful. He meant something like, "Immediate transport request."

And then we were suddenly, impossibly, on the Summer Camp's pier. I heard the water, lapping underneath it. I was confused, and couldn't tell if there was anyone with me, at first. Then I realized that not only was Thoyantir there, somehow, but that the three original beings that had brought me under the lake were there, too.

But I didn't bother paying much attention. I began stumbling back towards my tent, knowing only that there was someone there to lead me back to it, which was fine enough with me. I must have been barefoot, but I don't remember stubbing my toes.

The moon was up. Looking at it, I somehow found myself forgetting it all, forgetting everything except the golden light. They were telling me to forget what had happened, for now. It was so strange! I wanted to forget it, for now. I knew that I would remember it later, but right then, I was so sleepy, I hardly cared.

They took me back up the path and up to the tent. I kept yawning and yawning from sleepiness. I asked, "Is it going to be okay?"

They asked, "What?"

"Oh, I don't know, will I be all right?"

"Don't worry," they answered, "You will always be all right."

"Okay."

My parents were asleep when I came in. By a little light that came in from somewhere, I saw that my father looked very tired; he was sleeping with his mouth open. I usually never saw my parents asleep because they didn't want any of us kids in their bedroom, as much because our father didn't want us to disrupt his one clean, ordered place as from necessary modesty. My mother seemed to look happy as she slept, which I felt was nice to see.

I went back to my cot. It seemed suddenly very funny that I was still wearing my pajamas. All this strange stuff had been going on, and I'd been wearing my pajamas practically the whole time!

It must have been close to dawn because I began to hear birds chirping to one another in the trees overhead. But I was asleep again very soon: I felt so peaceful. I felt that I loved this place,

this Summer Camp, because... because it seemed so beautiful
here, and because I knew somehow I would be okay.

It was difficult indeed to leave the trance state when we were
done, as difficult as it had been to leave the Summer Camp for
the last time the following year when I was eight. We would
move to California in August of 1961. I would not feel such peace
in my life as what I'd felt here at the lake, both in and out of
"dreams," for many years to come

CHAPTER FIVE

Third Experience, California:
Age Thirteen

When I was eight, we moved from Michigan to California in 1961 because our father had been offered a new post as Unitarian minister for Marin County. He and our mother flew to California to check out the situation in advance and were very impressed. When they learned of the high reputation of the schools in the area, in addition to the excellent weather and the supportive people in the congregation, it was not hard for them to decide to move.

In California, we first were given a "loaner" house for a few months, generously offered by one of the members of the congregation; later we found a pleasant place high on a hill in Marin. It was surrounded by oak trees, having a broad deck with an acacia tree growing right through the middle of it, and a huge eucalyptus towering over the other side.

I believe the space people did see me in intervening years. However, Dr. Field and I did not look into this early time in California for stories of abductions, so our taped hypnosis sessions did not cover these earlier experiences. The "space people" probably came when I was sleeping. I do remember waking up in this house one night, and wondering if "the little guys" would be angry with me if I had to get up and go to the bathroom. Why angry, I do not know. But this memory almost surfaced.

As the kids grew, and wanted separate bedrooms, this pretty little place seemed too small, and so we found another. Our new home was a gray house just the next hill over from the first, even higher up than the old one had been, with an excellent view of the surrounding area. Our front yard, actually a shoulder of the hill the new house clung to, was overlooked by Mt. Tamalpais, the "Sleeping Lady," which rules in green and regal splendor over much of Marin County.

When this next incident took place, we'd been in the new place on the higher hill for about a year and a half. I was thirteen, just finishing seventh grade, and was about to enter the eighth at the new Junior High School. I felt positive about my life at the time: my first year in junior high had been much more enjoyable than most of my time in elementary school. In the new environment of junior high, I didn't meet with old expectations I'd experienced in grammar school: I wasn't picked on for being "weird" nearly as much. I was especially looking forward to another year with my favorite homeroom English teacher, whom I'd had in seventh grade.

The neighbors could not see our new house at all; we were surrounded for at least five or six hundred feet by oaks, laurels, and one lovely little pine tree near the front deck. As was usual in our family, both our parents still worked; our mother would come home at four thirty or five from teaching Spanish in another school district and start making dinner for us; our father came home at six. So, as before, I had time to myself.

When I wasn't reading or doing homework, listening to classical records such as The Fantasia on the Theme by Thomas Tallis (my dad's favorite), or to my mother playing Debussy and Bach on the grand piano in the living room, I would often go wandering in the wooded hills near our house, following the deer trails through the laurel and oak trees. Sometimes my sister and I would climb up the hill that we called "Mt. Baldy," to appreciate the beauty, peace, and solitude of the wilds. Some of this solitude was a method of avoiding my two brothers: the elder was abusive, and the younger teased us two sisters a lot.

Our home was a very isolated, secluded place, very peaceful and quiet. High on the hill as we were, even fog would rarely reach us. We woke many times to a magnificent surround of white clouds below the clear air of the morning hilltop. Seeing fogs like this, I would feel often particularly safe, somehow: we were apart from the world, but we remained in it. It was a wonderful spot.

And it was isolated enough for the "space people" to visit me after several years of apparent inattention. The incident began late at night: I was awakened by something I did not remember, and lay in my bed for a while, seeing the white light from the full moon come in through my window, and hearing the whistling of the cool wind in the trees just outside. The rains had mostly stopped for the year, and in true California fashion the tall wild-oat grass was still green and lush, but beginning to seed, soon to turn golden.

I lay in bed for a long moment but suddenly decided to get out of bed. I slept in one of the two bedrooms upstairs, my parents in the other. Both rooms opened up onto a short hallway with the bathroom on the left side; that hallway led into the large living room that took up most of the upper floor. Stairs to the family room, kitchen, and the other bedrooms led down to the right on the left side of the living room; the front door led onto a wide deck.

That night, I had no idea why I'd suddenly decided to come out to the living room after I'd been awakened; I had checked my alarm clock, and it was about 2 AM. So I wandered, bemused, out into the living room, and looked out at the moon. It was very bright, and I saw its light shining on the carpet.

Or: were there two "moons?" The windows in my room looked west and north; those in the living room, east and south. How could I have remembered the moon shining in through both the western and the eastern windows? And yet, although I said in trance that I saw white light from both directions, I did not think it remarkable at the time.

Then, I heard something, and I looked around, suddenly realizing I must have forgotten my glasses… and was quite surprised to see my sister there! Very little got her out of bed in the mornings in those days, much less up in the middle of the night, so it was no surprise that she looked grumpy standing there near the top of the stairs in her rumpled pajamas. She also looked disoriented because of it: bewildered, and completely inattentive.

While in the hypnotic trance, when I wondered about this mental lassitude, which seems such a frequent thing with UFO experiences, immediately I got a reply from one of the "space people" explaining this process: "We must sometimes 'translate' the body so that the person can enter the ship. Many people put fear and pain in their bodies, but it is not we who do that in the experience. The frequent stasis we project (like the "interrupted" appearance of my sister) is for your protection."

But at the time, I was worried, and asked, "What's going on?!"

Then, for some reason, I looked towards the living room windows and saw a face there, a big, white face, hanging upside-down in the living room window!

For a moment I was very frightened indeed: I couldn't recognize what this thing in the window was, because it just seemed large and strange, and the moonlight distorted its shape somehow. I stammered out, "What's that, what's that?"

Then suddenly I heard a voice in my head that said calmly, "Don't worry, don't worry, it's just us. You know, you remember us: it's been a while, but you remember us."

I knew who they were, then: the "space people." I quickly felt much better, my fear receding so that I became calm again. I replied, "I guess so. Um, what do you want?"

I felt very odd indeed. My thoughts seemed to drag through my mind, slow and fuzzy. But I understood their reply clearly: "Well, we want you to go to the door, the front door, and go out onto the deck."

I was no longer afraid. "Okay, fine," I said, "but what about my sister?"

They reassured me. "Don't worry, she's okay. But come on, we have to hurry."

"Is there something wrong?" I asked.

"Well, no, but we need to hurry, we can't stay here long. We have to go."

"Okay."

I could see them now; I must have moved forward while they were talking with me. They were the beings with big hairless heads that looked so round in the moonlight, and their eyes were large and dark. The moon, or some other light, was behind them, so their faces were shadowed and strange, looking as though they were wearing some kind of veils or masks. I couldn't tell for sure. But I felt their urgency and decided to go on out the front door as they had asked.

The grassy hillside in front of our house was full of light. Some of it was light from a bright moon and some of it wasn't. But I felt pleased to see this other, strange light. As I went across the deck from our front door, I suddenly began to feel very, very good. I felt so good I felt genuinely happy. It was good to feel that way because too often I felt depressed and unhappy in my daily life.

I walked up the cement steps that led to the path to the parking area. But instead of following that path, I turned left, up the slope of the hillside in front of the house, where the tree with the rope-and-tire swing hung, under the view of Mt. Tamalpais.

And, oh, it was so beautiful! There was a ship, hiding in the shelter of the oaks on the slope down to the left of that tree. The ship looked as though it was made out of light! I couldn't tell if it shone so brightly because the moon was shining on it, or because the ship itself was glowing, or even a bit of both, but the light from it was a pure, bright white light.

The ship was not very large: I guessed that it was about as big as the whole top half of our house. (It was roughly 30 feet in diameter, then.) It occurred to me that this was a pretty good place for them to land. They couldn't be seen here on the ground at all; even the light that might escape through the surrounding trees would not be seen well or might be confused with house lights. Although I do not recall any physical evidence of their landing there, I often had strong positive feelings about that area when I went by there later.

But they were hurrying me along, and somehow they were pulling me through the air! It wasn't as though I wasn't walking, exactly, but I wasn't conscious of moving. I was just looking at the ship, and admiring it: with the beautiful light coming from the ship it seemed marvelous.

"Where are you taking me?"

"Well, we've got to take you into the ship, and we need to…" The voice in my head did not use a word, here; rather, I remember a meaning: they intended to "wink out," to "travel" quickly, through some way other than normal physical means. Once they had me inside the ship, they would leave.

One of them, waiting near the ship as I came to it, seemed to know me, and I asked, "Have I met you before?"

"Yes," she said.

I suddenly knew that this one was a woman, although not a human being, but a female of her kind. And seeing her, and knowing that I knew her, I began feeling even better. Then suddenly, I was right at the edge of the ship. I didn't remember its shape very well, only that it was large, circular, and flat, like a convex lens. It opened up, somehow, though I didn't notice the mechanism, as I was much more interested in looking at the woman who had just "spoken" to me with her mind.

I asked her, "I thought you were wearing some kind of mask, before. Why is that?"

"Well, it's a kind of protection."

I felt doubtful: I couldn't see them needing it. "Well, what are you protecting yourself against?"

Her reply puzzled me. "We don't want other minds to see us."

If that had been a protection against other minds reading theirs, then how could I be talking to them with my mind? I protested, "Well, I mean, I can talk to you! I know that you guys, I mean, you're talking in my head, right?"

She replied with remarkable patience, considering her hurry, "Yes, but that's because of the…" She used some words that I didn't understand, but I knew then that she meant the little tracer in my head, the "spiky thing" they'd put in when I was six.

Perceiving my confusion with her terms despite her telepathy, she tried again. She gave me a mental picture, clear images of the memories of my abductions when I was six and seven. I remembered the tall healer with the golden visor and Thoyantir. I exclaimed, "Oh! You've been to the Summer Camp too!"

She laughed. "Yes, yes," and then added: "Because we have that tracer there we can communicate more easily with you. But we don't want to be found out right now." Feeling her urgency, I apologized for delaying them.

She was wearing a uniform of silvery gray. Despite her hurry, she seemed very happy about something. Coming out of the house I felt happy because she was happy but as I got ready to go through the door into the bright ship, I took a second look back, and saw how beautiful our house looked in the moonlight… and I knew then that I was standing there, that I was not imagining all this. I smelled the grass underneath us.

With firm patience, she repeated, "Get in!"

I had to duck my head to get through the door. I was never very clear about how the door worked. It was something like the various sliding doors into spaceships on TV: it slid into the body of the ship, somehow, and did not swing wide like a car door.

Inside was a wonderful humming sound. I paused to hear it. The space person encouraged me, saying, "Go on." But I was suddenly feeling annoyed and angry. All this wonderful stuff happening… and I couldn't see any of it! "I've forgotten my glasses," I complained. "I'm angry. I've forgotten my glasses!"

"Well, we'll take it slowly," she replied kindly. "We know you can't see too well without them, so we won't rush you. But just take it slowly. Go down that corridor and I'll follow you."

Okay, I thought, I guess I'll go on ahead as she asked. It seemed kind of strange to me. But hearing the wonderful humming sound in the ship again, I was still feeling very good despite my brief chagrin at forgetting my glasses *again*.

Yet as I went on down the corridor, I also began to smell a wonderful aroma, something I couldn't describe at all. It was very nice indeed: a wild, wholesome kind of smell. It was a bit like the scent of dry, clean air in the hills on a warm summer's day, or the smell of stones, or a bit like some kind of spice, but it wasn't like any kind of spice I'd ever smelled before.

The light inside the ship seemed to be blue and white together, although as usual, I could not figure out how they managed it. Nothing was ever so bright that I couldn't look at it directly, so there was no light source; nevertheless, once again there was light everywhere. So I walked, looking down at my toes… and suddenly it all seemed so funny. Here I was, walking along with my toes!

The inside of the ship did not feel cramped, although it was not as big as some places I seemed to remember. The corridor I was following led straight in from the door we had just entered. There was a railing on my right, and a large open area beyond, though there didn't seem to be anything in this area except for the bright, inner-ship light. The ceiling slanted over me on my left. I don't remember the air feeling either particularly warm or cool. I continued walking on by myself, though I felt that the space person was following me.

However, by now I was beginning to wonder: why did they want me? I felt suddenly a little defenseless and unsure: she said she would follow me, but I didn't see her behind me. I didn't want to walk ahead blind like this, and stumble into something, or go where I shouldn't go and get into trouble! So I stopped, disconcerted.

But nothing was going on around me except the humming sound and the light. A moment later, I got the impression that I should keep on going forward. It felt peculiarly as though someone was pulling at the point between my eyebrows where the tracer was, as though someone was pulling on a string and leading me further in.

Then, as I paid attention to this particular sensation, my mind suddenly opened up! It seemed as though not only was I what I knew but that I was also more than I was, and yet still only I. It was a feeling of affirmation, of wholeness and certainty, and at the same time a sense of strangeness, an extension of my sense of self unlike any I'd experienced before. I knew then, for certain, that I had been with them before; I knew that the thing I was on was a "scout ship," or a "flitter." It was a small ship, meant to be fast and inconspicuous, which could carry someone from place to place.

I also knew that we'd already left the planet. For them, movement of any kind was so very easy! For them, space was so very easy, because they didn't move through space at all. They could appear to go incredibly fast because, in a sense, they never moved at all.

I went further. The corridor now had walls on both sides of me, and the walls were becoming more interesting: I remembered lights, whole Christmas-tree-like collections of lights on the walls: soft colors, indistinct shapes, nothing very bright, only barely shining, but many, many lights. Sometimes there were solid patches or banks of light on my right, mostly, and some to my left. None of the colors were very intense, though each seemed very pure and clear as though they were fragments of hazy rainbows.

And then, as I followed the corridor, I suddenly saw a big ship, hanging in the stars in front of me, up in the ceiling! The "roof" of the ship I was in curved down in front of me, and there was a big screen-like opening overhead, about four feet wide and three high, which is where I saw the other ship.

Figure 8

As I marveled, I distinctly got the impression… not of laughter, exactly, but of a general delight from the beings that had taken me in. It seemed that they had wanted me to run around on my own a bit, and see what I would bump into. The merriment I sensed was not mocking or nasty at all, nor was it even the indulgent humor of a parent to a child. It was more a communication of appreciation, a gentle echo of my own wondering amazement at what I saw.

Looking at the screen, I had a brief impression that the little ship we were traveling on was moving through some kind of dust or another fine substance, though the brief distortion it had caused went away quickly. As we were coming closer to this other ship, I could see it was huge and shaped, incongruously, very much like a cough drop! Not the triangular kind, but the lozenge type, a sort of fat, squashed cylinder with rounded ends.

The ship was rather dark, though some light shone on it, making it look gray in places. But part of it was very dark, almost black. The closer and closer we came to it the bigger it became until it filled the whole screen or window.

I looked away, thinking, "What's going on here?" It was hard for me to accept anything that big. When I looked up again, we had come right up to it, right upon its skin. Then I turned around and saw that the being that had brought me here was standing behind me, smiling.

She asked, "Well, did you enjoy it?"

I whispered my awe. "Wow! It's so big! Such a big ship!"

She replied, "Yeah, that's what you call the mother ship. And we're about, oh, half an astronomical unit away from Earth."

I'd just learned about astronomical units in school, or I read about them somewhere: an Astronomical Unit is the distance from the Sun to the Earth, which is about 93 million miles. So we were now about half as far away from the earth as the earth is from the sun. Say, fifty million miles, traveled in the space of a few minutes!

From her, I understood that we'd "moved" straight up from the planet: in other words, we hadn't gone towards the sun, but out and away from the night side of Earth, out at an angle to a place directly relative to our original position on the planet.

"Why did you bring me here?" I asked.

The answer came back with the impression of more minds than simply hers. "Well, we need you to check on some things, and also we wanted to ask you some questions."

What, they wanted to ask me questions? Huh. What could I possibly tell them that they'd find useful? "Well, I'll try and help. I wish I had my glasses."

The being replied, "Well, we've found with others and with you in particular that sometimes a physical disability can enhance a person's mental development: because they are limited in one of their abilities they have to work harder with the others. And that includes your mental ability. This is one reason why you find it so easy to talk to us."

"Oh, hmm. Okay."

I had to accept what she said: she could not lie. She was a telepath: she could not lie. True, she could keep information hidden from me, but I was certain she could never tell a direct untruth without it being perceived.

I truly liked this telepathy stuff! I felt I could be myself this way, without having to wade through misunderstandings, misconceptions, or hidden motives: all those necessary evils of a society where only words can be used to communicate.

She had said they wanted to check something, so she led me down the corridor again to another room. There was someone else there. I almost asked if it was, the gray, lemur-like being in the picture they had shown me when I was six, and whom I later met.

But I saw that it wasn't he, even though it was also a tall gray being with large eyes. This one was dressed in something that looked amazingly like a white lab coat! He was fiddling with something in front of him, working very intently with something in his hands, though I couldn't see what.

This tall being and the pale, short one who'd brought me in made me sit down on a short, couch-like thing, something like a reclining dentist's chair, though I had hardly leaned back when they started beaming flashes of light at me, aiming them right at the point between my eyebrows!

"What?" I exclaimed. "Wait a minute, what!?"

The being that had brought me into the ship put her hand very softly on my shoulder, and said, "Don't worry, just try not to move. But don't worry: this won't hurt you at all: We have to…" Again I received silent words or meanings; I got the sense that she'd meant that they wanted to add something to the "tracer" somehow. How could they do that, with just beams of light? But that's all it was: just incredibly bright, colored zaps of light that stopped abruptly.

And then I heard a ringing in my ears, a loud, constant, insistent, chiming tone, ringing, and ringing! It wasn't coming from outside, but was in my ears, very, very loud. "What's going on?" I demanded, impatient and annoyed. "I don't know if I like this! I mean, you guys are great, but, um, I can hardly think!"

I didn't know then whether or not I had lost consciousness, but suddenly I was back in the chair, sitting up and blinking. Perhaps I did become unconscious for a moment, because the smaller being who'd been with me the whole time was standing at my feet now, looking at me with some concern.

I was suddenly struck by how short she was. Very short: she was hardly four feet high, if that, more like three and something. Of course: I'd grown. But she studied me with great care, and said, "Are you all right?"

"God," I groaned, "I think so! What was that?"

She replied, a little contritely, "Well, sometimes a backwash happens but don't worry, it's quite all right. But hurry up and get out of the chair now: we need to take you."

"Where are we going?"

"Well, we're taking… I guess you'd call it a conference room."

She meant just she and I would be going there, not the other being. But I felt worried: she sounded a little grave. I got the impression that this place she was taking me to involved something very important and very serious. Anxiously, I asked, "Will it be all right? I don't want to do anything wrong." Because I suddenly felt that I could do something badly incorrect somehow.

"Well, we'll see," she replied. I did not feel encouraged.

She led me on again, through some big, wide halls. I presumed that by now we'd left the "flitter" and had been on the main "mother ship" for a while. At any rate, we went some distance, beginning by going on a kind of catwalk, a flat thing with railings on either side, with a large space all around us. I could see other catwalks, too, and got the impression of a lot of bustle, a lot of activity.

As we went on I smelled that wonderful, bright clean smell of the air again that I could not describe. There was no perfume in the air: it just smelled fresh. We went a little further, and she took me up to a round patch of brightly white floor. "This is very strange," I said.

"Don't worry about it, just get on it."

The space above the bright patch was like a round cylinder: although the floor was bright white, the air was dark in the area above our heads. It seemed as though the bright patch on the floor was moving, spiraling around itself somehow. She got on it, and I said, "Well, all right," and got on it myself, a little reluctantly.

There was a whir, and I shut my eyes, thinking for sure the floor would start moving around like a superfast carousel. It was very strange. I didn't feel dizzy at all, as I'd expected, but somehow I knew that we were spinning very fast, and going forward, doing some kind of peculiar motion.

I couldn't feel the movement, though, and did not understand what was going on, though I was not too frightened. Even with my eyes closed, I knew she was right there next to me. She even put her hand on my arm to steady me. But I kept feeling how we moved on this thing without moving: it was weird! How could it go on like this, moving so incredibly fast without moving? I just couldn't fathom it.

But I could feel her hand on my arm, and her touch felt very solid. After a moment I opened my eyes again, and she was looking at me: her eyes… There was something about her eyes. There seemed to be a red light glowing from them. It wasn't as though she was angry; there was simply a soft red light gleaming from her eyes.

She said seriously, "Whatever happens, don't be afraid. This is important."

I asked her tentatively, "Am I dreaming? I mean, is this real? Am I dreaming?"

"Well, it is real, and in a way you're dreaming. But you're not." This suggested I was in an altered state of consciousness, like an out-of-body experience.

The spinning had stopped, and we got off. It had been an elevator of some kind, I supposed, except that it traveled in a much different way. It moved horizontally, at least, and probably in other "directions" as well. But only the patch on the floor moved. I was just as glad I'd kept my eyes closed.

As I was looking at her, I asked her what her name was. She replied mentally that her name was Cythromaa. (Pronounced sigh throw MAY, despite the double "a "at the end.) I didn't know what the name meant, but I always thought it had something to do with wisdom: something else positive and loving. I was already very taken with her and because of her encouragement, I felt safe with her.

Well, safe enough: I hadn't enjoyed the "ride" on the spinning patch on the floor very much at all. The device was just some "normal" method of getting around the ship but I found it most unsettling.

We had come out onto another catwalk. The railing only came up to about hip height on me and didn't seem very useful: it wouldn't have stopped me from falling, for I was five feet tall by then. But it came up to about shoulder height on her, or a little lower: a good height for her.

I looked over to my right and was amazed. It looked as though there was a piece of Earth there! A small, enclosed landscape, a piece of the world in the ship! It might have looked more like a real landscape except that I could see the walls of the ship far away on the other side. But there was living green and blue down there, to the right of the catwalk. I looked at it for a long moment, trying to puzzle it out through my poor vision, but I couldn't quite understand what it all was. Were there trees there, and water? It seemed as though there were…

I could see Cythromaa, standing next to me because she was close enough. But even this didn't seem to help: I was beginning to get confused, somehow, and a little worried: the situation felt tense. She reassured me, repeating, "Don't worry, don't worry," almost as though my anxiety was affecting her.

I tried to distract myself, and asked, "Is there anyone else here on the ship that I know?"

She replied, "Well, you know, you could… I'm sending you a picture."And she sent me an image of the two short black beings that had helped me when I was six. But she went on, "But I don't think you'd recognize them now; they've changed color."

Mystified, I demanded, "Why have they changed color?!"

"Well, we don't want to talk about that now." [1]

None of this was much help: I was stalling for time. I was frightened, for it seemed as though she was scared, too.

I asked, "Why do we have to do this?"

"Well, it's necessary." This explained nothing and hardly helped my mood. But suddenly we came to another room, to the left of the catwalk. It was a small room; all the walls were bright white, and the floor, too.

She went in with me and said, "Here, put this on." She handed me a filmy, gauzy, gray kind of something. Somehow she helped me put it over my head. It was like a blanket: she simply draped it over me so that it covered my head and face. It was made out of some kind of mesh, so I could see through it. I looked at her through it, and she looked very grave indeed.

"What's wrong?" I asked anxiously.

"Don't worry: I'll be there with you."

I was about to go through another doorway, to face something important... and unknown.

As we delayed at this second door, which led into the "conference room," I felt my anxiety increase. I suddenly protested fearfully to Cythromaa, "Hey, don't leave me! I don't... If you're worried, then this thing you're having me do must be something pretty big, maybe dangerous. I don't want to be left alone!"

She heard my thoughts clearly, and said, "Don't worry, I'll be here with you; I mean, you will always feel my mind. And nothing will harm you here." Perhaps affected by something in her thoughts, I felt suddenly better, relaxing a great deal. I was still worried, but I felt better.

The silver mesh she had me put on was not heavy, but it hung down straight and wasn't billowy. The doorway we stood in front of now looked just like a blank wall. This wall looked as though it was moving light: it was a very pale grayish fog with light in it. I knew there was a door there, somehow, though I could not see it. So, I stepped off the catwalk, feeling the deck with my bare feet as I walked.

I went in. I couldn't see anything. There was nothing but gray fog around me. And yet, I could sense that a large space surrounded me. After a few steps, I stopped. I still couldn't see anything but the fog. I could make out the floor, also a featureless gray, but solid. And then, in one place to my right, I could see a narrow, vertical rectangle of golden light.

I suddenly heard a sound like a thousand voices, all talking at the same time: I couldn't make sense of any of them! I began to get scared again, but instantly felt encouragement: it was Cythromaa, urging me to go on. So I moved forward, going towards the golden light, despite the Babel of almost-words and almost-voices.

The atmospheric, fog-like light had suddenly become a shape that looked surprisingly like a plain old doorway; the light even gleamed in a slanted shape across the floor, fighting its way through the fog. I walked closer: I could see the light shining softly on my feet as I came nearer, and the doorway became clearer.

I wasn't afraid of the fog, but I wasn't moving very quickly, either. The voices in the air were still talking, talking, talking, until they slowly faded away into noise, and became like the sound of wind in the trees. And yet it was like hearing a sound beyond sound, a silent roaring in my thoughts that never reached my ears. I supposed it was the sound of other people's minds. There were so many minds communicating all at once that I wondered how they kept track of themselves. How did anyone know what anyone else was saying or thinking?

Coming to the doorway with the golden light at last, I blinked angrily with frustration at being without my glasses. But I was committed. So I went right up to it… And abruptly felt a strange and powerful distortion of my sense of self. I had no other words to describe it: it was as though by stepping through that doorway, I was suddenly not only somewhere else, and somewhen else, but that I was suddenly another person! Yet I wasn't a stranger to myself at all: I knew who I was, even though I wasn't who I was!

After the original Babel of voices in the fog died away, the only thing I heard was humming, a bit like a motor running, though the sound wasn't clear, because this place in the fog was so very big. Bewildered, I felt suddenly that I was standing on the deck of a ship: not a spaceship, not a starship, but an ocean-going vessel. Or, was it? I didn't know: I felt completely disoriented for a moment, and Dr. Field had to break into my trance narration to urge me to come to myself and remember what I'd seen then correctly.

When asked to look again, I still saw the same image. The cabin was small, not much larger than a closet, and there was a lot of light. Everything was gold: the walls and the deck, and the two-part, flattish console underneath the two rectangular windows that looked out into the darker fog. The windows appeared to be nothing but flat panes of glass, angled back as though they were set into the prow of a speedboat.

This wasn't a speedboat, of course. I didn't have an explanation for it then at all, but later incidents in this strange place made me think that this "cabin" was probably a purely mental construct of some kind. But whatever it was, I was back to myself again. I'd just lost who I was for a moment. Now everything seemed normal enough, though the fog seemed darker now.

Figure 9

And out there in the fog was a huge eye: a round, bright yellow eye with a red rim, about three feet across that had no pupil. There was only the barest suggestion of lids or face surrounding it: only darker hints in the dark gray fog. I saw the eye through the two windows of the "ship's cabin." The eye appeared to be cut exactly in two by the center frame in front of the console.

The mind behind the eye informed me mentally that he was the Inquisitor. I was reassured that the name did not mean anything bad: he was simply here to ask questions. Fair enough, but I asked doubtfully, "Okay, but I don't know if I can help you any. Why do you look like that? You can't be that big!"

He replied, "No." His thoughts thundered in my brain: my ears heard nothing, but my mind rang with the sound of his "voice." When the Inquisitor communicated to me telepathically it was hard to follow what he was saying and understand it: his thoughts seemed to move so fast! As he thought "aloud" I received little glimpses and glimmers, only getting a partial sense of what kind of being he was.

I got the peculiar impression that the Inquisitor didn't have much of what I would call a sense of humor, seeming to be more a "natural object," like a stone or the sky. I also got the impression that he didn't care very much about how I appeared to him or how he appeared to me. This image was only how I saw him. The image had nothing to do with what he truly was. It was my own mind's reaction to what I sensed of him.

At last, seeming to have worked out the limits of my telepathic abilities, he asked me a clear question: "What is man doing here [on the Earth]? What is your race doing here?"

"I don't know, really," I babbled. "I mean, we're trying to live, I guess. I'm trying to learn, and I'm trying to… you know, I've got school, and so on." After all, what does one say to a huge eye hanging in a dark fog in front of the windows of a ship's cabin that is probably only a mental construct?

He asked again. "What is your race doing here?"

All at once, I began remembering all sorts of things: little things, like items I'd read in the newspaper. But these incidents and memories suddenly started going through my mind at great speed, becoming an incredibly fast stream of incidents one after the other! Some of the incidents stood out, like sitting in class and listening to my teacher, doing arithmetic, going out in the woods near my house by myself to enjoy the trees, or being teased by the other kids in school, and other things from my life, which all unraveled into the Inquisitor's mind.

And then, the eye suddenly turned a wonderful, deep sky-color blue with an almost metallic reflectivity, with a mottled, shining quality like that found in some amphibians' eyes. I didn't feel afraid. I suddenly understood that the being I was looking at did not have a body at all. The Inquisitor was only a mind. But he could embody himself if he wanted because the difference between "body" and "mind" was so slight for him that neither form nor formlessness made much difference.

He was trying to understand how humans related to each other and our planet. But with all my memories unraveled out of me as they'd been, I felt a little nauseous. Looking carefully to see where I put my hands so I didn't punch any buttons, I put my hands on the console to steady myself. The Inquisitor just took everything: all my memories, everything that had happened to me, and sucked it up like a strand of spaghetti leaving my mind empty.

I was breathing hard, and I gasped out, "What did you do that for? What was that?!" But there was no reply to my outrage. I even got the impression of, not exactly a mental grumble of irritation, but a sudden preoccupation. He was busy with something else. After he'd done all that, he was ignoring me completely.

"Hey!" I cried. "Hey! Listen to me! Listen to me! Hey, listen to me, um, you can't do that, you know! You, you… " He wasn't listening. There was nothing but blackness out there now, nothing but the sense of a big, silent mind. I suddenly realized that I had to get angry. I had to mean what I was saying for him to hear me. I got a mental image from Cythromaa somehow: she was showing me something with her mind, a kind of focus, something I could use. So I shouted to the black air in front of me.

I cried out, "Hey, you've got to listen to me: you've got to listen to me!" At last, I sensed a response, of sorts: the Inquisitor seemed annoyed. Determined, I repeated, "Hey, you've got to *listen*! I've got something to say! You've got to hear it!"

Eventually, his annoyance seemed to crystallize into a disgruntled thought, something like, "What's this person still doing here?"

I wasn't about to be deflected. "I'm still here because, well, I've got something to say!"

The image of the eye shifted back towards me, looking back at me indifferently. "This is important," I insisted.

His thoughts replied in a flat tone, "What."

I had his attention at last. He didn't seem at all happy about it. But I pressed on. "I matter," I asserted, my voice becoming more passionate as I spoke. "This world *matters*. What we do *matters*. Everything human is precious. It matters!"

The inquisitor inquired mildly, "How did you ever get the impression that it didn't?"

"Well, you weren't listening to me, you were ignoring me! You don't… you didn't… you know I… " I let out a very frustrated sigh. "I've got something to say!"

"Well," he instructed, "say on."

"Well, it's just that if you don't know… if you don't know that we matter, then there's no point in anything that we do. But even if we didn't matter, even if we didn't make any difference to anybody else, we would make our difference! We would find our ways to matter! We would find out ways to be… to mean something."

I got the strange impression of mental laughter, all around me. Not mocking laughter. It wasn't even amused. But it was a deep, rumbling sort of, "Aha!"

In the hypnotic trance at this point, Dr. Field inquired what the relationship was between this "Inquisitor" and the space people. Why was he on their ship?

I replied from my trance state, with a complete lack of notice for "past" and "present," that I could ask him. Whether then or "now," he replied that he was a visitor. He said that he tested what he came across because his tests were the surest methods of discovering the motives of those tested. Because with his method, he made you face your stumbling blocks and frustrations.

[Now, many decades later, I realize that he was engaging me in an area where I was vulnerable: I often felt ignored and overlooked, and sometimes devalued, in my youth, although have since found my ways to matter.]

As the Inquisitor had been answering Dr. Field's question, all the dark fog that I saw through the windows in the image in my memory had disappeared, as though someone had been slowly running water into a pot of ink as I had been talking, washing the ink away, making it swirl around and get lighter and lighter. The eye had also disappeared into the pale light, into the growing whiteness.

At last, the view out of the windows became the same pale gray I'd seen at the beginning, at the entrance into this strange mind-place. Even the mental construct, the golden image of the ship's cabin, was gone. It had seemed so solid, only a moment ago. But everything had become cloud white.

However, I knew somehow that the mind of the Inquisitor had not gone at all. I was also still aware of Cythromaa's attention in my mind, with such a clear impression it seemed as though she was standing right behind me, just outside the door.

So I asked, "What do I do now?"

The Inquisitor's mind answered, "Create something."

Huh. What did that mean? Could it be something like drawing, perhaps? That was all the impression I got: just, "Make something!" He didn't care what. So somehow, I started making an image of a horse. I'd been drawing them for years, having a great affection for them since I was five, and thought that it might be the easiest. It wasn't going to be a "real" horse, certainly, more like an idea of one. I drew the image on the fog itself, like lines of light on white air.

It wasn't easy. It didn't go together right, coming out in strange colors as well: blue and green, nothing like a horse. But perhaps the reason the horse kept changing as I worked on drawing it was because the Inquisitor's mind was working with mine.

I started talking it through as I worked, to help my concentration: "Okay, okay, all right: now, it goes like this, you see, and that's the way the head goes, and the ears are attached [this way], and then the nose… the neck goes like this and the shoulders… and then the front legs go down, and then the body goes back, yeah. And now you got a tail, yeah, lots of tail. And then the hind legs are always hard. Okay, yeah!"

And then my absurd blue and green horse image disappeared.

The Inquisitor said, "Create something else. Create a memory."

The first thing that came to me was to think of this spring's Easter Service, which we held at the Mountain Theatre on the slopes of Mt. Tamalpais. I remembered the flowers people brought, the rain that day, the rocks, and everything else I could recall. I remembered the oak leaves, trees, and the sky. I recalled the types of clouds in the sky and the seats made of green California serpentine that we sat on in the amphitheater.

The Inquisitor seemed to study this "creation" a little longer than the first, and then he helped me to recall it more clearly, so that I remembered even the little pebbles down near my feet, and what I was wearing that time (never a source of much concern for me). And then this image was gone as well! Now what? I wondered.

"That'll be all for now."

I was unimpressed. I asked very dryly, "What is this for?" I was feeling very skeptical. "What is all this for? You guys drag me out of bed for this? What is this?"

It replied, "What you're doing with your mind now is a fragment of what you're doing here. We amuse your mind for the moment because we're doing things on deeper levels. Have no fear; be afraid of nothing in your life, because you are inviolate, at all times in all places. I'll send you home, now, and you'll forget this until later, and you'll know when to remember it.

"But understand that Mankind has to work with the creative forces of the universe and not against them. As long as Man works against the creative forces of the universe, he will be forbidden to leave the planet. Because it would be like giving a child an explosive toy and having [the child] throw it around. When Mankind works with the creative energy, the deep creative energy..."

Here I got an impression of a profound breadth of space and being, of thousands upon thousands of songs and stars and beings and joy and light. It was just a huge kind of feeling. And yet in all the vastness, everything was noticed, nothing was lost in the size of it. Nothing was ignored; there was nothing that was not known. There seemed to be no "Something" doing this awareness because reality *was* awareness.

The Inquisitor continued, "Until Humans understand that, they cannot progress."

As though the Inquisitor was in my past and the present at the same time a part of the hypnotic trance, I recalled some other things: When I was young and went on one of my first zoo trips with some friends of the family (it rained, and we had a picnic of fried chicken in the car) I was struck by the strange thought that the whole world was a zoo. Not in a negative sense, but in a positive one, because Mankind was being protected to some degree from itself, from the results of our mistakes.

Wild animals kept in zoos are protected from each other: Lions are not put in with zebras, nor are leopards with antelope. They are also protected from humans in a variety of ways, as well: a human feeding an ape a peanut can give human salmonella to the ape, for instance, which can kill the animal.

But it is not clear how we are being protected from ourselves, except in hidden, subtle ways, in terms of a nudge here and an encouragement there. I believe this is because any greater action on their part would be a form of interference unacceptable to them, and to us. Human beings feel very free to interfere with the lives of other living creatures on the planet (did anyone ever ask a Dachshund if it wanted to have the body it has?), but we are quite intolerant of the idea of any similar interference in human life: we can give it out, but we can't take it.

For me, their non-interference policy is one of healthy respect towards us. We are being protected from the "outside" as well. But Earth was a "zoo" because we and the other beings were separated for some indeterminate time, to protect us all.

After explaining this last concept in the hypnotic trance, my voice became very slow and measured, speaking one word at a time as I repeated the Inquisitor's thoughts, given to me within the hypnosis session: "But it [the separation] is temporary, it is very temporary. It is only what is needed right now until Man works with pure Creative Energy, and this will not be long from now. But until that time there is much pain yet."

I replied, somewhat astonished, "Thank you. I didn't think I'd get so much answer!"

"You are worthy of it," the Inquisitor assured me. "You are worthy of it. Remember always, you are worthy of being noticed."

The rest of the experience with the "Inquisitor" seemed anti-climactic. The pale fog gently turned me around and I went back out through the entryway in the corridor wall. Cythromaa was still outside, waiting. I looked at her and had to stop.

Her eyes were just indescribable. It was as though I could see her mind with more clarity now. There was such extreme love there, and such caring and concern. It was a sense of constant joy and delight in just existence. Just existence! Not necessarily her existence, but the existence of everything.

This sense of caring was a constant, ongoing kind of delighted joy. Cythromaa, as a creature, as a being, had great delight in being, joy in what was, simply because it **was**. No judgment, no attachment, no other reason needed, just because something existed. The walls of the ship, the floor, the deck, the railing, or even the little knobs or buttons on the walls were precious to her just because they existed and for no other reason.

Then suddenly I exclaimed, "Oh!" and blinked. "Oh, my head!" It felt as though some kind of mental rubber band had snapped back into my skull and gave me a peculiar feeling of vertigo. It was not painful, but it was unsettling.

She reassured me gently, saying, "Yeah, it happens that way sometimes. But you did very well in there! You made very few mistakes and much fewer than some because you went straight for the light, the love, and for knowing. And that was very well done."

I replied emphatically, "Thank you! But I want to go home!"

She laughed. "Yes, yes, yes, you know that we'll do that, right now. Take off your 'net' (meaning the gray, gauzy thing she'd put over me)." Did that net-thing have anything to do with any of the effects I'd experienced? Could some of what I experienced have been technological, in addition to being psychological?

I wriggled out of it somehow, and said, "Where do I put it?"

She pointed to the wall, which was dark, swirling gray again, and said, "Hang it up there."

Following her instructions, I put the gray net on the wall, and it simply hung there, even though I didn't see anything to hook it onto: it was as though the fog just held it up.

Then she suddenly asked, "Do you want to see some more of the ship before we go?"

My earlier desire to go back home forgotten, I enthused, "I think I'd like to if we can. I mean, it just seems so beautiful in here!"

She replied, "Yes, that's because you see a bit more than you did when you came here." But then, as we started going on, I suddenly wondered whether or not I had the time to see the ship, now. It was the middle of the night, I guessed, and maybe I should be going back now.

Cythromaa replied with a mental communication that was hardly words, just a meaning: "Well, we have plenty of time here."

I understood her. It wasn't that we were outside of Time in their "Mother Ship:" for us, time went on normally. But there was some temporal relativity going on. She and I could take many hours doing something here, and then she could return me to where we'd started, and perhaps only half an hour would have passed.

She explained it to me in an offhand way, and at the time it made perfect sense. I asked, "How big is this ship?"

"Well, you would call it about half a mile long, and between a quarter and a third of a mile wide. And, it's a... we call it one of our 'Home Ships.' It's more a combined mental construct than it is a physical object, do you understand?"

I commented dryly, "Well, seeing what you guys can do with your minds, I'm not surprised!" Impulsively, I changed the subject. "You know about our science fiction, don't you?"

I was walking next to her, now, and could see her face. She smiled slightly. "Yes."

I had been enjoying science fiction for the last few years, ever since the librarian at the local Children's Library suggested I begin reading it, correctly guessing that I would enjoy it. Andre Norton was my first love and in my opinion, there are clues in her books that suggest that she might have been a contactee too, although her experiences seem to have frightened her. But she wrote about telepathy in a great many of her stories, which made me feel comforted.

I continued: "Well, you know, there are all sorts of wonderful stories, and I was just reading some stuff by Andre Norton. This thing about telepathy, is it that normal?"

"Yes. You humans have for so long engaged yourselves with other things that this ability within you has atrophied to some extent. But it's more that you don't pay attention to it much, even when it happens. Some of you humans, like yourself, are comparatively gifted in it. And, of course…" she reached up and touched the spot right between my eyes in a companionable gesture, a very friendly gesture "…we have the tracer!"

She smiled and seemed to find this very funny indeed. I giggled, though I didn't know why, and then I laughed and asked, "You mean we're cheating?"

"Yes!" We both laughed, and her gentle smile got a little bigger. "Well, what would you like to see?"

"I don't know!" I exclaimed. "I mean, I have no idea of what's here. Unless there's some sort of place where there are a lot of different beings? You know, where some different space people are?"

"Well, sure!" And she started to lead me on.

But I hung back a moment. "Um, do we have to go in that spinning thing again?"

"I could tell you didn't like it," she said, "but it's nothing to be afraid of!"

I was not convinced. "Well, I'd kind of like to... I'd rather take it slowly, right now. I just want to feel my way through things a little bit, you know?" Then changing the subject again before she could answer, I commented, "It's such a wonderful smell on this ship. How did you do that?"

"Well, I... it's very hard to explain. But it has something to do with the quality of the minds here. There's a special kind of resonance."

I knew what she meant because when she was communicating with me, I understood what she told me with her understanding. Only later did I find that I hadn't understood something as well as I thought I had.

Returning to the subject at hand, she said, "Well, you can just go and find what you see, because of course the ship will change!"

"What!?!" I exclaimed, flabbergasted.

"Well, you know, I told you that this home ship is as much a mental construct as it is a physical thing..." As she stood there on the catwalk looking at me, she enumerated by touching one finger to the others, much as a human being would to emphasize what was being said.

Her movements were not quite like a human being would use for counting, but I got the impression she had a lot of human mannerisms, and that this time she was just joking around by pretending to be an academic, pontificating teacher as she explained. I received such a feeling of delight from her. I understood then that she liked Humans. She delighted in learning from us, and that was one reason why she and I worked so well together.

She explained: "The laws of physics are different here in the sense that you can go walking, and you find what you're looking for." I supposed one could call it magic: the magic of another kind of physics than we know.

I shrugged. "Well, why don't you show me something?"

"Okay. Well, I've got to check on something, so why don't you come with me?"

As we went further from the "wall" where I'd had been examined by the "Inquisitor," it occurred to me to ask, "Hey, um, the Inquisitor: is he living on this ship somehow?"

"He's one of the minds that have constructed it."

"Well, okay, that's very interesting." I felt doubtful. "Um, what're you guys doing here, anyway?

"We're learning. You have a lot to teach us, just because you are what you are. It's like…" She paused. "You Humans will look at rocks. Now, rocks don't say anything to you, but you feel they teach you a lot about how your planet was formed or other things. But if you learned how to listen to the rocks directly they'd teach you even more. Well, we're learning how to listen to you, in ways in which you don't even know that you're talking!"

I understood what she meant, with that same kind of easy acceptance I'd had before. It wasn't as though I was dreaming, but I was in a receptive state of some kind. Perhaps this was because we were friends, and we got along. The method of "understanding rocks" she'd meant was a purely mental science, akin perhaps to some of our psychic abilities.

She continued leading me along the catwalk, up against the side of the ship. I understood that she was going the long way on my behalf, of course, because I so disliked the spinning "transport." The catwalk was roughly three feet wide and the railings came up only to about mid-thigh on me. The catwalk was made out of dark gray metal with a light brown cast; the railings were more silvery. All the colors inside the ship were very soft. A lot of areas looked just as though they were made out of white light.

On our left was the curved wall of the Home Ship's skin; on our right was the vast area, arched over by the "roof" or the bulkhead. I got the impression that there was a great deal going on in this vast space: I could guess at the shapes of the other catwalks on the opposite side of the ship, and a lot of movement. It seemed as though there were a lot of other beings there, and I heard soft sounds from across the way, as though there were people doing things.

But all of a sudden Cythromaa and I were at this place on the catwalk where there was this strange "curtain," a bit like one of those hanging, "beaded" curtains of macaroni, except that the "macaroni" seemed very large.

I felt puzzled by it and had a hard time describing it in the trance for some reason. The shapes that made up the curtain looked a great deal like the marks of tire treads in a dusty road: flattened "S's" or "Z's," rounded zigzags, hung in neat rows. The color was a peculiar mixture of yellow and green together: not very bright, but not an ugly color, either. The curtain seemed to move a little bit, on its own. I asked Cythromaa anxiously, "What is this?"

She replied, "Don't worry about it. It's just a…" She used some kind of word I couldn't understand, even with our apparent telepathic contact. "Doorway" was the closest equivalent I could come up with.

"You've got some strange things on your ship!" I observed.

"Well," she teased gently, "you've got some odd things on your planet, too!"

Going through the green and yellow "curtain" was like going through water, somehow, although I was never wet. I was so struck by the feel of it, though, that I held my breath, much to Cythromaa's amusement. I grumbled at her, annoyed, projecting a feeling something like, "What do you think I am, a country rube?"

"Well, no," she said gently, "it's just that the ship affects others differently." (A diplomatic reply, if I ever heard one!) It seemed that there had been other beings who'd come to this ship, and they hadn't responded to the "door" the way I had.

I wanted to make up for my complaints, so I said, "Well, I certainly seem to be having fun here, mostly!"

"Yes, yes: we're very glad you enjoy it so much."

But we hadn't gotten through the whole doorway before I suddenly closed my eyes because they didn't seem to want to take in what they were seeing! It was as though lines of light, fragments of lines of light, were coming at me, all shining in the dark, greenish-yellow "matrix" of the "doorway:" red and blue and turquoise and white and yellow and green, all of different shades and widths, different shapes of light.

All of these colors were moving without moving, hanging in this "non-space" of the inside of the "door. They moved towards me with a weird perspective, so they looked as though they were focused on me somehow, and yet they weren't!

It was as though I was seeing too much at once, or perceived too many perspectives at once. There were no mirrors in this "door," although I thought at the time that you might be able to get some of the same effects with a series of reflecting mirrors with their illusion of infinities reflecting infinities.

I didn't want to look at it much: it hurt my eyes. But after a long moment, we finally got through and came to a vast space: the area in front of us was a bubble-shape, and the walls were light golden brown. We were still on the catwalk. By looking over the railing I could see that there was quite a drop down the floor of the area below us and that the ceiling was very high.

Down below us, about fifty feet or so were these white shapes that looked very much like paper airplanes! They looked as though they'd each been made out of two flat triangles placed together on their sides, so that their longest sides formed the outside edges of the wings, and the remaining short sides formed an inner "V."

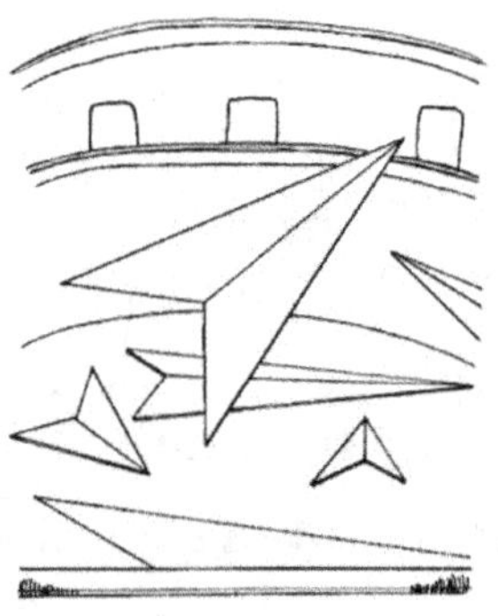

Figure 10

I laughed when I saw them. These chevron shapes appeared to be hanging from the ceiling on wires, or perhaps they were just hanging in the air, spinning slowly in the open area below.

Several people were working on the ships. "Space beings," I supposed, though they were too far away to see. I asked Cythromaa what the white shapes were, and she replied, as though it was completely obvious, "Well, they're the ships!"

I got the impression that these "ships" were not meant for travel through outer space, as such, but were some other kind of transport that could be used to take someone from one Home Ship to another instantaneously. They were conveniences. She went on to say, "But we're making them."

She could very well have said, "We're thinking them," too. I felt that they didn't manufacture things as we do, with bolts and rivets and whatnot. Rather, when making something, they seemed to "en-corporate" whatever it was from carefully controlled thoughts within a receptive matrix. She'd come here to see how things were going with the forming.

Forming the ships was almost like growing crystals. You had to "grow" them in certain conditions. She showed me a silly image of a very large space person like herself, with a little beaker and a stirrer, looking down into this solution in which little tiny ship-shapes were growing, like crystal seeds. I laughed aloud at her thoughts and felt her enjoyment.

Unquestionably, she had a sense of humor. Because she just loved all of existence, she seemed able to laugh at just about anything. She directed my attention to another part of the floor below us quite some distance from us to our left where there were some very large dark things. They looked like molds shaped vaguely like the white "flitters" we'd just seen.

There were beings of her kind working quite closely to these darker shapes. But in the center of the dark "mold" was glowing red and quite bright, as though there was something very hot in there.

Part of the process of making these small ships was to focus energy so that this energy took the form of the mold. It wasn't like pouring the energy into a fixed shape, as you would do with molten steel. These "molds" seemed to be like a series of magnets, say, or something set in a certain pattern around the energy. There seemed to be two lobe-like shapes above the bright area where the energy was being patterned, and a similar pair on the bottom, and the new shape was being formed in the "empty" space between them.

Figure 11

The energy looked as bright as I imagined molten steel might, but I didn't see any sparks or any kind of ladle for pouring any kind of liquid.

Receiving my image of hot steel, Cythromaa told me that if I wanted to imagine sparks, there would be some. "Go on," I said jokingly as I laughed again, "quit teasing!" Because I knew she was right if what she'd said earlier about the ship was true: the whole ship seemed to be "amenable" to mental energy. I had better be careful with my thoughts!

We watched the process of the ships forming for a while, and I found it thoroughly fascinating. In the molding process, the energy was getting patterned with some of the basic "laws" of the way the universe was put together. I didn't understand how this could happen, but it was as though the bodies of the ships were being impregnated with a specific set of basic universal constants in their formation.

It sounds here very much as though her people might be more deeply aware of the interchanges between the "implicate" and "explicate" orders of reality: in other words, they were using a kind of physics that understood the "ground" of reality that "becomes" both matter and mind. Her people might be more deeply aware of the interchanges between different orders of reality: they were using a physics that understood both matter and mind.

The "universal information" in her mental communications came across to my mind as patterns of color and light. I said, "Do you see this the way I do?" Meaning the color-based patterns of information, and the way these lights seemed in my mind. I saw fragments or strings of lights, much like what had been in the "doorway," but paler, and more convoluted and complex.

She replied, "No, I see it much more complexly: that's why I wanted to see how this was going because the ones working there are not yet masters of the art of shipbuilding.

"I'm one of the 'supervisors,' you'd call me, and I'm checking to see how it's going. I see that process that you're seeing as lights differently. I am aware of much more intricacy and many more dimensions. And I don't see colors the way you do. We see them more as 'tones' because we don't have that same kind of brilliant acuity of color that you do."

"Gee," I said, "that's very interesting..." And then I put my foot in my mouth by saying, "I guess you don't miss it [this color vision], or anything?"

She did not seem offended. (This is another one of the advantages of telepathy: mental communication is a protection against the worst effects of foot-in-mouth disease. If no offense is intended, then none is taken.) She said, "Well, no, but that's one of the reasons why I find Humans so delightful. You see things so vividly that way because you're so attuned to really fine gradations of light angstroms. What we would consider…"

At this point, Dr. Field stepped in to caution me that our time was nearly gone for the session. I assured him that she was almost finished, and continued for her:

"What we would consider information, you would consider color. So [the information] is what's being worked into the body of the ship right now, but you read it as color."

I stopped there. Following this session, Dr. Field and I dealt with other concerns for a while, and we didn't continue with this recall for about two weeks.

But as the tale continued, we discovered that this "experience" when I was thirteen ended up being a very full night for me. There were places to go, and beings to see… and I still had to get back home to bed!

[1] I know that a color change in the small beings is also mentioned in Whitley Strieber's book, "Communion," which I had read some months before this hypnotic session. In the semi-consciousness of my light trance, I resisted saying this, even as I remembered her having said it. Surely, I thought, this was my imagination, or some kind of cryptomnesia, where you know something, then forget it, and then remember it again without realizing that it is a memory. At the time, I couldn't accept it as confirmation. I don't recall ever seeing the little black beings again, though, so I can't say I ever saw their color change.

CHAPTER SIX

Age Thirteen Experience, Continued

As Cythromaa was describing the differences in our perceptions of the shipbuilding, I watched her as she looked down into the work area below us. Suddenly she said it was time to go: she had seen what she had needed to see. I asked, "Are we going to go through any strange doorways again?"

She replied, "Well, um…" and then she laughed. She didn't find the doorway strange at all, and she seemed to enjoy the fact that I'd had such trouble with it. To her, the door was as simple as a mechanical can opener would be to us: something she used daily, hardly worth noticing!

"Why was that door so hard for me?" I asked.

She replied, "Well, Humans have gotten out of practice seeing into the dimensions that we generally use."

"How can you see into other dimensions?"

"Well, it does take a kind of a quirk of mind to do that but we're used to it. There are other things that Humans can do that we can't."

"Like what?"

"Well, Humans have studied emotions far more than we have and you have also…" Here her thoughts seemed to stutter to a stop, and she extricated herself lamely, "Well, there's not too much I can say right now. It's… we don't want to interfere. And sometimes Humanity will hide what it is doing from itself so that it can do what it needs to do without getting distracted."

Affected by her sudden caution I suddenly worried about how long it would take. I wasn't worried about school because it was so close to summer vacation, but I didn't want to wander about groggy all the next day from lack of sleep and told her so.

But she did not respond to my anxiety. She seemed abruptly preoccupied with something else, and then said suddenly, "Come on, just one more thing." Which I supposed was kind of an answer.

We continued along the catwalk, with the curved bulkhead at our left, and an open space on our right. But after a moment, we entered a corridor. I was peculiarly enchanted with that corridor. It was just a passageway, another everyday kind of thing, with straight angles and a ceiling tall enough for me to feel comfortable.

Yet there was something about the shape of this particular corridor, or the feel of it, which seemed very pleasant. The walls, ceiling, and floor were all white, but there was an atmospheric shimmer or shine of blue-white light in the air itself. I could hold up my hand, and my hand was not tinged with blue at all. But looking at the walls, there was a definite haze of blue: very strange.

The whole corridor just felt nice. It felt clean, in a way, with a handsome elegance of everything fitting together with everything else excellently well. There was such a sense of beautiful harmony and balance in the place that it felt good just to walk there. The blue light was very pleasant and fine, a pale sky color. The corridor was quite short, and at the end of it was a dark place. "I remember this!" I exclaimed, thinking suddenly of the strange dark place I had been taken through when I was five.

Cythromaa corrected me, "Not exactly, this is a little different." I got the impression that this gray surround we were coming to would move me "faster," somehow, than the other one had. I found it difficult to describe in trance what I understood from her at the time. How could one move more or less "quickly" through non-space?

"But we're going off the ship now," she finished.

"Off the ship! How… how…" I was amazed. But as I stuttered, I understood that this Home Ship somehow had several ways to reach different worlds directly, and she had said earlier that the Home Ships were as much mental constructs as they were "physically real." This was probably part of what that meant.

The Home Ships could be used as reference points for "inter-dimensional transportation." There were exit points at various places in the ship where this kind of "leaping out" was easier, and the white corridor with the blue light seemed to be one of them.

The actual exit was the dark place ahead of us. The corridor seemed to "fog out" into it: there was no sharp line of demarcation between one place and another. But at intervals, along the same level as the corridor floor in this dark gray area ahead, were these bright squares, like white tiles in a dark floor. They were very large, about three feet by three, glowing white.

I asked if I had to jump. "No!" she replied. "Don't you remember? You can get pulled along." She showed me, and it was very strange indeed. I saw her, just for a brief moment, as she suddenly "became" on one of the white squares, and then she was elsewhere! I got pulled along after her, willy-nilly. But at the same time, I received a very strong impression of reassurance. It was almost as though she were holding my hand, even though she was not close to me at all.

"Traveling" in the dark space felt as though there was something solid supporting me even as it pulled me along. I did not feel restrained. It felt very much like sliding down a kind of chute, with a forward movement on tangible support. I hardly noticed when I stepped out of the exit. My feet had just seemed to brush against the white square, and then I was in another place!

"This is neat!" I exclaimed in my trance. "This is so neat!" For a moment, I felt Cythromaa's mind, still guiding me. And then, the darkness changed and became rich golden light: a very warm color, earthy like yellow ochre rather than the flash of pyrite.

As we continued "moving" forward, I began to hear voices, many different voices, and I was delighted. My mind seemed to swim in the golden light, and I heard her thoughts very clearly. "You told me you wanted to see a lot of the different space beings. Well, I wanted to show you this place, and you'll get to see some of the people who are working with Thoyantir."

For a moment I was confused because I'd forgotten who Thoyantir was. But I barely began to ask the question, "Who is that?" when the answer was clear in my mind again, through the telepathic image.

Telepathic communication is so easy! I love it. You can understand so much, so clearly, that you hardly have to work at it. Granted, Cythromaa was a skilled telepath of no mean ability, who'd had practice working with me and with other Human beings. But I reveled in the elegant sureness of this form of communication.

I asked, "Why isn't Thoyantir here?"

"Well, he's still working on something else. And… but he'll see you next year."

I had no objections to this at all: remembering him again, and how much I liked him, I thought that would be fun. I realized that a part of me had never left the "space people." Seeing them again was like seeing old friends, catching up on old stories that we've told each other again and again through time.

I felt Cythromaa's ability to guide me through the "transport:" there was a specific ability needed to do this kind of "travel." It took some concentration. But once you understood the proper method you could just slide right through the transport space, and arrive easily.

We arrived at a place where it looked as though it might just be another part on the far end of the Home Ship, even though Cythromaa said we were going off the ship…

I suddenly realized I was alone. However, she had told me with an impression of intention that she wanted to go somewhere else, and that someone would meet me here, so I wasn't worried.

I stood a moment, rubbing one foot against the other because I was not clear about what I should do next. I suddenly thought of the others who might be here. What would they think, seeing me standing here, dressed in my pajamas? Hilarious! But I was curious to see what was ahead, so I moved forward a little.

The whole place seemed to be made out of gold. Straight ahead of me was a large, round space, with a wall quite some distance from me. There were catwalks here, just as there had been on the ship, going up about three or four levels above the floor. There were lights in the ceilings of the catwalks, and

corridors leading off from them: a surprisingly Human
architecture.

Figure 12

I heard voices, too, though this time, I was hearing them
audibly: they weren't in my mind, although I also sensed a
presence in my mind, as though there was someone aware of me
and how I was doing. So, I did not feel alone, and I did not feel
frightened.

It felt wonderfully alive in this new place with the golden
walls and the catwalk corridors outside the Home Ship. It felt as
living and growing as a forest might: even the air smelled fresh
and alive, with a cool humidity. I stepped forward carefully,
coming to the low railing at the edge, and saw that I was about
one level up from the main floor. It wasn't a great height, no more
than ten feet or so, about a story high.

I looked to my left, and experienced a disorienting visual
effect: the corridor I was standing on seemed to curve away from
me forever towards the left, like one of the infinite reflections in a
pair of mirrors! On the right, the curve was the same, until the
wall slanted, and the catwalk turned with it. Further on, the
catwalk slanted back again, though I couldn't see where it went
from there, just the corner of the railing. The railings here were as
short as the ones on the Home Ship (about 26").

I looked around again and got the impression that there were
many people here, working together on something, though I was

frustrated with my poor vision. I was just beginning to wonder whether or not I should go on and explore as I had on the Home Ship earlier when suddenly Cythromaa stood next to me again. "I've brought someone," she said. I turned to look, and standing there was this amazing being! He was very tall, somewhat over six feet, and had a face very much like a wolf's!

Hearing me compare this being to a wolf, Dr. Field asked me what his skin looked like. I replied that this new being had very dark fur and that he was wearing something like an extra-long vest: two pieces of cloth that hung over his shoulders, joined at the front and the back in a V-shape, but not joined at the sides. His face was fascinating: his eyes were large and milky white. He had a sort of muzzle, and large, pointed ears. It was the ears that made me think of a wolf or a dog, but the rest of the shape of his face wasn't like either a wolf's or a dog's.

Figure 13

As I was thinking all this, I got the very clear impression that he had no objection to being compared to a wolf. He thought they were marvelous animals. I stuttered, "Why… how do you know about wolves?"

He replied, "I've been studying Earth for some time. Cythromaa is one of my colleagues."

All I could manage was, "Oh! Um…" and a hundred questions came to mind, like, "What's your name?" and, "What are you doing here?" and "Why am I meeting you?"

His mental reply was very clear and easy to receive: it was quite delightful. "You couldn't pronounce my name," he said. "You can call me 'Snarly,' if you want."

It didn't suit him. "I don't want to call you 'Snarly,'" I protested, laughing at the notion even while in my trance. "You don't look snarly at all!"

"Well," he replied, teasing, "it would go along with being a 'wolf!'"

"You're not a wolf, but what can I call you?"

He chuckled silently in amusement. "Well, I've done a little work in Russia. I know there's one human word I like, and it's 'samovar.' And I happen to like the name 'Samovar.' If you don't mind calling me 'Samovar,' that will do nicely!"

I giggled. I said, "I can't imagine calling anyone a 'samovar!' What's a samovar?"

"Well, actually it's a kind of a teapot."

"You don't look anything like a teapot!" [Later I remember liking the word 'samovar' too… for no apparent reason.]

Our thoughts were just scintillating delightfully between mind and mind, easily and rapidly. It seemed as though we understood each other deeply at this first meeting, as old friends sometimes will on the first day they meet again after lifetimes apart. During this conversation of mental handshaking, we became friends.

We could communicate, he and I, better than I ever had with anyone else, except perhaps Thoyantir, but that would be a different kind of relationship. It was so much fun! [I found out later from a psychic that I had also met d'Barni, one of the current ET members of The Lodestone Bridge, on one of my other trips. But as D'Barni was still relatively young at the time, he looked quite human, although his face has changed with time, which makes him seem a little more alien now.]

With the easy quickness of our telepathy, asking Samovar his name took perhaps three seconds. I then asked him what he was doing here on Earth, and he replied, "Well, I just told you, you know, I've been working in Russia here a little bit; I do better in the cold than some of the folk here."

"What are you doing here in this place with the golden corridor?"

"Well, this is where some of my work is."

"Well, what's 'here,' anyway?" I asked as my communication with him still proceeding as fast as I could think. "What is this place?"

"Well, you might call it a university. It's kind of 'educational complex,' because all of us here know something already: it's not like we have to learn from the beginning."

I enthused, "This is marvelous!"

"Yes, I know. But we wanted to show you this thing."

I'd seen a lot on this trip already, so I asked, "Why are you showing all this kind of stuff? I mean, it's been wonderful, she's been showing me all these neat things, and I've been seeing all these strange things, and all these weird things have been happening to me…"

"Well, you'll know what to do with it when the time comes."

I couldn't possibly leave it at that! "Okay, when is that?"

Hesitating a little, he said, "Um, we're not going to say. Because we don't want to…"

He stopped, and I felt him suddenly become very reserved, almost withdrawn; his thoughts only implied the rest of the sentence. He did not want to "frame my framework." He did not want to interfere with my free will or my intentions for my own life. It would be up to me to choose, to find the best time to use this information, if ever.

But although he would not tell me when I would use the information, I felt that he knew I would, because he knew me, and he knew the circumstances of my life and the inner intentions I possessed. He had confidence in my judgment.

My inquiry stymied for the moment, I backtracked, "Um, what do you want to show me?"

"Well, will you come with me?"

"Sure, fine!" I agreed, and then looked over at Cythromaa, to see if she was coming too.

She replied, "No, I just wanted to make sure that you met him. I've got other stuff to do right now, but I'll see you off the ship. Do you want to do that?"

"Sure, I don't mind."

So I followed Samovar off to the left. Dr. Field broke in to ask the being's name again, which I told him, and then added, "He wanted to be called 'Samovar' because he liked the sound of the word, not necessarily because of any other reason. He felt it was a very 'Russian' word, and he enjoyed the Russian language, the people, and the whole experience very much."

As I was explaining this in the trance to Dr. Field, I was following along behind Samovar, and wondering whether or not he had a tail. It seemed logical, after all: such a wolfish being! But the vest-like garment he wore hung down behind him as well as in front, coming down to a long point behind, with a kind of embossed metal decoration down near the tip of the point. I suppose it was to keep the garment properly weighted, as it was not joined at the sides.

But I could not help wondering about the tail. His form was very human otherwise, the usual bipedal hominid shape. He had a straight back, though I could not see how his shoulders were, as they were covered by his orange-gold "vest." His legs seemed to work a little differently than Humans' legs. I kept wondering about that possible tail, not sure whether or not he would be offended.

His mental reply took full advantage of my discomfiture. His thought, very dry, admonished me, "What would *I* do with a *tail*?!"

I giggled.

"Do we have to go very far?" I asked in a moment. "I got the impression Cythromaa said I could come back sooner than I left if that makes any sense... or, not quite... oh, you know what I mean!" He did, and I knew he did, despite my confusion. "But, um, I don't want to hang on your hospitality too long. I don't want to bug you guys."

"Well, on the contrary," he replied mildly, "we're bugging you, uh, to use the vernacular. But don't worry about it!"

I couldn't see very much of the corridor ahead of him, because he was very tall and I followed close behind him. His body blocked the view, and the corridor was narrow as well. I looked up and saw lights in the ceiling. They were bright squares, just like in many hallways on Earth. I remarked, "This is the first time I've seen anything that looks like lights around here! That isn't just glowing air!"

He didn't seem to think the lights were even worth commenting on. "Yeah, we just thought we would do that here," he said, in an offhand manner.

I had been following him for some time now. "Where are you taking me?"

"Don't worry, the next few doors down we'll let you in."

I realized suddenly that we'd been passing "doors" in the corridor. They were nothing like human doors, but were more like specific areas where the walls were permeable, certain places where the walls would permit entry and exit: "doorless" doors.

"Okay," I replied to Samovar's last statement, but I was beginning to feel a little overloaded. "God, I've had such a busy night!" I exclaimed. "I've seen so many things, and this is almost too much!"

"Well, don't worry. This won't be much more."

He seemed preoccupied again, as though he was using his mind to work with something else. So I kept following along, wondering what was going on, until he announced with his beautifully clear mental communication, "Here we are!"

He nodded to something in front of us, and I was puzzled. It was not a door. It didn't look like anything at all, just a gray space. But I knew there was a way into it. I suddenly resisted the idea. "Ah, ah, where are we going?"

He didn't want me to delay. "Well, come on!" He reached out with his arm, and I saw then that his hands were not very human. The fingers were very long and narrow, and seemed relatively inseparable, more like the digits of an animal's paw than the fingers of a human hand. They were not paws: I was sure he could use each finger separately. But he gestured out into the gray space in front of us, as though he was theatrically sweeping a curtain aside with one movement and then bowed his head to tell me to go on.

"Well, um after you," I temporized.

"No, we can't do it that way: you have to go with me. Otherwise, you might get lost."

"Lost!? What do you mean, 'lost?!'"

"Lost." He stumbled a bit over the explanation of the way we were about to go through. "This is… you know, the way one's mind is, is what one finds. When you're linked with me, you can go where I can take you. But when you're by yourself, we're not sure what could happen. We don't want to take a chance on it. You would have a hard time getting back to your planet, and getting back to your body."

This suggests that I was, or would be, experiencing out-of-body travel at this point. I understood from Samovar that if I went on my own into this next space, I'd leave my body behind, and then they'd have a fine time trying to find me to "put me back." But if Samovar took me though, then I would be safe.

So we both went through… I paused a long time in the hypnotic trance before I went on to describe what was happening. Going through the "door" felt like swimming, like being in the water. And the area within the "doorway" seemed suddenly immense. I felt like a microbe, floating in the sea of a drop, something floating in a great ocean, an unbounded place between where we were and where we were going.

I asked, "What is this place?"

Samovar answered, "Well, you have to go a little further."

"Okay," I managed. "Are you still there? I can't see anything! It's kind of gray and green in here!"

"Take my hand," he replied. I did. I remember: it's almost as though my flesh remembers how that hand felt. I could feel the bones of his fingers. They were very pronounced, as though he didn't have a palm, or that part of his hand was very hard and narrow. The long, closely parallel bones of his fingers seemed to go down clear to his wrist. This was truly fascinating.

I also very clearly recall that he held my hand from underneath the outer edge. He did not slip his hand in between my thumb and forefinger as my palm faced inward to my body but from the side of my little finger. It seemed an unusual way to take another's hand. Samovar was not human but I felt more secure and comforted at his touch. His strange touch was an anchor in this oceanic space.

"Where are we going?" I asked, still seeing nothing but the gray-green space.

"We wanted to try this," he replied. "We don't know if it'll work, but don't worry, nothing bad will happen because I'm right here with you. And we just wanted to see how well this transport worked."

I complained. "What do you mean, 'transport!?' I've been through so many transports around here… "

I got the impression that he was thinking, not directly to my mind, but still "loud" enough for me to hear, "Don't worry, quit complaining: it's all right!" Then he added, "You'll like it."

We took another step forward and then, I was standing on solid ground! I was standing on the earth. I could feel it with my feet! There was grass under my feet, except that it looked nothing like grass at all. I bent down to look at it, and each blade was very thin and pale, almost white. I have seen long, furry molds that look like that, except that this "grass" was not mold.

I looked up, and the sky was incredible. There was more than one color in it! Our sky on Earth is just blue, blue from end to end. But this sky was made up of dark blue, purple, and turquoise, all blended into one another like the shades of color in a sunset. It was darkest straight overhead, and lighter towards the horizons, but no one single color. I just had to stare at it, because it was so beautiful!

The quality of light was different here, too. I looked over at Samovar. He didn't seem to be doing anything special, but I noticed for the first time how strange his mouth and nose were. They weren't like a tapir's snout, or a dog's muzzle, but seemed to be a little of both, and yet like nothing else I had ever seen before. I got the impression that he had no lips, no edges to his mouth to smile with. It seemed very odd!

I saw some of the colors from the sky in his pale eyes, and the "vest" that he was wearing picked up some of the sky's light too. I looked away from him and saw that there was a group of buildings or a small city in front of us.

Or was that what I was seeing? There seemed to be something very much like low stone walls in front of us. I felt a wind blowing, and then saw colored banners, or something, flapping in the moving air. I could feel the wind: it was cold! I was astonished at what I saw. "How did we, where did… how did we do this?" I stammered. "Where are we?"

Samovar replied, "I'm very glad: it worked perfectly fine. It…" again, he stopped, but I got the impression of his continued thought: "Now it is apparent that humans can manage to go through this transport to get to other planets." This was important to them because this kind of transport did not only involve movement through space but mental transference as well.

I was still amazed. I just stood there staring, not moving from the spot where I'd arrived. The buildings did look as though they were made up of well-dressed stone, left naturally unpolished. There was one large, white banner-like thing fluttering and flapping in the breeze from the top of one of the buildings right in front of us. Behind the buildings were tall things that looked very much like trees, but they were a brilliant lemon yellow.

Over to our left were streaks of clouds in the sky, white clouds, which looked like cirrus. Near the one very large wall or building directly in front of us was a road of some kind. I knew were right on the very outskirts of this place, on the edge of the city in front of us.

Figure 14

I soaked it all in, thinking, "*Wow!*" I looked down and saw the earth again, a russet and yellow ochre mix of colors at the root level of the "grass," real and alive. It was so wonderful, but at the same time, it felt very strange. Because I suddenly knew this was alien. This was not Earth: this was an alien world: a real place.

Then Samovar said, "Look at me." I did. He had to bend down a bit to look into my eyes. Somehow when he focused on me, I became unusually aware again of the point between my eyebrows, where the "tracer" was. "Go to sleep, now," Samovar commanded.

"What do you mean 'Go to sleep?' We just got here!"

"Go to sleep now," he repeated, then explained, "It's easier, on the transport back, to take you if you're disengaged from your body just a little." [Disengaged? Did they take my mind and my body, to this other world? Or was it just my mind?]

"Aw, come on!"

He said firmly, "No. This is important. We don't want to lose you. I risked… I believed that this would work and I'm very pleased that it has, but right now you have to go to sleep."

You can imagine my toe digging dejectedly into the alien earth. "Oh, pooh," I muttered.

He brought his hands down in front of my eyes, and they closed on their own. But because of his continued mental contact, I could still see his face clearly in my mind. I could still see his eyes, looking into mine. He said, "Yes, that's correct; just allow me to bring you back. It's easiest if we do it this way."

I woke up a moment later, and it seemed that no time had passed. But I knew that something had happened. It must have, because now I was standing on the edge of the "airlock" of the original ship, back on Earth and ready to go home again! This was not the Home Ship, but the original "scout ship," the "have to duck your head to enter" traveling saucer.

Cythromaa was there, and she was laughing. "Well, what did you think of Samovar?" she asked through her mirth.

I replied indignantly, "Did he play a trick on me?"

Still laughing, she replied: "No, no, no, no: but he does like to give surprises!"

"Well, I don't know what I think of this surprise!"

Finished with her laugh, Cythromaa said, "Listen: we have to go, and you have to go, and we will see you again. And don't worry. We'll see you again. If nothing else you'll see us in your dreams, but we will also see you again soon, and many times afterward. But when you…"

She paused, but I got the impression that the only time I'd see her for quite a long while would be when I was asleep. This would have something to do with my "tuning," my attunement with them. My various experiences were only one part of a greater, inner work with them, carried on mostly in my deeper mind.

I got the impression that I should not expect to see a UFO while I was standing around awake for quite a while. They wanted to continue to work primarily with my unconscious, in the deeper levels of my being.

I was disappointed to hear I would not be able to remember them. How could I know if any of this was real if I never saw it consciously? She insisted, "It's okay, you can go home now."

"Okay," I replied. "Where's the rest of my family, by the way?"

"Your mom and dad are asleep, and your sister's gone back to bed; she didn't want to spend much time with us."

"You mean she goes on the ship, too?"

"Yes, but that's not her work."

I said, "Okay," again, and then wished her goodbye. I stepped back away from the little ship. I could see her in the doorway, and although she wasn't waving, I knew she was saying goodbye too.

I went down the hill towards my house and then went in the front door. It was unlocked, as always. High on the hill as we were, we were rarely bothered by anyone. I yawned, stumbled my way back into my house, and thankfully went back to bed.

Once again, I remembered nothing of the experience in my conscious mind, and would not until I was fourteen, and asked to remember, when I saw Thoyantir again.

CHAPTER SEVEN

Non-Physical Experience:
Age Fourteen (1968)

This experience occurred in the middle of July 1968. My school had been out for at least a month, and summer vacation had sunk deeply into the days. When I was fourteen I often went off to be by myself one afternoon, going to sit down under the trees on the wooded Marin County hillside very near where I lived. One of my favorite walks was to go down west of our house past the neighbors, following deer trails to a fire road and then into a wide canyon with a gully fed by the winter rains.

Although surrounded by houses in the area, the land was wild, with scrub oaks, laurels, the occasional madrone, and poison oak. Because of the trees, the streambed was hidden from the few houses on the opposite hill. Since California is dry in the summer, there wasn't much water in the creek. The moss on my favorite rock was drying up but was still lush enough to be comfortable as I sat on it, looking downstream and watched the trees move in the gentle wind.

It felt like Saturday: in summer vacation, every day is Saturday. Maybe it was a Friday, but it didn't matter. The woods had their own time. I would say it was about two o'clock in the afternoon. There were trees all around me. They were thinner and less dense on the hill to my right, which was dryer. But this was my place and I was happy to be alone.

However, this new experience began when the hillside on the other side of the creek opened up! All at once a hole like the entrance into a tunnel was there, small and dark. A gangplank of some kind extended out from it horizontally. Standing on it were two of the pale, small, round-headed beings, dressed in blue.

Their skin seemed a darker gray than I had remembered it being, though I had no idea why. They seemed very intent, moving as though they didn't want to waste any time. Watching them, I felt dreamy and dissociated and felt no fear at all. It was like watching two television programs at once: one reality on one screen, another reality on the other, only I was in both.

One of the beings was standing a little further out on the gangplank. He asked me to come and I did. There was no sense of movement. I don't believe I ever "left" where I was physically. But by responding to his call I was standing there next to him all at once. I did not completely understand what was happening, but they wasted no time. I was to follow them: that was all. I was too relaxed to feel annoyed. I even remembered that some of these beings liked to talk with me. But these two seemed too preoccupied.

We went into the hillside, into a tunnel made up of segments of darkness and light. Each area of light seemed to be some other reality. This was like several other "transport corridors" in the earlier experiences. Each area of light seemed to be a doorway, an impossible step from one reality into another. But the corridor still felt safe. We walked normally. I had no fear of falling into any darkness.

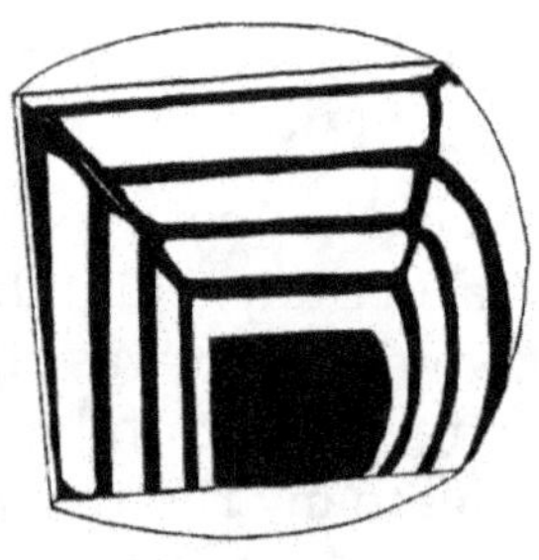

Figure 15

One of the small beings walked in front of me, the other behind me and we flickered through the light and darkness in perfect calm. In the areas of light, several bright, enticing "secondary doorways" stood closed. There were so many doorways!

Suddenly I was in a small room. Because it had a curved ceiling it was likely on one of the "space"-ships, although I knew somehow they hadn't come through the atmosphere to get me: I felt certain that some of the ships or carriers didn't travel in or through space to get where they were going. Rather, it was as though they could materialize instantaneously at various propitious "nodes" in space-time.

From the small alien's mind, I could see that there was a latticework, a "net," throughout the whole universe. I understood this corridor was a transport linked with the "net" that interwove our universe of space/time. The links of the "net" were outside of Time. This "network" provided roads between an infinite number of places and nearly infinite times. If you knew how the lattice was "built" (though this structure had not been manufactured: it was part of the nature of space itself) and understood the structure of the "net," you could travel within it, and space, almost anywhere.

I felt that this particular "ship" had somehow insinuated itself into one of the hillsides near the stream, though for some reason it could not stay there long. However, even though it was shaped in one of the conventional saucer-like forms, it wasn't a UFO in the usual sense. Rather, it was more like a "movable place." Perhaps the saucer shape was simply the most convenient one for some reason.

When the session with Dr. Field began, I began describing the experience from the middle again. This session seemed to involve a great deal of "implied" information. There were many things I knew without knowing how I knew them. The doctor and I soon understood very clearly that this was not a physical abduction, unlike the somewhat confusing one of the previous year that seemed to contain both physical and non-physical aspects.

I tried to pick up the narrative from a clearly remembered image: there were three people there in this "ship." One was Cythromaa, from the experience before when she and I had gotten to be such good friends. Seeing her again, I described her as a darling, darling person, full of life and a kind of cool wisdom.

I remember working out how to spell Cythromaa's name one afternoon at home, even though I didn't quite remember who this person was, except that she was beautiful and wise, though also strange. She seemed to be someone I knew, although she was *not* someone I made up. I began writing in earnest when I was fourteen (see below), and I could *tell* the difference between memory and imagination: remembering something is not at all like making something up.

There was a very tall being with her, though I could not make out his form well at all: his body seemed to be made from planes of light, as though someone had taken a variety of pieces of clear, colored glass, then layered or strung them together somehow into a roughly human shape. He seemed to shimmer when he moved and I had the peculiar impression that he was somehow in more than one reality at one time! He didn't look very human; there was hardly a suggestion of a face on his head, and he reflected light as he moved.

The third person looked completely human, but I knew she was not. Her body was very close to our human norm but she represented some type of parallel humanity. I understood that each sentient form and each planet had its specific lessons and that the universe was so vast that duplicated forms were possible. Surely, the human form's lessons were worthwhile to many and I felt that this woman's "humankind" had arrived at its shape and state of being through methods different than ours.

She certainly looked human enough, and I supposed that if one were to put her down here on Earth to get medical tests, she would test out pretty normally. But she was not a person born on or from Earth. She had reddish brown hair, a pleasant chestnut color. Her eyes were a striking, dark blue. I felt that she was also extremely intelligent. I liked being with her.

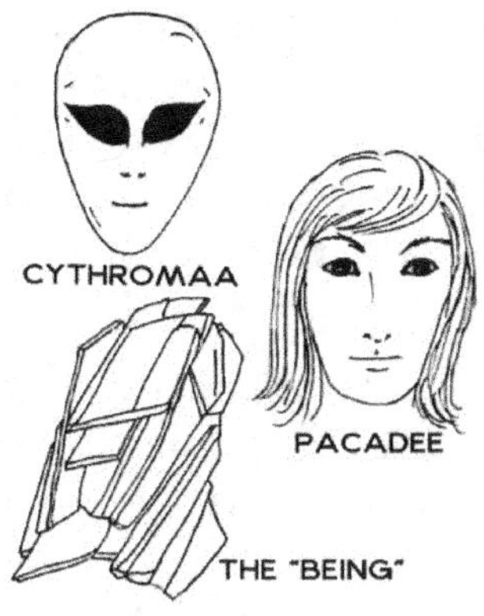

Figure 16

The three of them were showing me something I had seen years before, though I did not remember it then. They were standing around a circular area of the floor that had been sunk about a foot below the main level, creating a large, pit-like area with a wide, simple railing around it. The "human" could rest her elbows on it easily, the being whose form shimmered didn't seem to want to try, and Cythromaa was hard-pressed to look over the top of it into the pit. Behind the railing, near where they stood, was some kind of narrow console. Cythromaa got hidden behind this sometimes.

I couldn't quite understand what they were showing me; it was something in the center of the pit. Then when the "human" woman talked to me it seemed as though she spoke in a language that used sounds my ears could not quite make out. Another phoneme set, perhaps, that used different sound qualities for words.

Nevertheless, I could understand her meaning well enough, probably through telepathy. She said that I could call her Pacadee, pronounced much like "chickadee," even though that was not quite correct. She told me [possibly with help from Cythromaa], "Well, what's happening there in the center is that this is how we assess what's going on with Earth. So we have a lot of channels of information being put into this."

The thing in the center of the pit, raised about three feet from the level of the floor, was a bit like a hologram., though of course in 1968 I had no idea what a hologram was. The closest metaphor my mind could make of it then was a world globe that might be covered by other, concentric globes made out of clear plastic, perhaps with weather systems or the constellations painted on the outer layers, with a world globe in which you could see the constellations, countries, and oceans over the globe beneath them at the same time.

This thing in the center of the lowered circle of floor had layers like that: it looked like a spherical map, written on the air; at the same time, there were images of various points on the planet. And there was something else surrounding the "globe." It looked like fog to me, but somehow I was sure they could read information from it.

Figure 17

They told me that some of the information was actually in the fourth physical dimension (like a tesseract) and that they'd trained themselves to see this dimension. So a lot of what I saw seemed confusing and senseless to me because I could not see into the extra dimension that would have made it more comprehensible.

Perceiving my puzzlement, they said, "Don't worry about it!" so, as usual, I didn't. After all, I liked these three beings. It was good to be near them and I felt at home with them: they were quite delightful and I felt they cared about me. I was also certain that they were never going to hurt me just to hurt me, as too many human people in my life had done.

However, they were showing me this "information globe" to reassure me that they had sources of information that we did not and hence they had a more complete and accurate picture of what was going on in the world. This did not automatically make them better than human beings, but they had a broader view of the forces and patterns affecting the world.

So much was happening right now and in the future that would seem to be wrong in the short view that would create much good in the long view. It was in this experience that I developed the utter conviction that we would NOT blow the world up with atomic bombs: it just wasn't going to happen! I retain that conviction to this day.

It was as though they were giving me a prediction that much in the world that seemed to be going very badly would work out for the best in the end, even though there would be great difficulties sometimes. They reassured me that even though sometimes I wouldn't feel as though I knew what I was doing with my own life, or as though I wasn't doing what I needed to do, it would be all right. Even with my weaknesses, frailties, or those times when I would make mistakes or do poorly would somehow add up to better. (Considering my negative adolescent perceptions of myself this was truly welcome encouragement.)

Certainly, the layered "information globes" were fascinating and wonderful to watch: I joined the three beings studying this display companionably for a long while. At times, it seemed as though tiny points in the moving surface could contain galaxies of data: I felt that I could almost catch glimpses of that fourth dimension they had mentioned.

I suddenly asked, "Why am I here?"

"Well, we wanted to show you this, and remind you, because there may be a time when you'll need this information." One of them continued, "I know it'll help you right now, even though not too much of this experience will become conscious."

The information in the "globes" was so complex, so comprehensive, that there seemed to be too much of it. But by watching it, I could have understood how things worked at a very deep level: how things remained "in tune" and how they were put together. This didn't make much logical sense. Yet I knew I could have understood how one blade of grass grows as only that particular blade of grass and no other, how things worked on a very fundamental, causal level.

I felt then that part of the reason why I'd been born was to learn from them as they would learn through me. Yet, although they were learning from my learning and seeing from my seeing, I was not learning *for* them; they had never forced me, not in anything. It was as though what I experienced in my life was a part of that very information that they read from those incredible, concentric "globes!"

Paranoia might call me their spy, but I was certain they had no intention of harming anyone or stealing information. They wouldn't need to steal anything, anyway: they could get what they needed through the information in the "globe." They understood how things were put together at such a deep level that they didn't need to pry out "state secrets" from anybody because they knew something better than those secrets: they knew how the universe *worked*.

They laughed: they must have caught my image of a spy and thought it quite humorous that we Human beings were so anxious about our secrets, especially when what was going on was something much deeper than what we thought was going on. I got an image of a little kid putting a paper bag over his head with eyeholes in it so he could "see everything" and then say confidently, "Well, no one else can see *me* now!"

Needless to say, the paper bag over his head would make such a child more visible, not less. I never got the impression that they wanted to do anything about or with our "secrets," even if they were able to discover them. That kind of stuff just didn't seem to concern them.

As I heard their mental laughter I felt how much I enjoyed these beings, even the strange ones, very much: there was such beauty in them. When I was away from them, something in me missed this beauty tremendously. When I was with them I could be certain that kindness and gentleness truly were the nature of things, and that no one had to hit and hate and hurt. You didn't have to be afraid and hurt others from fear or make someone else afraid. Fear was not the way their universe worked!

Even as I received these impressions from them, I kept watching the globe spinning around and marveled at the amount of light that came from it. I also felt that the globe was sentient as well. It wasn't a "person" and wasn't "alive," yet it was not simply an object. It might even be a manifestation of their living intelligence so that it *was* alive, in a strange way.

Reacting to a question from Dr. Field, I remembered asking them about fear. They replied, "Well, fear is one of the things we've tried hardest to understand. We can understand some kinds of fear. When an animal is being attacked and needs to run: that fear we can understand.

"But the fear that generates anger we don't understand, though we're learning. We're just beginning to understand and this is something completely new, a fascinating lesson that God has put before us! But that you can attack out of fear seems very strange to us and we're still trying to understand. That's why we have the human representatives."

(Yes, they used the word "God" here. After all, to talk with me they had to use the contents and concepts of my mind. My experience with Cythromaa's mind when I was thirteen, however, suggests that their concept of a "Divine Being" is very different from ours, if indeed they have a notion of a separate "Being" at all. I believe that for them, there is only *being*, a constant awareness of what *is*. I feel that this contains the immanent and the transcendent: both the all-pervasiveness of consciousness and the utter uniqueness of each, all, and the *All*.)

I understood there were a number of these "human representatives," on Earth now: people like myself who had been linked with them in some deep way, perhaps acting as ambassadors or emissaries. Through us, the "star people" were trying to understand what it was to be human. For them, Earth was a unique form of existence. Other planets in the universe had a similar vibratory level to Earth's but many more didn't. To these beings speaking with me, the universe seemed to be levels of realities made up of different vibrations, rather than physical planets.

For them, everything in the universe was a matter of "tuning to pitch." Once you knew how to tune to one specific pitch, you could go anywhere and "any*when*" in the universe you chose. Once you learned how to tune properly, space and time were never difficult. Indeed, the star-beings laughed when I called them "space people." They joked, "Well, there isn't any 'space!' How can you call us '*space* people?'"

Without being prompted by Dr. Field, I suddenly remembered being in another place in this experience where everything was white and indistinct; there didn't seem to be much to see. But when we entered this new place, one of them got on one side of me and the other got on the other side, and then we went through a final door. And then the beings that had led me here had disappeared.

Yet I was not alone. Thoyantir, "the big guy," was there. I understood that he'd always kept what he called a "thread-connect," a tie of the mind, to mine. I knew that sometimes the tie would run deeper at various times in my life, and I would feel Thoyantir interlock or "inter-phase" with me. At times I'd be conscious of him specifically, and at other times I would be aware of "star people" through the point between my eyebrows where they'd put the "tracer."

It was very good to see him. I felt safe and happy with him, as though I did not need to worry or be afraid. His love was that of a known friend. However separate in our bodies, our minds were close enough to touch each other and I felt no threat whatsoever. His presence in my mind was so distinct and strong that I hardly noticed his physical presence, even though it was certainly imposing. A tall, long-limbed being with gray fur, large round eyes like a lemur, and "teeth" reminiscent of a saber-toothed cat's would be hard to ignore… unless you're not afraid of him.

When he led me away from this white area earlier, Thoyantir had taken me to his little ship where it was parked. He said, "You can sit there on the passenger side. This is unusual; I usually take the ship by myself. But I can ask the ship to take other shapes if I need it to because there are some planets where certain shapes are needed and other shapes are not needed. So I asked it to give you a seat."

I was surprised, and exclaimed, "You mean, you can talk to your ship?"

He said, "Yes, certainly: it's no trouble. Just get in." So I did: it was a nice, comfortable seat. It was fun! Even though the ship was not alive the way a plant is, I could feel the ship being aware of me and I had the feeling that it welcomed me.

"We'll be taking a very quick trip here. But don't worry if anything strange happens, because we're going to be flipping through different dimensions. You may want to shut your eyes."

I did. There was no real sense of movement, only a little tremor, and then somehow I knew we were out in the middle of space. The space around us was so big and at the same time, I felt as though I could hold all of it in my hand: a huge space that could be contained.

Curious, I opened my eyes. In the hypnotic trance, I found it difficult to explain what I was seeing. It was as though there were areas of white and black, but the contrast was extreme. That white made our "whites" look like grays, and our blacks like darker grays. There seemed to be shapes. There was a white arc against the darkness, like a curving road… but after only a little while I had to close my eyes again.

I said, "Just let me know when I can open them, please."

He said, "Sure: that will be fine." His legs were bent so that his knees were up to his shoulders as he leaned forward to work, very intent on what he was doing. Yet he was not operating a control panel: my side was the one who had a control panel. It was as though the ship itself was being humorous with me, conforming to my idea of a spaceship. I didn't see very much, because I mostly had my eyes closed. But his side of the ship was noticeably different than mine. His side seemed more amorphous, or "fuzzy." Was it different dimensions again?

When I looked, the view out of his ship's forward "windows" was so strange, big, and wonderful! It was full of colors that had sound and other things I simply could not describe. I got such an incredible sense of beauty and integrity from the images that I *could* understand: everything seemed to know its place in the universe and how it related to other things. It was like a dance where everyone knew the movements.

We arrived at another ship. He said, "You've been here before. This is one of the Mother Ships."

I said, "Oh! I guess I have, haven't I? That was that other time when I was a kid?"

"Yeah."

"This place is very big, isn't it? I've had dreams of it."

He said delightedly, "Ah! You've remembered it! We've taken you here in different states of consciousness."

I asked him, "Well, I'm not conscious now, am I?"

He replied, "Well you are, and you are." I couldn't understand what he meant. It seemed as though I was not unconscious but conscious, and yet it was still an altered state of some kind.

Although I didn't remember how he did it, Thoyantir took me to another place: we suddenly stood at the edge of a vast, well-lit room. I could only guess at the size. Was it a fifty-foot ceiling? It reminded me of the inside of an airline terminal. There were several small groups of people, beings, here and there in the huge, echoing space. There were also several tables, counters, or consoles of some kind, reminding me of the information booths at an airline terminal.

Shortly after this, I met with the three people I described at the beginning. I believe Thoyantir and I went to another room to meet with the three because I had no memory of any other beings near them, as might have been if we'd still been in the "airline terminal." But shortly after we were in that large space we came to be where Cythromaa, Pacadee, and the being that seemed to be made of shimmering planes of light. As before, they were standing behind the lowered, circular area of floor with the "information globe" spinning in it.

As I remembered earlier, Cythromaa was dressed in a gold suit this time; when she saw us she made a gentle smile and said hello. We were close enough for me to see that her eyes revealed what she was. Was this enhanced perception because Thoyantir was with me?

I got very few impressions of any kind from the third being that looked as though he had been made of glass, other than this impression of "maleness." His body's colors were mostly light blues, whites, deeper blues, blacks, and perhaps some colors beyond my visual range. The other two did not explain his presence, and he never spoke with me directly.

"Hey, it's good to see you guys," I said cheerfully.

I received a mental impression of multiple replies, all meaning something like, "Yeah, it's good to see you, too."

Then Cythromaa herself finished, "I'm glad you could come."

I asked, "Why am I here?"

"Well, we wanted to show you this," they replied.

I looked at the spinning thing between us. "What is it?"

"It's how we understand how the world is going," Cythromaa explained. "We wanted to show it to you because we know that you will understand it, that the world is going very well, and that things are developing better than we'd hoped."

As she spoke, I got the impression once again that Cythromaa found human beings quite fascinating and impressive because we'd been given challenges that almost no other race had. Things are happening so badly in our world so often because, when you are carrying a great weight any slight misstep can mean disaster. Yet if you can carry it successfully and reach your destination, it is something excellent.

But when I had seen what they wanted to show me and learned what I could, I turned back to Thoyantir. His face was very beautiful. His eyes reflected the light around them with large, clear corneas, much like a cat's.

His body always seemed more than a little odd, though. There was something about the angles of his arms and legs or the smallness of his body to the length of his limbs that startled me. Perhaps it was because he felt so human to me and seemed so human in my mind that his alien body could be something of a shock. Sometimes it seemed almost difficult to look at him, except for his face.

But just then I had something of a bone to pick with him. I was tired of forgetting my experiences. I complained, "Well, you know, I've been working with you guys a lot, haven't I?"

He didn't smile a human smile, but I knew he was amused. "Yes."

"Well, what is all this about?"

His reply was very calm. "Well, we mean for you to work with me."

"Well, can't I remember something of this? Can't I bring anything back? Because we've been doing this for ages! And I'm fourteen for goodness' sake! Why this delay?"

Unperturbed by my complaints, he said, "Well we'll do what we can. Here, I'll show you something." We suddenly seemed to be transported somewhere again. But although I felt a brief moment of disorientation, my link with his mind made the process relatively effortless.

Now away from the room with the "information globe," we'd gone to an even smaller room, very bright and cozy, but with the same, peculiar lack of edges, many of their rooms had. I only *felt* the walls: I didn't see them. However, we both sat down, companionably close.

"I want to show you this," he said. It was a book. Of course, what he held in his hands looked almost nothing like a book, but I understood when I saw it that its purpose was the same. It was small: he could hold it easily in his hands and it had writing in it. He said, "This is my planet and my people as they used to be, long centuries ago. Let's see if your human mind can retain this kind of information."

I looked and realized that somehow the writing itself was telepathic! I didn't see letters or words or even pictures in the book, yet somehow when I looked at the book, it communicated to me whole, deep images: complete ideas, like the supercharged thoughts of inspiration or dreams.

One single "word" of this book about a planet or its people was enough to provide a kind of mental gateway into the whole depths of the subject being described. You could perceive everything about an area, from the types of rocks and plants, to what the people were doing there and why. These days, you might call this "telepathic hypertext."

The information in Thoyantir's book was very condensed, "stacked up" on itself six, ten, perhaps twelve layers deep. There were meanings under meanings, with images under images. And yet its telepathic structure allowed a depth of comprehension beyond anything but imagination or inspiration, where full comprehension can be almost instantaneous.

As I studied his book I realized that he was using this as a method of teaching me his language, or at least *a* language. But more than that, by being aware of my perceptions he was trying to see whether or not I could encompass an entirely different way of "framing" reality.

(That is what languages are: structured points of view and ways of thinking. If you don't have a word for a thing, a concept for it, it's difficult to even *see* it, so that something outside of your framework of expectations (your language) can remain completely invisible. Conversely, once something has been labeled, it takes a special effort of will to see the thing as though for the first time, with an unprejudiced view.)

It was clear that Thoyantir was trying to see if my mind and brain could assimilate this type of multiply encoded information. It was a very positive experience: the richly layered images were incredible and very beautiful to me. There was so much living knowledge in the book that my mind nearly blanked into one large astonished "Wow!"

I suddenly wondered whether or not this was just a primer or something. If this were the easy stuff, how would it be when it got harder? But Thoyantir reassured me, "Don't worry about it: you're doing very well indeed! It seems that my overlaying my mind with yours has been of real assistance."

So his experiment was a success. I understood from his thoughts that this had also been an inquiry into how far the human mind and psyche could reach. He felt that dealing with multiple levels of perceptions could be Humanity's greatest skill if we wished it. I felt my mind getting awakened at deeper levels, as though it were stretching into something it hadn't realized it could.

However, at the time my reaction was entirely unambiguous. "Hey, that's neat!" I cried. "I feel so good."

Thoyantir replied, "I'm glad you do. This is some of what we'd hoped for."

When he said this I could see that he and I worked in dreams a great deal. But I wondered why I couldn't see a little more when I was conscious (such as UFOs in the sky). "Well," he said,

"We can have… I'll make you see a little more when you're conscious. Dreaming this information won't hurt you.

"However, we still need a little gap between what is experienced at a deeper level and what is experienced on the conscious level. Too much too soon could put too much power through the undeveloped brain cells." (Remember, this is in 1968 when I was only fourteen.)

I grumbled to myself, "Gee, my brain cells aren't that flaky!"

I had a feeling of humor and encouragement from him. And then he said: "I want you to help me with something."

I was surprised. "How can I help you? It seems funny that you need my help."

He replied a little hesitantly. "Well, there are many of us here [on Earth]: many of us from many different places and different realities and layers of realities: some from the past, some from the future, and many from the present. Some are very alien and some not so alien. We are learning from you and others like you [the other "representatives"] how to inter-communicate with Planet Earth."

He continued, "This is a fascinating source of study for us because we can learn so much from what you learn and from what you know. But there are those… who want to harm us."

Thinking of those who harmed others was difficult for him: it was very hard for him to talk about them. It wasn't that he was afraid of them or the subject, or that he hated them. His diffidence seemed to be because he desired to give no mental energy in this direction, so as not to give the harm or the ones who harmed mental "weight" by thinking of them more than necessary.

He repeated, "There are those who want to harm others. And some of them have attuned themselves to certain lower vibrations in the Earth: lower in pitch, not necessarily negative, do you understand?"

I did. As I described earlier, it seemed that he also perceived planets to be "areas of combined frequencies" rather than physical places. Our planet was working at a certain "pitch," and there were certain harmful beings that could come closer to our vibratory level.

Yet at the same time, there was some kind of instinctive, protective ability within my mind that he and I could take a moment to invoke and reinforce. He could also use this protection for himself as well, but first, he needed my permission for his telepathic action. He did not want to simply take what he wanted from me without respect. So, he asked for my consent.

My agreement was hardly given but the change was done. I felt no different, mentally. But I somehow knew that the consequences of our actions were very far-reaching. At least, because of this shift, his mental link with me became deeper and stronger, and yet at the same time he disengaged some of his very close watch on me. I was no longer a child: I could handle my mind with more maturity.

He told me then that it was time to return. "Trust in what you remember," he assured me, "because your mind will protect itself from knowing too much too soon. Trust in your creativity because that's partly what we (the "star people") use. Trust in what I give you because I mean no harm and I give it to you without harm.

"And trust in my love, because we have known each other before, and we will know each other again, and we know each other now. And because we know each other now, we will know each other again and have known each other before." He meant that there could be "connective" moments that can affect both the past and the future simultaneously.

But I wasn't in any hurry to leave. "Can you show me anything else? Can you show me anything of your world?"

"Well, I showed you that in the book."

"I mean now. Where are we now?"

He replied, "Well we're in the..." and he used a strange name, something like "conjunction point," or "confluence point." I understood that where we were was a function of the "net," the interconnecting links between realities. This was the center: all the "points" of the "net" met "here."

He said that this place had been called Star Seeso [As in The Andreasson Affair, by Raymond E. Fowler.] And yet, Star Seeso was not a place, exactly: it was as much a state of mind as much as a place because it was everywhere and nowhere at the same time: it was the center. You couldn't reach this "place" by traveling through space at all.

I asked him again if I could look in other places here if I could see some other things. He cautioned me, "Well, if you looked now, in the receptive mental state you're in, you would see almost whatever you wanted to see, rather than what I and my fellows would see. Do you understand?

"Human minds are very agile, and they would see many things. And sometimes humans fear us because they see their fear. We do not mean to cause them to be afraid. But because their minds are so agile and fluid they see their fear instead of what we wish to share."

It was difficult to end the hypnotic session with any clear finality. Remembering the state I had been in when I was with Thoyantir tended to re-engage me in that state and it was hard to juxtapose the differing realities. I suddenly felt these altered states were altered *realities*.

We're so used to the notion of an objective reality that is discrete and separable from our perceptions that we're not used to thinking this way. But right then, it was clear to me that a subjective change of mind was also a change in "objective" reality itself.

I felt suddenly that I'd had a very full day, and closed the session. We had intended to do more, but although we did one more session, it did not record properly. But I had the main story at last.

Some months later, true to Thoyantir's promise, I remembered some of this book. The opportunity to recall this memory of the book came about because of an assignment for a World History class in my first year of high school.

That year, I had a truly delightful teacher. She'd arranged the classroom with tables in a circle, two chairs to a table, to facilitate discussion. She started our year by giving us the basics of anthropology, an overview of the scientific method, a short study in ecology, hands-on experience with chipping arrowheads (not easy!), and a variety of other fascinating projects.

One project was to invent an animal and its ecological niche, and back up its existence with soundly based "scientific research" invented for the purpose. The other project was to invent two countries that were having a war of some kind, and to describe the reasons, causes, costs, and potential outcomes of this war.

(She was one of the best teachers I'd ever had. Of course, somewhere around the middle of the year she suddenly realized that we hadn't covered Asia, Africa, Australia, or either of the Americas, India, China, Russia, or the rest of Europe... So she quickly invented several three-week crash programs covering each major landmass, resulting in a somewhat more "normal" curriculum...)

But the information from Thoyantir's "book" found its way out into my daily consciousness in two ways. First, I'd started evolving my own "alphabet." Not for any particular purpose, but just because I knew that such a thing existed, somehow. The second way this hidden information revealed itself was in response to the World History project about the two countries that were supposed to be at war.

My response to the assignment was to invent a whole planet! Some of the details were inspired by a dream with a wonderfully clear image of two beings standing on a rocky plain: they were carrying implements that looked like hunting weapons. One of the beings was pointing at a campfire. [Figure 18]

Remembering the dream, I peopled my invented planet with beings that looked a lot like otters with saber teeth. I evolved their customs, language, culture, sub-races (the furry ones were in the North), continents, and even poetry. But it was poetry in another language, an "invented" language I didn't understand, even though I knew it meant something.

Figure 18

My World History teacher took this wild response to her assignment with great aplomb: she had me show my drawings on the overhead projector, and even read some of the poetry aloud to class! Needless to say, we all thought this planet-stuff was my imagination, however privately convinced I was that it was somehow "real." Sometimes I thought it'd better be my imagination. If it were real then for sure I was crazy! But I knew it was real, too.

The telepathic protection Thoyantir created for us together was another one of the incidents I remembered later. It was also shrouded in the images of a later dream, as the memory from the book had been. In the dream, a space person had crash-landed on Earth, in his small ship. He had been trying to escape from another being that intended to murder him. The space-being that was trying to escape searched with his mind; when he found me he asked for my assistance. Hearing his call, I found where he was, and helped him heal so he got away safely

This dream was an absurd, romantic bit of nonsense to be sure, though of course it mattered to me at the time. But I had reason to be proud of it. I turned the dream into a short story, all of a single-spaced typewritten page long. It was the very first story I'd ever finished. So, I owe the "star people" early encouragement to become a writer.

However, I remembered very little else because, when I turned sixteen, our mother died, quite suddenly, of a cerebral hemorrhage. There was virtually no warning: she woke up one morning and was dead that same morning. We were all unprepared and deeply shocked. It felt very much like slamming into a brick wall at seventy miles an hour. Only, we all kept going on, waiting for her to come back home through the front door.

However, I found that after her death, remembering her just as she'd been yesterday, or the day before… or even the year before, or two years before, was just too painful. So I dealt with my deep grief by forgetting: I forgot almost everything of the two or three years previous to her death. It was easy enough to remember things already well past. These memories were cushioned by the distance of time. But my recent memories became frozen and forgotten.

Thus, my memories of the "space people" were also lost, hazed by the pall of shock for the longest time. I began to forget them, even though I'd had frequent dealings with them. This is why I needed to use the help of hypnosis to pull the early memories back into my consciousness. But they did not forget me and indeed have been with me all of my life.

My Journey Continues:

Nikola Tesla & The Akashic Records

CHAPTER EIGHT

Conscious Channeling:
Nikola Tesla & More!

Around the time I moved out of my family home at 18, I first heard about Sufism. The Dances of Universal Peace, circle dances done while chanting names of God and other holy phrases (presented by the founder as "Joy without drugs!") were being held in various places in the SF Bay Area. Being a Unitarian, I was intrigued by their open attitude towards all religions. I went, enjoying the dances, and the friendly people, quite a lot.

When I was 24, I met my first serious boyfriend in that community. His father was an archaeologist very much in the spirit of the Ancient Aliens theorists: indeed, his father was a contactee, having seen a ship at Desert Center in CA with George Adamski.

"Phillip's" father could channel various beings, an ET as well as a past life from Egypt, and when Phillip and I went down to the LA area to visit him, I asked Phillip's father to show me how he channeled the entity. It was a fascinating experience.

But as Phillip was first telling me about the extraterrestrials, my reaction to his stories might seem surprising: I thought that we human beings would hardly be worth their time! I did not doubt that they were real and had come to Earth, and could come freely and easily, without worrying about the distances, but I wondered why they would go to the trouble.

I had put them out of my mind, partly because of the shock of my mother's death This must have been hard on Thoyanntir, Cythromaa, and Samovar, all of whom were still connected to and with me. But Phillip's interest and fascinating stories started me thinking about them again.

This boyfriend was friends with another fellow, who also attended the Dances of Universal Peace. Phillip's friend was interested in UFOs too; indeed, as I still did not have a car, this friend drove me to see a UFO conference in San Francisco, presenting, among other things, the story of Betty and Barney Hill, which I remembered from a fascinating read of the article in Look magazine… Unfortunately, shortly after this, my first boyfriend and I came to an irreconcilable impasse, and we separated.

Philip's friend would eventually become my husband, though we took a long time to get engaged, so we lived separately: he sometimes with his mother, and I wherever I could afford. I cleaned houses in the morning; in the afternoons, I made rocking horses and other animals out of wood and papier mâché that were strong enough to hold an adult. I had a good deal of help from my dear intended, who made the rockers with his band saw for the many creatures I crafted, from dragons to carousel horses, flying horses and lions, tigers, and a wolf.

So my life went on for several years, and I stayed in the Bay Area Sufi community, learning a lot, drumming for the Dances, and making friends with several people. One good friendship was with a darling woman, a pianist, who, in 1984, gave me a Seth book by Jane Roberts.

I found Jane's and Seth's collaboration fascinating, and the things they were describing about the nature of the universe inspired me! When I came to channeling on my own, her marvelous works served as a shining inspiration for my later works with Nikola Tesla's spirit. When my husband and I married at last, this same woman played the music for a delightful small wedding at the house of a friend.

But while pursuing more initiations with the Sufis before our wedding, I was given the Sufi practice of attuning to my teacher's teacher. While doing this practice I had an experience I did not expect. The method I used was to walk "in the manner of" that teacher, who had been an energetic, quick-minded, large-hearted man.

At the time, I was living in a rather run-down apartment, so my quick walking was noisy, and I felt sad for the tenant downstairs. So I did something his teacher had done as he was dictating letters to his students: I played solitaire the way he had, still attuning to this man's energy.

And my teacher's teacher started dictating to me! Of course, I wrote it down and showed what I had received to my teacher, but he did not react well. It took me years to figure out that my teacher may have felt angry and disappointed that his teacher wanted to talk to me, but not to him. But I also came to feel that this teacher could not handle either the idea of my ability to channel, or my interest in UFOs.

I left the Sufis shortly after that, in 1990. The same year I saw an offer for a magazine called "Spirit Speaks," and subscribed. It was a low-cost magazine, with no advertising, that presented anywhere from 15 to 18 channeled articles on the subject of the month. I wanted to be a part of this!

Engaging the meditation I had learned from Betty Bethards so many years ago, I asked mentally for someone to work with: the personality that came was Constance McDerwin, a witch in Bath in the early 1500s: I had been her friend and one of her coven members. She lived in town, and her husband traveled a lot, so we would go to her house for our meetings.

When she told me from the Other Side that her husband had been accidentally shot to death in a tavern brawl, I was surprised because I didn't know guns existed back then. Yes, alas, guns were in use even then: to me, this confirmed that I was communicating with someone real.

When I channeled her or some other being, I almost always also asked the test question for spirits that I had learned from Betty Bethards: *Do you come of God?* "To which the spirit had to answer "Yes, I come of God," or they were rejected as being not of the Light.

Constance's coven name was Obehon: together we wrote several articles for the magazine, and together we invented a newsletter, "Familiar Spirits." It was through this Newsletter I was contacted by a man who asked me to channel various people for *his* newsletter.

One of the people he asked me to channel was Nikola Tesla. But when Nikola's article was complete, I told him to stay where he was: I knew he was telling me the secrets of the universe, and I wanted to hear more. He obliged, helping me write several articles for my newsletter. It was joyful and fascinating.

Then, in the year 2000, I met another person at a spiritual retreat, whom I will call "Elaine". Elaine recognized me immediately as a soul she knew; I knew she could be a trusted friend. Elaine had not wanted to go to that particular retreat, but her intuition kept insisting that she do so. She and I both feel that the Goddess brought us back together: we have been friends for countless lifetimes.

Elaine and I did several kinds of spiritual work together: having a great deal of experience with the Tarot, Elaine was joyful to be around and she liked many of the same things I did. She had quite a positive attitude.

However, during this time, the distress in my physical body was dragging me down: my mind became less clear, and my body became harder to manage as well. On a very hot summer day when my husband and I got out of the car, I found that I could hardly walk! I mentioned this to my chiropractor, who told me to see a neurologist. It was good I did: the neurologist was able to tell me what was going on and how to help me deal with it.

As part of a test, this neurologist gave me some cortical steroids: with these steroids, I suddenly remembered some things. They weren't particularly special memories, but they were memories that I realized I had forgotten, and they were *mine*. Only then did I realize how much had been buried under the brownout; even now there are still some years I am unclear about.

So, much of my work with my beloved ET's was put aside again. However, once I learned how to work in the Akashic Records and then went back to channeling Nikola Tesla, my life would still lead me to open the ET connection even more.

In the early 2000s, Elaine brought me to see Lee Carroll channel Kryon, the non-physical being that introduces himself as "Kryon, of magnetic service." Having channeled Kryon for decades now, Lee Carroll is called "The Pollyanna Channel" by some because of his consistently hopeful information, and sometimes called worse by others, but he is a man of great integrity.

Sometimes he has others speak in the Kryon gatherings: in the seminar that Elaine brought me to, the speaker was an MD, Dr. Todd Ovokaitys, a true genius who has done much good work in Africa to solve AIDS there. He has also worked with Life Extension and created the Lemurian Choir, where people are taught to sing in the original Lemurian language.

When I saw him speak I was so taken by his intelligence that I just had to ask if he might be interested in the material I had gotten from Nikola Tesla's spirit. He said yes, and so I shared some of the material from my Familiar Spirits newsletter. In time, Dr. Todd gave me several questions to ask Nikola: this created a lovely and unusual correspondence via emails.

Dr. Todd most graciously asked me to channel Nikola in person at one of his presentations. I was quite honored but made myself so nervous that I asked him to request that no one come to speak with me after the channeling was done.

However, there was one woman, Linaya Hahn, who came to speak with me because she wanted to ask Nikola something about the nature of light. Nikola and I gave her an interesting article, and we kept in touch: they continued to stay in touch.

When Linaya published a book on good ways of balancing PMS some years after this, I asked her who had published it; she told me, which connected me to Candace Stuart-Findlay and Empowered Whole Being Press.

I was delighted: this was a way I could publish some of my children's stories! Inspired by my mother, who told us stories when we were young that she made up on the spot rather than always reading from a book, I had collected a few of my own stories from years before, when I went to a women's Thursday morning group. In this group, each of us shared what was going on in our lives.

Candace said she was interested, and so began *Auntie Duck's Story Rhymes* ™." (I used "Auntie Duck" because I didn't want to compete with "Mother Goose...") Both books are still available at Amazon. Candace was so pleased and intrigued that she illustrated the first book, published in 2015, *Auntie Duck's Story Rhymes for Hatchlings*; the next book was *Auntie Duck's Story Rhymes for Ducklings*, which I illustrated.

But one summer, when she went to the International New Age Trade Show, Candace overheard some of the distributors complaining that they kept seeing the same kinds of material. Candace mentioned that she knew someone who channeled Nikola Tesla, and there was such avid interest in response that Candace suggested that I work with him next.

Thus began several unexpectedly challenging and exhilarating years. The spirit of Nikola Tesla still cares for Humanity a great deal, and this shows in his wide range of topics. In the five books of *Nikola Tesla: Afterlife Comments on Paraphysical Concepts,* he has articles on subjects from physics to magic; meditations to open chakras and how to center in your Divine Self; articles on DNA, stem cells; the Human Paradox; The Offset Angles of Life and Light. Three of these books have won awards from COVR, the Coalitions of Visionary Resources.

For the first book, Nikola and I put in the article we did for the other newsletter years ago, entitled, "Real, Wild Magic!" In that one article are many hints and suggestions regarding a new type of physics he is presenting: not one based upon particles and the "zoo" discovered with linear accelerators but rather a combination of frequency and vibration with multi-dimensional geometries.

I trusted his genius and his heart-centered wisdom and would write what he wanted; in some of the articles I interjected a few questions. I felt a little inadequate at times: despite my interest in science, I was never trained as a scientist, much less a physicist, and it bothered me that I was, it seemed, all he had.

But he would chuckle benignly and say that I would listen to him, and get the information accurately enough, and he enjoyed working with someone whose mind was not already made up regarding the nature of the universe. Essentially, I wouldn't argue with him!

Candace read a few of the articles, and was impressed, as she is also fascinated by the natural, and quantum, world. She reached out to William H. Terbo, who was the Founding Director, Chairman, and Executive Secretary of the Nikola Tesla Memorial Society. Although Mr. Terbo has since passed, we were quite pleased when the articles we sent to him to review met with his approval so that we could use the name Nikola Tesla on the cover with integrity.

The whole process was delightful and fascinating: when I learned about String Theory, particularly the idea that there were hidden and expressed dimensions, Nikola exclaimed, "That's *it!*" and so we evolved the concept of the Enfolded and Unfolded dimensions of reality. He presented many other new concepts just in the first book, from Para-light, which he later described as the light-core of the universe that is without vibration; the fact that gravity is such a comparatively weak force because it intersects Physical Reality at a multi-dimensional "slant;" that Time has many hidden aspects, such as "Frozen Time," and "Compressed Time."

The most challenging work, and the most fascinating, was the true nature of Manifestation Magic, which we covered in Volume Two, along with the articles from our "correspondence" with Dr. Ovokaitys. Magic was quite a challenge, as we were working on the very edge of what consensus Reality accepted at the time.

Nikola Tesla's spirit described many meditations, the dearest of which to me was how to find your soul's Core Tone. [See the Appendix.] He offered short meditations and longer ones; there is much meditative work involved with creating Spiritual Enzymes, and how to evoke manifestation Magic; he created mediations for working with Luminal Intelligence and the Dimension of Primordial Chaos.

That Dimension is one of the Three Essential Dimensions, which are: the Zero dimension, which is in every place and no one place; the dimension of Identity, which is the only dimension that acts upon and affects all the other dimensions, even the Zero dimension; the dimension of Primordial Chaos. This last dimension not only includes the amorphous, undetermined aspects of Reality, and the inner framework of all chaotic systems from clouds to veins and tree branches but is also the source of the "Creativity that Creates Itself:" the Source of all Mystery and Wonder.

One of the most fascinating sets of concepts arose from a question from Dr. Ovokaitys: Torsion Fields! These Torsion Fields, such as Numeration, Proportion, Formation, Translation, and several others, including the dimension of Identity, are like the para-genome "switches" that allow a particular gene to be suppressed or expressed: these fields allow the three Essential Dimensions to create physical Reality.

In later books, I followed Nikola's thoughts to the point where I realized that the smallest particle (which we called, borrowing from Jane Roberts with a grateful nod, the "units of consciousness") is not dualistic at its core but triune! This surprised me. But I could see what he meant when he showed it to me: the three in one and one in three.

Working with Nikola Tesla's spirit, I often feel like a telephone: the messages come through, and I am aware of the words as he impresses them upon my mind, but I am so involved in the process of receiving that I do not pause much.

Sometimes I check to see if a word he uses is correct, and I find that it always is: he is quite precise in his meaning and uses all of my vocabulary. Much as I do with Thoyantir's poetry (see the following chapter), I understand the concepts as Tesla presents them because he imparts his understanding to me. But often when I re-read the material afterwards I am astonished by what we did.

Candace has been unfailingly helpful and full of very good ideas. When, in Volume Three, Carl Jung wanted to speak, she tried many times to get permission to use his name but could not. So, we have presented what Jung told Nikola Tesla on the Other Side instead: for surely all of those in spirit meet with, and can enjoy, other people of like mind. Like the phrase from Herman Melville: "For genius, all over the world, stands hand in hand, and one shock of recognition runs the whole circle round."

This led to further opportunities for other discarnate people to speak, either through me or with the help of Nikola Tesla, so there are two books full of articles from writers, actors, statesmen, scientists, philosophers, and spiritual teachers; Presidents, and other rulers; abolitionists, musicians, lawyers, and healers.

I feel quite privileged to work with these people! Abigail Adams had a lot to say; indeed, she is in both Nikola Tesla Presents: Afterlife Lessons from Famous People and the second book, Channeled Human Wisdom for Modern Times, which Nikola and I consider some of our best work. There are so many that still care about Humanity on the Other Side!

CHAPTER NINE

Deep Diving into the Akashic Records

Every so often in the SF Bay Area there are various spiritually themed Expos: chances for the spiritual community to gather and see many various presentations, find out what skills and tools others are offering, and buy books. In 2008, my friend Elaine and I went to the Expo presented in San Francisco, looking forward to the possibilities.

We were all given programs, not only for free talks but also for lovely and expensive lectures from famous people. But when I saw an entry about someone presenting how to read the Akashic Records, it was as though that person's picture lit up, shining, so that I knew I *had* to hear her speak!

Graciously, Elaine came with me. The speaker was vibrant, intelligent, and slightly nervous, but what she presented was utterly fascinating to me. This was a way of opening up my personal history of past lives, soul agreements, my relationships in this life… and, as I found out, the love and wisdom of my Akashic Record Keepers, along with a new community of friends.

I took the beginning classes in San Francisco, as did Elaine because even though I finally had a car, I found driving in SF quite difficult, and Elaine was very good at it since she worked in the City. And I was so happy to sign up for the Akashic Records training! Elaine was tremendously helpful: she not only took me to the training classes she also joined the Akashic Record Study Groups that our teacher, Lisa Barnett, of Akashic Knowing, presented in Marin County.

We all practiced working in the Records there, doing readings for each other, sharing each other's new abilities and friendship. However, after two years of getting wisdom and information from my Record Keepers for me, I suddenly realized that I was supposed to use this knowledge in the service of others. After some more training, I became a Certified Akashic Record Consultant with the Akashic Knowing School of Wisdom.

Working this way was a joy. I had been channeling Obehon, and would soon channel Nikola Tesla's loving spirit again, but reading the Akashic Records is *not* channeling. Nor is it being psychic the way I understand it. Instead, you enter into the realm of the Records and are granted permission to receive the answers to questions. But for me, the best part of it was that I could finally get true and accurate information...

That was very important for me. You may remember that, in 1968, my sister and I went to see Betty Bethards, a woman who had some remarkable experiences after a friend of hers died. From Betty, my sister and I learned how to meditate and about our spirit guides.

One afternoon soon after I learned how to meditate from Betty, I was expressing how wonderful it was to connect with my guides. Someone I knew very well at the time challenged me to a test: he knew what he had already decided regarding whether to present something in one venue or another, so he asked me to have my guides tell me what his choice was.

Trapped, and not in meditation, I guessed wrong.

"You see?" he said, "That means this isn't real," or words to that effect. Understandably, I was crushed and never shared my joy about these kinds of things with him again. However, despite my failure, I could not tell him that I *knew* that the inner realms, and the beings in them, were real.

The final test of this was my mother's death: I could not believe that the amount of love and caring she had could simply disappear as though it had never existed. I did have dreams of her, and once she told me how to cook something: she was an inspirited cook when she was alive.

What I learned years later was that I am not psychic in the sense that I am open to discarnate beings all the time, or able to read past incidents in a house, for instance, or see the future: I am a clairaudient channel. Being psychic and being a channel use different areas and frequencies in the brain. And reading the

Akashic Records is yet another skill: it does not appear to be a gift, such as being psychic or clairvoyant: to enter the realm of the Akashic Records needs training.

So, in 2010 I began reading the Akashic Records for others, and *finally*, I was able to get accurate information if I listened correctly. I have had several people work with their Akashic Record Keepers through me more than once, and that means a great deal to me. Indeed, I tell my clients to give me as little information as possible before their reading so that I can just listen to only what the Keepers know about the client instead of what I thought I might know.

Working with others in the Akashic Record community I learned that each Consultant has specific strengths: some would work with the Record Keepers to help a client clear the energy in their auras, their homes, or their lives. Others are superlative at pulling in angelic healing energies, sometimes being able to clear large chunks of old emotional and psychic wounds free from a person's deepest Self in one session. I found I worked best at discerning a client's past lives, and the lives of their family members as those lives related to the client, as well as the present dynamics of the client's family.

THE LODESTONE BRIDGE:

ET Communication & Cultural Exchange

CHAPTER TEN

The Lodestone Bridge:
The Time Is Now

During the mid-1990s I also evolved The Lodestone Bridge. "Lodestone" was Thoyantir's suggestion: he said he wanted the name to be attractive… quite a pun, as lodestone is magnetite, which is naturally magnetic enough to collect iron filings. Magnetite was called lodestone when it was used for compasses.

It was then that the various members of the Bridge made themselves known to me: they represented a wide range of physical forms, though several of them were remarkably human in their responses, desires, methods, and intentions. I started feeling their presence but they never pressed: they offered me their emotional support and companionship

Then we found out that my husband's mother was not well: she had diabetes and was not taking good care of her blood sugar, so she had developed multi-infarct dementia. We went over to visit her, and then we lived for a while at her house in San Lorenzo.

One evening in 1993 at her house, I suddenly got the distinct instruction: "Go outside! Go outside now! Hurry, you'll miss it!" So I went to the backyard and saw three bright lights in the sky, mostly white but a little pink too, on one side of the backyard. They were arranged in a very specific formation, and hurtled across the sky in that same formation, taking perhaps five seconds to go from one horizon to the other. There are a lot of airplanes flying around the Bay Area, and I knew these were *not* planes…

When my husband and I bought our own house in 1997, I dug a pond in the backyard for goldfish and water lilies; laid down some lovely greenstone rocks in the front, and planted many things like heat-resistant lilacs and lots of bulbs. My beloved cat, Theodore, whom my husband had helped me choose the same time we went to the UFO conference in San Francisco, came with us and lived until he was 19.

Over time, though, I realized that I wanted to share my dear and special Extraterrestrials with others so much that I found a couple of people to work with me. With the help of the two women, I did my best to have "ET Evenings" at our new home. I would make sure there was tea and chairs for everyone, and that I was ready to channel any ET being or beings people wanted to hear from.

What I had envisioned for presenting the ET's was a chance for people to hear from, speak with, and generally meet beings from other planets through my channeling. Because of the extra protection that Thoyantir had given me when I was young, I could trust that I would only bring through the wise and civilized ones; the loving and shining ones. Thus they would all be representatives from civilized cultures.

I thought that people would be *interested* in other worlds and the beings in and on them; I thought people would be fascinated to hear from a member of the Sirian Council, say, or someone on another planet they had known in a previous life.

However, at that time, most people saw the evening as an opportunity to hear "some expert from out of town" give them advice about their lives, thus treating these extraterrestrial representatives disrespectfully as though they were some kind of "Ann Landers from the Skies!" Alas, I did not know how to control the meetings effectively, and so more than one person took over the meetings with their agendas.

In addition, although I did not realize it, I was starting to lose some of my health too, which caused my body and my brain to work less well. My concentration was beginning to suffer, and my body found it harder to do things. So, the ET Evenings collapsed. It was, I suppose, not the right time to present them.

However, one of the women I had been working with suggested that I ask the ET's some questions. I interviewed the members of The Lodestone Bridge telepathically, getting some intriguing answers: you will see the information I got from each member in the following chapters.

Around that time, I met another person who was not only interested in the ET's she was a channel too. She was a woman of firm opinions, but very intelligent; she had a special light about her that intrigued and fascinated me. I will call her "Doris."

An ordained priestess, Doris gave me many gifts: she channeled several of the Egyptian gods for me, including Anubis. It was dear indeed to see and work with him again: I remembered that when I was in Egypt, I knew him and Nepthys, who was the twin sister to Isis, and Anubis's mother. Nepthys is the Hidden One, who works in the shadows, not for harm, but for healing, enlightenment, and spiritual gestation.

Considered in modern times as a god of death, for me Anubis was the god that carried the souls from Earth to Heavenafter they passed the judgment of Ma'at, the Spirit of Truth and Integrity. She weighs your heart against her feather, and only when it is clear that you have lived well and done no terrible wrong do you gain admission. Anubis, and Horus the god of spiritual insight, made sure that the balancing scales of Ma'at's judgment were properly calibrated. In his integrity, Anubis never dropped any of the souls he carried Home.

I had once encountered a past life in Egypt in a group setting with a hypnotist: in this past-life memory, I was a girl of about 7 or 8, going outside with my teachers to see the nearby town. I was delighted and fascinated by everything I saw: the little shops in the souk; the donkeys and the goats (I thought the goats were delightfully absurd!); people moving everywhere and talking about everything they were doing.

The memory was truly vivid. I found out later from a good psychic that I had been an Adept in that life. According to the psychic, the temple priests would keep the Adepts in seclusion until they reached a certain age, and then they would let them see the world and the people they would serve in the Temple. The memory I had was of my release from training.

I was so happy to find Doris, who could channel, who seemed to know so much and had so much to offer as a teacher! She was an excellent astrologer, and when, after reading The Unknown Reality by Jane Roberts and Seth again, I encountered another self's lifetime in an alternate reality, Doris was psychically open enough to create that other self's astrological chart! Not only that, but she did a chart for all the members of my family in that reality.

I had discovered this alternate self by wondering who I might have been if my mother had married someone else. I did not know it then, but the same soul that is my main contact from Sirius in The Lodestone Bridge, Mir Tarr, was that alternate life father's soul, and the soul of the mother in that life, and my mother's soul in this life, was a Sirian woman named Eliadanna, his Sirian wife.

In this way, Mir Tarr was my father twice over, because when I first came to this galaxy from another (a barred spiral), I came in through the Orion Gate, but Mir Tarr and his life-partner Eliadanna agreed to be my parents from Sirius and give me a physical body as their child on my way to becoming a human being on Earth.

I worked with Doris for nearly three years. I had the delightful experience of listening to Thoyantir speak through her, and Mir Tarr, as well as D'yet and D'Barni and *her* main ET contact, Artonn from Vega. He was Vrrtvv Vxx's partner in the Rangers, and you will see more of Vrrtvv Vxx's story in the following chapters.

It was with Doris's help that D'Barni got his name. His brother, D'yet, was the elder by several years, and was a famous and accomplished empathic poet; D'Barni's name was originally given to me as "Dey'too." Doris had objected that this name sounded like he was considered an afterthought by his own family.

Once when I was channeling him and his brother off and on, she said she was having trouble keeping track of which one was speaking. Since Dey'too had golden fur, and D'yet's fur was black, she said, "We might call them D'Fred and "D'Barney so I can keep up with which one you are channeling!"

I cracked up at the time because Dey'too told me that "D'barni" actually *meant* something in his language: a "d'barni" is a natural stone column in the desert, carved by the wind like the cliffs near it, but standing alone. It was a symbol of courage and veracity, and he decided to take that name in honor of our work with him and his brother.

Doris helped me become ordained in the tradition of Auset (Isis); I still work with the four goddesses of that ordainment. Doris also taught me how to do a pencil sketch with shading and highlights, so I did some portraits of Thoyantir, Mir Tarr, and D'Barni: I still have them on my wall in my meditation area.

I had a sense of community with the others who read the Akashic Records, although I did not forget the ET's. Because of the work I had done those years ago with Doris, I often spent time meditatively with Mir Tarr, D'yet, D'Barni, and especially Thoyantir. The Lodestone Bridge and its members worked with me gently and lovingly, in particular Toh Ka Schei, Shambeytas' assistant.

It was so much fun working with these beings, and learning about them and their worlds! I often invited these friends in Spirit to join me in my daily life. D'Barni liked to connect with me enough so that he could enjoy what I was eating: his people are mainly vegetarian, and he truly loves the taste of cilantro.

D'Barni and Thoyantir loved going on walks with me. When my husband and I saw the play "Cats" in San Francisco, my ET friends were there; when I walked in the woods or went outside just to think, they were with me. Never pressing; never pushing; never insisting, they are ever-present, loving companions.

I made portraits of them too, with colored pencils. I had already drawn Shambeytas, and Toh Ka Schei told me how she wanted to be posed, and then patiently told me which color to use a little at a time, until I had what I thought to be a quite beautiful rendition.

Originally, I drew Sssssss Ssit with a cat's face: this was only to show that she could be loving, but enigmatic at the same time: she is a being who thinks long thoughts, so to speak. But in truth, she is as we have her drawn now. Sey Seyaraek asked to have a human face because, although she has a very diffuse form of consciousness, she considers her feelings to be very human.

I have definitely depended upon the protection Thoyantir placed around me to keep me away from "those who would harm us:" I and others believe that there are entities, and negative ET's, who feel that the end justifies the means and that many of these entities are quite skilled in abuse and misdirection.

Like the angler fish of the deep sea, the light in the lure it waves above her toothy jaws is real… but the promise of that light is not. This deception is like the thought-forms in alcohol and many other drugs: we human beings naturally have so much light, so much spirit, of which we are too often utterly unaware, that alcohol wants to get drunk on *us*! So it convinces us that we love it, and love it using us. Heroin wants to find restful peace with us; cocaine wants to feel our focused joy… and so on.

These thought-forms are not wise, but they are as cunning and as insidious, crafty, and seductive as the most agile parasite, and they have caused tremendous loss and grief. There is one parasite that lives in a bird's intestines. When a snail inadvertently eats the bird's droppings, the parasite infects the snail's brain and makes it think that climbing up onto the highest grass stem it can find is the most excellent, wonderful thing it can do… where it gets eaten by a bird, so the parasite continues to live, quite happily, in another bird.

The parasite is only concerned for itself: if has given the snail or the bird any sense of joy it is simply incidental. But the parasite, or thought-form, does whatever it needs to do to keep living. There are thought-forms that live on fear, despair, misery, pain… But we do not have to listen to them or be coerced by them as long as we keep our wits about us.

So, my beloved ET friends, colleagues, and family members were always within reach of my thoughts, particularly Thoyantir, both D'yet and D'Barni, and often Mir Tarr. It was sweet to have them brush against my consciousness to remind me of their intelligence, kindness, and understanding. They were involved in my life: there was one time when I was watching an original Star Trek, and in that particular episode one of the character's voices sounded so exactly like Mir Tarr's in my mind that I was astonished, and so was Mir Tarr.

In the middle 2000s, Elaine and I would go up to the house I had asked my husband to buy near Mt. Shasta: he and I thought it would be a fine place to retire to until my health made it less likely that I could manage there in both the heat of summer and the snow and ice of winter. We have it rented out now, but I had many quiet and beautiful weekends there, sometimes by myself, working in the lovely garden, feeling the energy of the mountain.

As Doris had gotten me ordained in 2000, I also used a back room in this house near Shasta as a temple. I still work with the 4 goddesses I chose: Nepthys, called "the Lady of the House," the dark twin of Isis and the mother of Anubis; Bast (Bastet), the Cat-Goddess, Isis (Auset) and Gaia. I work with them when I have some especially meaningful prayers to do. Elaine also came up to the house (we would share the driving) and often we would work in Nepthys's temple.

When I work in the Akashic Records, sometimes, as I had in the original ET Evenings, I can discern when a person came to Earth from another star system, and who they were on their home planet. Some people are surprised when I bring this up, but some others were very happy to know that their constant feeling of "not quite fitting in here" had a reason behind it. Doing this gives me tremendous joy in addition to all the other help and grace I can offer through the wisdom of the Akashic Record Keepers.

Working with my clients, I have seen the possibilities regarding people's future lives, and that is fascinating. Even though I remember almost nothing of the reading after I close the Records, I have the distinct impression that there are a lot of people thinking of returning to clean up the Earth in the future and that the Earth will respond very well to such care.

There will be a lot of healing and cleaning of areas, ecosystems, cities, and oceans. There will be animal communicators that will heal those animals that have been brutalized by human beings. The same kind of healing will be available for those human beings who have lost too much; are still haunted by past-life nightmares; are burdened by the traumas in their genetic heritage and so on.

Also, many people are going to come in with special gifts such as telepathy, healing, and perceiving invisible things such as ghosts, Earth spirits, and places where negative energies collect and warp the space around them, so that this energy can be cleared out.

In some ways, the Earth will resemble a fairy tale, where there are helpful animals everywhere that respond to kindness, and give themselves willingly when asked politely and with respect. Animals understand predation: it is not always necessary to become vegan to be compassionately spiritual, though human beings can definitely be more gracious in the way they treat other beings on this planet!

Human beings are omnivores, as are several of the extraterrestrial races. For instance, Thoyantir's people eat meat; Ka Cha Seika's people eat crustaceans, fish, and similar creatures; Vrrtvv Vxx and his family go hunting now and then: their bodies are big enough that they need animal protein.

However, more and more Earth humans will leave meat-eating behind for several reasons. Many have already seen this happen to them, their children, and other family members. And now there are many Starseeds who, because of love for this planet, have come down to help, knowing that the only one who can speak with authority about a situation is the one who has lived through it, and learned things from the ground up. This way, the Starseeds can tell the subtle differences between a wise man and a wise guy and explain this to the rest of the galaxy.

There are still a lot of fear-based people on this planet. But I still remember the lovely image of Earth on the starship that Cythromaa, Pacadee, and the wonderful glass-like being showed me, telling me that it will be impossible for us to blow up the Earth again.

The more people that choose: "When in doubt, do the loving thing;" and, "Do *not* do unto others what you would *not* have them do unto you," the more sure I am that we will not only succeed in creating Peace on Earth and Heaven on Earth but that our future will be astonishingly beautiful and loving.

The Record Keepers, wise human beings that are passed but still present, and the members of The Lodestone Bridge love Humanity and want to help the Starseeds so that they do not feel so alone. We are all angels, after all: we are the angels who can pay rent, and take their son to soccer practice at the same time we deliver a box of vegetables to the local Food Kitchen. We are the angels that can forget ourselves, forget others, and even forget love so thoroughly that we cannot imagine Love is real, and yet we turn around again and embrace love with strength and wisdom.

I know that we on the Earth will succeed.

CHAPTER ELEVEN

The Lodestone Bridge:
Mission Statement

The Lodestone Bridge is dedicated to promoting friendship and beneficial communication between people of Earth and several extraterrestrial worlds. We are also dedicated to re-portraying Earth to the galaxy to break Earth's long centuries of isolation from other worlds. To do this, we are voluntarily increasing our mental, emotional, etheric, and spiritual contact between Earth and the galaxy. Under the auspices of the Galactic Federation, we work with only those beings that have agreed to communicate with mutual respect.

Many of these beings have expressed interest in sharing the human experiences of culture mentally and emotionally, including stage plays, movies, and other things such as reading books; sharing time on vacation trips into nature; museums, and similar areas of human experience. Many of these beings are excellent telepaths and empaths. The other forms of contact are meditation and channeled information.

We offer several methods of participating in this cultural exchange of experiences and personal friendships. The main methods of contact provided are etheric travel, either through the "Ladder and Line" method of meditation or through the stargates, under the auspices of the Stellar Representatives: Mir Tarr for Sirius, Shambeytas for the Galactic Federation, and Chetrun Tohyyan, an EhnKrahn, of the Galactic Center Council.

The Lodestone Bridge stands emphatically apart from those who promote confusion, paranoia, distrust, or who have malicious intent. The beings we include in our group, as in the Rangers of the Galactic Federation and related groups, desire to work responsibly with human beings, to protect all concerned.

By creating the Citizen Ambassadors, we hope to begin another phase of human consciousness with our Lodestone Bridge of understanding. The authenticity and honesty with which you choose to approach this form of contact is the honesty and integrity you will receive in return, from those who would communicate with Humanity again.

CHAPTER TWELVE

Lodestone Bridge ET Members:
Interviews

THOYANTIR

Personal note: Thoyantir was the first of the members of The Lodestone Bridge that I met, in my own early contact experiences. We were dear friends even before I was born, and he has been a part of my whole life. His home star, Altair, is a little over 16 light-years away from us, in the constellation of the Eagle.

One time, when my family and I were at a diner, Thoyantir was quite fascinated with the décor, what I might call "1950s Futuristic," somewhat Art Deco, and particularly streamlined. Of course, I didn't say a thing about this to my family: by then they knew I was weird, but my parents would have worried about me if I started talking about aliens!

Meanwhile, when I could, I spent some time connecting with Thoyantir mentally. Soon, I got various groups of phrases from him that you might call poetry, though they were meant as little teaching aids for his people's children.

Francesca: Why are you a member of The Lodestone Bridge?

Thoyantir: I am a heart-friend to you, Francesca, as you know: we retain our deep contact. I have been working towards renewed contact with human beings and the other members of the galaxy for nearly my whole life. My people have strong connections with Earth, and many of my people trained here on Altair live on Earth now, in human form. I can offer the people who wish to work with the Lodestone Bridge a different view of what humanity means, as well as my telepathic and empathic contact.

I would offer some of my ability to heal long distance but I know I cannot make any such claim, as I am certainly not an accredited doctor by present Earth standards! But I can offer communication, and some protection regarding other ET contacts, as I have created for Francesca. It will depend on the person, the degree of contact between us, and on what is desired.

For me, the Bridge is the joy of engaging my telempathy with other beings. If one has skill at singing in your world, surely he loves to sing? So also I love to communicate with my telepathy. I have the potent joy of evolving a gestalt with the other Lodestone Bridge members. This is something quite wonderful.

Human consciousness is becoming more adept and able than it has been for centuries, even millennia. Many in Egypt, as well as in many of your more "primitive" cultures, could communicate with star beings. Those abilities were nearly lost to you around 4000 B.C., when many of the human perceptives were killed or shut themselves down.

Now, you have returned to your original potential and more. We Altarians remember some of you very well, and with love. We relate to you as equals, though our cultures and species are very different in form and expression. Some of us remember you as family, friends, or teachers.

We are calling on those connections now because friendship outlasts both time and space. I have learned much about love from human beings, much about emotions, and more than I care to know about the damage that the lack of human love and emotions can create. I have seen the cost of human pain directly and learned a great deal about healing emotional wounds, and how to avoid them. I have also learned a great deal about beauty in the face of despair, courage in the face of loss, and determination in the face of tremendous obstacles. I have learned a very great deal from human beings!

The most important thing about the Lodestone Bridge is the engagement of a living being with another living being: re-gathering of the families of being. The members of the Bridge seek to remember, rejoin, and renew those ties of friendship, affection, and the genuine love that you and we once had between Earth and other planets.

Francesca: Please tell me a little about yourself.

Thoyantir: I am a husband, father, and mentor, from Altair's fourth planet. I live in a wholly etheric body but I consider myself a physical being. My planet, Altair Four, has a wildly eccentric orbit, with a year that lasts for ten of yours. Even the etheric forms must hibernate for two to three years every cycle, but we are often still subconsciously aware and active.

Hibernation is a "dead" time, when all is slow, including our thoughts, although we usually retain enough awareness to act if our lives are threatened. I have known three families who did not survive hibernation because of predation. Those most skilled among us can sleep during hibernation in an "aware" state of dreaming, like your human lucid dreams, and can keep communicating with many other minds. Even though I am not as physical as a human being, my form derives much from the genetic material of your Earth lemurs and meerkats. We live for 90 - 150 of your years, 9 - 15 of ours.

I am a Mind Surgeon. Because we allow the other predators of Altair to remain part of our ecology, our people are both hunters and hunted. You would call those who hunt us animals; to us, they are our strength. When someone is harmed, whether through misadventure or by being hunted, I have been trained to take the pain of the wound and use that pain as energy to repair the hurt. This is an action of deep telepathy and empathy, and I take much satisfaction in it.

For most other healing, we are herbalists. We understand how trace compounds in living things give benefits, from fungi to even the fur of certain species. We are aware of the many methods of dispensing herbs, from poultices to infusions; some of these concepts we have gotten from Earth, some from other places. Some herbs are activated with water; some with oil; some with blood; and some with other fluids. I do some healing with herbs, though in your terms I am an emergency room doctor, since I am called immediately after someone is hurt.

Usually, though, when someone has been pursued by a predator, and damaged beyond a certain point, they yield and die. I am rarely called to act in these situations, because we feel that once death has been accepted by the one who has been hurt, they should be let go; most often, the outcome has usually already been determined by the one injured.

Francesca: Can you tell me a little about your home world?

Thoyantir: Although we do not slaughter the predators in our world, as human beings do, we are not careless and do protect our children. And we do not have fast cars that can kill people, or houses that are flammable, either. But long ago we understood that predators keep us strong, even though there is always a price. I have had some of my loved ones killed, such as my first mentor, and a sister. I used to hunt alone until I was nearly killed on a hunt several years ago when my two new children (twins) were born.

Now, because I am part of The Lodestone Bridge, two Rangers from the Galactic Federation have insisted they come with me when I am hunting and strongly suggest that I stay with my family as much as possible: they feel that my ability to talk with human beings is so essential at this time that I am too important to lose. I still chase after small things, for I like the quiet solitude of the forests. We have extensive wild places and live most often in caves, hollowed-out burrows, and sometimes on the sides of cliffs. We are quite able to stand upright, using our tails for balance.

I hunt by sight and by telepathic awareness. There is often some scent of the prey, but it is not my primary means of perception. Although I have no visible ears, I guess I hear audible sounds about as well as you do, though my main "hearing" is telepathic and empathic. Yes, I do use that empathy to sense my prey, but we are taught to never use our empathy to call the prey, to coerce it.

As a hunter, I am not as scrupulous as your wolves that hunt mostly the sick, injured, and weak: there are some illnesses in the prey that we cannot assimilate. But I do look out for those who have chosen to be prey that day. We do not often hunt as a group, except in the spring, when everyone still living after hibernation has ended is hungry!

Sometimes several friends will travel together, hunting or visiting other families. Our culture is matriarchal and in some ways as complex and full of protocol as some of your finest Occidental or Oriental royal courts. Because the woman chooses the partner for her family, and the men must show themselves off somehow, the males often dance. Usually, two will dance together, whether spontaneously, or in planned, regular bouts.

These courting dances have a lot of leaping in them, and sometimes singing, so it is very much like a martial arts demonstration while the participants are singing opera, for we do sing with wordless cries much as the indri lemurs do on Earth. This can be quite a show! It can be like a mock battle, for some dancing has become a very stylized art, though it is usually just for the joy of one's own body moving, and the exhilaration of dancing with another in a synchronous pattern, whether between men, men and women, or just women.

Learning the leaps and mid-air changes of direction certainly keeps us safer when we travel in the woods. My people also have musical instruments: drums, sounding boxes with strings, and reed instruments. We also make what we call Gift Circles: spheres of wood or stone, with little scenes inside, so that they are something like your Easter eggs or ships in bottles.

Many of us like to fly in outer space, in our small ships. With them, we study many places we could not survive, even with our etheric physicality. I have been inside my sun several times, this way. I am there, but the ship protects me. It is enchanting!

Thoyantir: Oddly enough, our telepathy began as the physical empathy needed to encourage both mother and child at birth. Because our children also have large skulls, birth can be at least as difficult for us as for human beings. During birth, the father holds his wife and enters a kind of healing trance, a very profoundly loving act. She and the child must both feel safe from predators and welcome to the place where the birth is happening.

However, if a woman is pregnant during hibernation, mother and child can become so tightly bonded it is unwise. We try to avoid pregnancies at this time. A woman can "hold" a barely developed fetus, and put off full gestation for quite some time. This might be done when famine or other stress makes it clear that the child will not be supported, or if her mate is killed just as the seasons turn from deep fall to winter.

But this delay has several costs to her and her child, some social, some physical, and some mental. Once the child or children have been born, in the first years of lying in with her children, the husband does most of the hunting. We hunt the equivalent of rabbits, deer, fish, land eels (not quite like your snakes, more like large, amphibious lizards), and whatever else we can find and bring down by chance. We do not cook our food, and bring home what we can carry. We are not wholly carnivorous, as we eat fungi, some seeds, and herbs. We don't have farms.

Francesca: I know you have a family. Can you tell me about them?

Thoyantir: Although I did not wish to create a family at the time she asked, as I already had a daughter, my present wife O'ero chose me as a husband, and asked that I be the father of her children. I was touched and flattered both: she is a woman of high standing. We have not regretted that choice: our two new children are growing strong and well.

Chessan, my daughter through O'ero, is working on refining her telepathic abilities so that she can become a Translator; Chessan's twin Lirayes is a good hunter and is already training with his mentor to be an exhibition dancer.

Once Chessan has perfected her telepathic abilities as a Translator, she may become a healer much as I am, or an administrator, as is O'ero. Planetary administration involves communicating with more than one person at a time over greater than usual distances, as in a conference call: we do not have your technology and do not feel we need it.

I have another son and a daughter by another woman who still lives near me; the twins spend a lot of time with their mother too, which is only appropriate. O'ero also had a daughter by another; that daughter is grown. My father is still living, and both my wife's parents are also still alive. I still enjoy spending time with my present mentor, a wise woman with unusual, all-white fur, rather like my new son; his twin sister's fur is black. We live in a hilly savannah-like land, much like hills in central and northern California.

We let our children go to their mentors when they are about 15 Earth years, or one-and-a-half Turrun years (as Turrun is one of the names of our planet); generally, the child will have had enough experiences in his or her life to decide what craft or calling they will pursue. The child chooses the mentor, though there are exceptions. The mentor becomes the child's second family, and all the old ties change then.

You might say that the parents launch the child, and the mentor helps it to fly. The child learns the nature of her telepathy with her mentor, which needs careful, personal work. My mentor taught me the ancient method of writing telepathically-encoded symbols, and I shared some of them with Francesca.

When a child must choose, or change, her mentor, or an adult faces changes in her life, they go walking, alone. Not all of us return! Some find new places to live, others get caught by predators. This is not something that frightens us. It is understood, and accepted, perhaps much as you accept that driving on the freeway, or being in a culture that allows or even encourages firearms, might lead you to an untimely death. As I said above, many who are ill, or heartbroken, will offer themselves to the wild this way, as did my first mentor. If that offer is not taken, the person must find another way to heal.

We learn how to shield ourselves from others' thoughts and emotions around five Earth years old. Some telepathic training between mentor and student is done in hibernating sleep. Some truly excellent telepaths or empaths can share dreams. That is what my student wishes to do: he intends to find healing answers within the dreamer's dreams.

Since we are creatures primarily of the mind and emotions, we have sciences of telepathy and cultivate the wisdom needed to understand relationships. We describe chemistry as natural affinities, resonance, and deep similarities, rather than a simple view of electrons and valences. Our ships, which take us between worlds, are alive.

But our personal ships have an order of life nothing like your technology: instead of a mechanism built of disparate parts, the ships are the manifested patterns of an idea, a focused telepathic structure. This must be so because each ship is directly responsive to our thoughts. One of our sciences is writing, as in the telepathically embedded glyphs I studied; we also do work with sound, though we do not have quite the voices you do.

By your standards, our culture is far too disorganized to have any standard religious observances. We do not give much thought to religion because the Presence within life is so obvious, and we feel that the relationship to every created being and its Source is very individual. I am aware that there is an Intelligent, Feeling Presence in all that is, which is the Life that manifests in myriad forms, and is beyond form altogether. I have a deep sense of trust in this common Awareness, and I know that I act within its Being.

Families are the only groups that keep close to each other geographically, as even mentors move on after their students have learned what they wish. However, a mentor may find several places of special beauty, or wonder, and bring her student there, to discover the meaning of each place individually. We rest in such places when we have the opportunity to enjoy special solitude.

Those of us who are particularly good at telepathy have ranged our minds far within other worlds and cultures. In this, we have been luckier than Earth: your planet unfortunately lost its connection to the star-worlds due to the breaking of the lines of communication between the stars when your world and your race were young. Though it has isolated you all, this systemic breakdown was no fault of yours. We of Altair retained enough awareness to continue communication, despite the barriers presented by the lack of the network.

*****

When I was in High School, Thoyantir shared some of his language with me. Here was the first poem: Note: all the vowels are like in Spanish; the emphasis is usually on the second syllable; the accents on some letters change the emphasis and the meaning:

Nekete dán bar ift ana

mithan delu nepthanen

anam mulen

Du reccecht thianuu sulen

rianuwán lukuth taban

meketh rialsu kan

…rilili s'un beketh…

menkaman mjemet nuruun tsankécth.

The will of Love stands in the center place,

Delight eases wounds;

there is balm in the secret door.

In the heart, the Window, shining.

At the vast edge of Form is the formless,

each [thing] finding its own homeplace in the

harmony

…beloved children laughing…

All That Is, touched by the Inner hand,

 finding completion in praise.

He gave me a great deal of this, and I loved working with him. There were a few phrases that, when he gave them to me telepathically, I could understand them, but when I tried to

156

translate them I realized that I had no human equivalents for what the words meant.

I did not share it much, as I realized that most modern people don't care for poetry at all, and trying to interest people in poetry that they had to work to understand, well… I knew that was not worth the trouble to share. But the process was delightful, and expressed our love for each other.

MIR TARR

Personal note: As I mentioned earlier, Mir Tarr was one of the first beings I met when I came to this galaxy from another, a long, long time ago: he and Eliadanna gave me a form suitable for this galaxy, and I still consider him my star-father. I first sensed him in this life when I was 14, but did not truly know who he was until I reached out to create the Bridge.

One of the things Elaine and I worked with was the Sirian Council. There are three Councils that human beings can visit in meditation: the Sirian Council is not a physical place, so it has room and time for everyone to speak. It has the semblance of a tall, elegant building with an indoor amphitheater; there is a podium in the center, and any being who has something important to say can come… including us from Earth.

Through Elaine's psychic perception, she felt that several on the Sirian Council had rather limited and negative views of Earth people. Indeed, my star-father Mir Tarr was looked down upon by some because he, too, had lived on Earth in Roman times: He was a senator at least, though Doris felt he was the soul of Emperor Trajan.

Mir Tarr is the one to go to if you want to speak at the Sirian Council. His eyes seem blank because there is so much light in his people now: they had a time when they fell from Grace, but they have been working at becoming more and more compassionate.

Francesca: What potentials do you see in The Lodestone Bridge?

Mir Tarr: The Lodestone Bridge can create the exciting possibility that human beings can become at last the great beings they have wanted to be. You can do this on your own, and we will watch with love and fascination: the growth of something wonderful is always dear. And you can do this with us, as equals, and we will take those joyous strides beside you.

I relate to human beings generally as one who has been human, and so understands, but also as someone who is not human now, so must keep on understanding. I relate to The Lodestone Bridge itself as I would any group of like minds, especially those creating a goal. I help create the place in which realizing the goal may happen. Relating to each being individually, I do not forget the strength of the ties of the friendships.

Working with The Bridge also offers me a profound sense of wholeness, because it calls on both my human self and my Sirian self. The thought that I can present that wholeness to human beings moves me very much. I am communicating with you now through the Lodestone Bridge because I feel I can be heard now, because of what I am, and because of the Bridge itself.

When I was human, I learned much about love. Love has a cost, and so it is precious. Love is also a gracious gift, and so shows the powerful and joyous nature of the All. I learned the value and cost of having integrity. I learned the paradox of being human, which is sometimes to throw everything away for trifles, and yet to make those trivial things actions of deepest meaning.

Working with you, I have learned courage and patience, honor and wisdom. In this Bridge adventure I have learned strength and beauty from the human beings and the beings of the other worlds. I am eager to work with those who are willing to communicate with others unlike them, when the love shown by those others is real.

I want to work with those who remember how it was when Earth felt a part of the community of the stars, and those who can respect their own wisdom as well as that of others. I want to see that the old, loving bonds of friendship can be forged again, through earned trust, discovered truth, and personal integrity.

I come where I am invited. In all of your minds, there is a space for the spaceless, and time for the timeless. I enter there. Because I remember Earth Time, I know how to enter that timeless place in every mind that freely admits me. Because I know the architecture of minds, I know the doorways into the minds that seek communication with me. I have a fifth-dimensional form and come here by taking up no time. I come on the wings of your consent and stay in the warmth of your friendship.

Francesca: Tell me a little more about yourself.

Mir Tarr: As a Sirian, my form is primarily energetic, although I have some physicality. If you saw me you might call me an energy diatom, or "space amoeba." I was a Roman senator once, and that is the form I like to appear in for the Bridge because the experience was so important to me. I call myself a Mind Architect. From my multi-dimensional Sirian perspective, I see the shapes that minds take. With their permission, I can help beings create new structures in their minds that allow their thoughts to flow more smoothly.

As you have said above, I have recently been appointed to the Sirian Council in matters where humans are concerned, because I have learned from some of my own human mistakes and errors, and can save someone the trouble of making the same ones. I value human beings very highly and can reflect that value to star beings. I illustrate integrity, loyalty, and honor for those human beings who feel they do not see enough of that in their own lives.

I can certainly offer love and how to learn from it. I also joined the Bridge because I desire to re-engage humanity with the galactic community. There has been so much lost in the separation, both love and knowledge! As it is with the Altarians, many of you who are human now have also been Sirian. Sirius and Earth are very close in more than spatial distance. I have been human more than once, and still greatly value the lessons of love I have learned on Earth.

Francesca: What things interest you?

Mir Tarr: I am fascinated by how the form and the formless meet one another and create being. I find forms of all kinds alluring and fill my experience with them. At times, the intensity of my pleasure cannot be described! Working with minds is artistry for me, and is as absorbing and rewarding as any art can be.

We of Sirius have learned some sharp lessons about arrogance: we had to give up our physical forms because of it. Rather than having just two parents, we now gather in groups of several to create new souls' forms. There were so few left of us after the downfall we created for ourselves that we swore we would never again make the mistake of birthing a child without a community of family members to support it because only community support would train us away from our hubris. We have not been perfect in this and were recently humbled again by human contact.

I feel we have much yet to learn about love and caring. To this end, I welcome lessons from human beings. In my opinion, friendships create the best families, whether they are of blood or heart. Passion, which is the impulse to create a freshening of life, waxes, and wanes, but friendships endure.

I keep my days of rest and my celebrations. I enjoy it when others enjoy with me, and I may ask others to be with me. I remember several holidays from my times on Earth and sometimes in fits of nostalgia try to re-create them. From my work with human beings, I believe that you do not take time enough to celebrate. You have your special days, certainly, but you do not celebrate yourselves enough.

Look into your own eyes in the mirror sometimes and celebrate their color! Celebrate how you have grown, and how your perceptions have become more valuable over time. Watch life celebrating itself. Your forms, all of them, are songs and stories. Listen! They are laughing, rich with merriment!

For me, watching other beings is to have restful fun. I go to one of the main Gates in the galaxy, Arcturus perhaps, simply to study those who go by. I might engage one or another in conversation, and so learn things I did not know before. I also spend time "outside."

This "outside" is the edge of form and the formless: some call it mathematical chaos. When you see those fractal constructs, the ones that have infinities inside of other infinities in fantastic shapes, you have an idea of what I mean. I watch the swirl of infinite possibilities. This is like watching leaves dancing in the sun might be for you, only more so. I also simply let my mind slide into a kind of random state, and watch it create ideas and visions, memories and imaginings: they are all part of my dreaming play.

Francesca: What sciences do you have on Sirius?

Mir Tarr: Our sciences have three categories: Patterns, Rhythms, and Movement. You are already aware of your psychological patterns. And you know that when you are aware of the interconnected natures of these patterns, it swiftly becomes as engaging and complex a task as solving your "three-body problem" in physics. Rhythm is the same.

We know that nothing occurs in isolation, without relationships to other things and this is also true with time and timing. Movement can be seen as the expression of both Pattern and Rhythm, though it also creates them. How these three areas of study interrelate brings us directly to the edge of Mystery, which is the true mastery of science.

Healing is a matter of perception. Sometimes illness can be cured by engaging the injured one in utter stillness. Sometimes illness can be set aside within ourselves as we take actions in other directions. But in all cases that I know of, no illness can be cured without the person's full permission. If it only seems to be cured, then the energies that have made it up will return in another form, held by the defiant will of the one who has been ill.

Sometimes we must first discern the benefit hidden within the illness or the misunderstanding behind it. If medicine can be seen as that which promotes, creates, or re-establishes natural and desired patterns, rhythms, and movement, then certainly we Sirians work with medicine. We have discerned much of what removes blockages and restores flow. We have discovered what may revitalize significance, and what promotes relationships that have less strain. We are aware of what sustenance truly is, and what it is not. We learn from complexity and simplicity.

As to how we relate to That Which Is, the forms or rituals are not nearly as important as the intentions. Is the intention of your relationship with the All, one of self-discovery, or is it the imposition of will? Is it joy, wonder, love, or peace? My spirituality reflects my experiences very directly.

While on Earth, I learned the tremendous values of integrity, honesty, loyalty, and the ability to endure, to persist with stamina when needed. I feel I have a true awareness of beings greater than myself, and the Principles of Being that create That Which Exists. I have a deep respect for both Time and Space. Still, in a human sense, we Sirians are dreams. Dreams that have fled from what has held us, and gone on to discover what we are.

As I said earlier, I do "randomize" my thoughts now and then, seeking the pleasure of finding that which is not me, which I may choose to make part of myself. Sometimes I make myself as utterly still as I possibly can so that I might discern my nature in contrast with other things going on. I can rest parts of myself while other parts are still active. While I am doing this, my perceptions have been known to change remarkably.

KA CHA SEI KA

Personal note: After Thoyantir and Mir Tarr, Ka Cha Sei Ka was the first being to present herself specifically to the Bridge when I sent out the original request for contact. Although her form seems like an ant to some people, to me she is much more like a lobster type of being, though most people see her and think she is an "ant-being." Their whole world, it seems, is very swamp-like.

Her planet, unlike D'Barni's desert world, is mostly heavy jungles, rather like some of the swamps in the American South. This is where her chitinous carapace can help: with her mobile, finely segmented arms, she can reach out whenever she needs to, and not many things can bite through her armor. In several respects, her life-cycle is similar to Vrrtvv Vxx's people; both are related to horseshoe crabs.

Ka Ca Sei Ka has since confirmed that her people visited the Hopi Indians centuries ago, and the Hopis called them "ant people" too, and I am not surprised: despite her appearance, Ka Cha Sei Ka has a very human attitudes, aspirations, emotions, and intentions towards life.

She also told me of a story of some creatures in her world that looked rather like abalones when resting: they can, however, extend the edges of their bodies outward, until they looked rather like pizzas with bowler hats, the shells in the center of the circle these extended edges created, and they can glide from place to place. They are celebrated in her world because, when a certain type of tree gets infested by some particularly nasty burrowing worms, these "flying abalones" search out the trees and dig into the bark with some sharp mandibles and remove the worms.

A few of these unusual animals get so involved with digging that they risk burrowing under the bark too deeply, and become trapped there. But the trees that have these special creatures on them thrive. Consequently, these "flying abalone" are regarded highly, and their sacrifice is seen as quite special.

I imagine that once true contact is made, her kind would have a great number of useful things to say about reclaiming wetlands. I had not met her before the Bridge, but I have found her humor and enthusiasm quite delightful. Her name is pronounced as a loud stage whisper, without using your voice box, as they have no larynxes.

Francesca: How would you like to work with The Lodestone Bridge?

Ka Cha Sei Ka: Working with the Lodestone Bridge has given me a good grade on my graduate thesis! And it offers me a place for my wonder and my enthusiasm. It offers me a community, too. It offers me an opportunity to see who you are, which can be different from the galactic images of you.

With the Bridge, I see a chance for a new community, one that can fill the empty spaces that some of you have. If love is absent in the beginning, it does not mean that it cannot find its way to you and others later; it just takes more time. I think of human beings as tremendously heroic because they face this separation, this loss of connection sometimes for your whole lives. I hope I can present you with a different set of methods that are similar enough to your own to be comprehensible.

Even though I must confess there are long hours and days when I hardly think of any of you because my own life demands my attention, I do study your human feelings, drives, emotions, and your habits. I can relate to you as I might to some of the more unusual people I know: waiting to learn what is real to you and then enjoying the differences. I study and enjoy your humor, bravery, and your paradoxes.

You human beings are patient and impatient, loving and unloving, joyous and then tragic in your sorrows. Your humor can be bought from joy, pain, or both. Your bravery makes you loyal to others, and loyal to what is most true and human in your selves, but sometimes you can give your loyalty to something that is very much not like yourselves. I've learned that important things take effort and time. I had known this before intellectually but had not understood the significance involved.

There are other beings amongst the galactic races that already have ties of friendship, or at least recognition, with some of you who are now human. These beings can see into your depth of character and are not made anxious by surface appearances of emotions or culture. And, there are those other planetary races that love and know they can love even the most bitter or dangerous or vicious human beings.

Francesca: Who do you think might most enjoy working with The Lodestone Bridge?

Ka Cha Sei Ka: Those human beings who might be interested in working with the Bridge are probably those who are suited for it: that is, they became human while remembering how to be who they are, who feel comfortable with the reality of their timelessness, their infinity of expression. Those who like inner adventures are welcome!

The most important thing is to feel the connections, the loving bonds that can be created in this work. When we engage deeply with another being, we remain engaged, whatever the changes in circumstances. Time or space can blur the intensity of that engagement, or change its expression. But, once we know another, we do not forget.

You see, some on other worlds feel that you are vicious and dangerous. Others think you are merely very strong and feral animals, driven by abuse. Still others despair of your ever becoming intelligent: i.e., telepathic, adult, aware, compassionate, and perceptive. Some see you in a very poor light, thinking there is nothing of value in you at all. Or, if there were any value, it would be like the amount of gold in the poorest kind of ore: it would take far too much work to extract.

What many have missed is that there is value in you despite the abuse, the danger, and the fear. Your value is your capacity to love. Not only one another but to love Life itself. That is of tremendous importance. Many of us here are counting on the strength of your love.

I have enjoyed myself very much, telling others what I know of your world, and there is much anticipation for your growth into truly civilized beings. We may come to you, or Earth may prefer to find a way to meet us halfway. I haven't visited you physically, at least not yet, although of course my people have.

But I feel sure we shall meet each other in a hundred years or so when Earth allows itself more visitors. We need to increase the range of our ships a little, too, since we are about a hundred and eighty light-years from you. We're on the galactic rim, as you are, but in the direction of the galactic center. But as there is a very positive, mutual resonance between our two worlds, I can be with you mentally fairly easily.

It is like when you sometimes have sister cities in two separate countries, exchanging ideas, goods, and sometimes people: my world shares friendship with yours, though on the whole most human beings do not realize this. Some of your scientists communicate with ours in dreams and reveries; we exchange perceptions, though again they do not clearly remember the source.

Francesca: Please, tell me a little about yourself.

Ka Cha Sei Ka: As you have observed above, my planet's people are very human-like. We call ourselves the Vauntu nri. Although our forms might seem strange to you, I feel our cultures are very close to Earth's and we are very similar in our likes and dislikes. I was even trained in what you would call a university as a psychologist or psychiatrist. I am both curious and enthusiastic about other people and beings, and I love to share good ideas, the ideas that expand things, illuminate what has happened, and help people understand themselves and others.

I am married, with several children. I met my husband in the course of my work with the Bridge, and we are delighted with each other. Marriage is something we can do any time within a 20 to 40-year period after maturity. Childrearing is considered a career, for which formal training is usually provided. Once we are married, we tend to stay that way, because there is a lot of personal latitude as to how that marriage is expressed. We are often monogamous, but there have been some inventive quadrads and triads as well.

When we are born, we are curled up in a transparent shell. We are left, all together, in a place of warmth, until our shells harden and eventually crack us free. Then we swim in salty water until our new exoskeletons harden. When we are perhaps several months old, we look for parents. Sometimes our body-parents will be there, and sometimes not. There can be many there that day, or there can be few.

Usually, the body-parents want to take some child or another, and usually it is theirs; in any event, there are a few left. Some are too fragile to grow; others do not choose parents at all, and live for a while in the nursery. Perhaps nine out of ten grow out of the nursery; perhaps half of those survive childhood.

This may seem careless, or dangerous, to you. But we have a different view: we believe that it is the child's choice to grow fully, or not. There are also several stages of growth to go through, and several molts. Some do not make it. It is not our way to worry. There will always be enough to love.

We see the world around us with infrared light. It is somewhat more difficult to see by day, especially when it is hot. But we manage. We do not have teeth, but rather some serrated ridges that lead down into our throats. We are not hunted, unlike Thoyantir's people; in this, we have a somewhat fortunate circumstance in our evolution. According to my research, most races in the galaxy are omnivorous, and so are we.

The animals we eat are small, like grubs, or insects that live in our non-animal foods. Reeds, seeds, tubers, and other roots are enjoyed. We are particularly fond of the protein-rich skins of some water plants, which "bloom" with a red "fur" when ripe. We eat worms, eels, and similar. Not a nice diet for a human being, but it has enough of what we need. Most of our animals have exoskeletons, as we do. Some are armored, like pill bugs on

Earth, or like your sturgeon; nearly everything is amphibious to one degree or another.

There are some animals to be avoided. Some of these you might call chain-snakes, with spiked segments on a long body that moves very quickly. Others are parasitic. I told you about one of the species of animals I very much admire, the "flying trilobites:" they are the equivalents of hawks or eagles in your world that know when some of our trees are being ravaged by parasites. They go to the trees in flocks, hunting the parasites by hanging on the tree and becoming part of it.

Francesca: What kinds of things interest you?

Ka Cha Sei Ka: Inventive ideas that take the whole situation into account gladden me. But what fascinated me with the Lodestone Bridge was to understand the contrasts between your people and mine as well. Not simply the cultural differences, for there are many of those, because each culture builds itself on its sense of what is important. But I am also interested in what human beings want. I think the largest difference between human beings and the Vauntu nri is the level of human fear.

When fear becomes so prevalent its source cannot be perceived, then it demands an object upon which it can crystallize. But even deeper than fear is human loss and loneliness: you are so alone. You are barely telepathic, and empathic usually only in special cases, or with training. And even deeper is the loss of love itself. Human beings have been divorced from themselves, and from a sense of community, for a very long time. It is this separation that paradoxically drives love further and further away.

There are enough sheer numbers of you to help create a kind of communication field, even though most of you are only semi-conscious of your true mental and emotional natures. Also, many of you have now created a shift of being. Your human dance of being has its rhythms, and the proper steps, and because you know your dance, you anticipated the recent Shift. Make no mistake: this Shift was watched in several galaxies.

Francesca: Is there anything else you would like to say about your world?

Ka Cha Sei Ka: We tell a lot of jokes, although they're not human in form. Our jokes are closer to your "shaggy dog" types, with a long story that allows the listener to empathize with the character, and then feel his perplexity when things don't go as planned (mainly because of the character himself). Swimming is a pleasure because it reminds us of childhood.

We swim well, but if the water is over our heads, we prefer to scuttle along the bottom. We can hold our breaths for about a minute and a half even when young. We enjoy our food, and we enjoy our friends. We have much pleasure in discovering things, which is why there are so many scientists in our world. Since we are very nearly as physical as you, we make love for pleasure, we sleep for pleasure, and we play for pleasure. I'm also finding my work with human beings a pleasure, both in this opportunity and in others.

The diversions in my world are many, some of them very human, and some of them you would think odd indeed. For music, we move the various parts of our outer skeletons, rubbing them together as Earthly crickets do. A good musician can control the flow of air between the shell-plates so well that wonderful tones can be produced in sequence.

Food entertains us, both the eating and the presentation. Sometimes we tell stories about the food, though these stories look more like one of your Noh plays. These presentations are full of condensed movements, built on chains of long-standing meaning. I remember one quite impressive show, where the hostess came out, made three distinct movements, and had her guests laughing outright for several minutes. In three strokes, she had told us the situation in the kitchen, the situation in her marriage, and a joke linking them both!

We take every third day as a rest day. About every two weeks, we take two days of rest at least. How we spend those days is very individual. There are particularly special days for us too, but they relate mostly to beginnings and endings, celebrations of successes, good news, and self-discoveries: they are all given time to be honored.

We decorate when we celebrate: many of us have collections of party supplies, which can be mixed and matched depending on the mood we want to create. Families evolve their little rituals of arranging these decorations. Rather than having steady, prescribed methods of celebration, we are constantly inventing new ways of making days special. We find creativity quite stimulating and enjoy being inspired by others' good ideas.

Francesca: What about science and medicine?

Ka Cha Sei Ka: We are not highly skilled telepaths or empaths, like some races I know, so we tend to heal in ways very similar to your own. We do know a little more about how our bodies work, chemically, so that we can sidestep an illness by knowing which compounds to use to rebalance the body with itself. In some ways, our medicine is like your acupuncture, though it is a risky thing to puncture our exoskeletons. Perhaps because of our exoskeletons, we are not as skilled as human beings at repairing some aspects of wounds or breakages.

Several in the galactic community have heard the truly interesting things human beings have done with skin grafts, bone grafts, and similar. Yet to force a body to take something that is not its own, as in a liver or kidney transplant seems very strange indeed to us. If you recover from damage only because you can take on that which is not a part of yourself, this means that there is another that must give that part to you.

To justify those who can be repaired this way, there must be more hazards, more damage, and perhaps even war, to supply the bodies so that the parts of those bodies can be used. This idea has been tossed about like mud in the air on our world and others and hasn't come down to land yet.

For us, the sciences are fields of study, training, and fascination. We have come to a few of the same conclusions as you regarding, say, magnetism and its so-called "laws". But we do have some pursuits of thought which are very difficult to explain. For instance: how would you utilize the vertical flow of time to discern the layers of sequences within a single moment?

I believe our sciences are well balanced between the physical and the non-physical, what is perceived and who perceives it. But it can take too long to explain. Our spirituality is Love. Our metaphysics is another thing. How many eyes see the world? That is how many views there are, and that is how many the world is viewed through.

The Vauntu Nri people agree on a few things, which we have learned by sheer practice, through a harmonious gestalt of experience: that there is enough harm by misadventure to go around already and that intentional, deliberate harm injures the harmer and the harmed too much.

We have learned that when confusion or partial perception is passed on to following generations, it takes so much effort to correct, that the effects of the original misperception border on the exponential. That joy does not care what form it is in. Nor should we care, as long as we can recognize it as joy, and that things viewed from the opposite sides of a spectrum look opposite indeed.

D'YET AND D'BARNI

Personal note from Francesca: I had a fascinating experience with Doris once: as we were working with D'yet and D'Barni: we were tag-teaming, both of us getting into an open state where we could "visit" with them while remaining in our bodies. At that time, D'Barni was very interested in his herbs. He was very fond of succulents and healing herbs that lived in the shadowed crevices of their planet's wind-sculpted mountains.

Doris and I did our best to see the same things that he showed us: a plant like a white-edged spider plant; a tangle of leaves with remarkable veins the same red as rhubarb; a plant with soft, pointed leaves that looked very like a lamb's ear plant from Earth.

Unfortunately, D'Barni put some leaves on Doris's dream-body arm, and she suddenly had an allergic reaction to them! He tried several other plants to nullify the effect, and finally, she felt her psychic body recover, but he was most chagrined. We kept working with both of the brothers, though.

For D'yet's and D'Barni's people, stage plays are very important. They are not only stories about people: they are another way of showing someone's skill in communicating and taking on the feelings of another. For many reasons, D'Barni truly enjoys one Earth actor, David Suchet, who played Hercule Poirot because, if you have seen the actor as himself, and then compare it to how he is as the character, you can see how deeply he shifts his energy to truly become that character.

D'Barni was also fascinated by a particular Star Trek: The Next Generation show about a race of people that spoke in metaphors: it is as though we might say, "Juliet on her balcony," to mean longing, perhaps, or hope, or "Rosebud" to mean an unrecoverable loss. This is not to say that his people speak that way, but he was quite interested in the idea and could understand it.

But when I was reading some Jane Austen, D'Barni commented that there are times when his own culture seems as socially complex and occasionally fraught as the most detailed and complicated Regency novel you could imagine! The families and their alliances matter as much as the careers and avocations of the people who are to be married; where everyone will live together matters too and this can create some adroit maneuvers to accommodate everything that is wanted.

Nevertheless, his people have a relaxed attitude about sexuality: sex is not shameful in itself: however, if for some strange reason it is being used to harm someone, then it is unacceptable. Sexuality is such a fraught subject for so many human beings, but not so much for most extraterrestrial beings.

His and many other ET cultures do not suffer from the grievous human convention of securing masculine priority by demanding that the male lineage be guaranteed. In the usual course of things, every child knows who his mother is! Or if not, certainly his community remembers. But the human method of securing the male lineage by demanding that all women must be virgins, or else they are considered "spoiled" has led to a tremendous amount of shame, pain, misery, and grief on Earth.

Francesca: Why do you want to work with The Lodestone Bridge and human beings?

D'yet: Earth is a world of passion, emotion, and poetry. What more could a poet like me desire? But more, human love is like no other in its courage, depth, and loyalty even in the face of pain, betrayal, or disappointment. When you learn to love unconditionally on Earth, you can be confident that you have learned love well.

In our work with The Lodestone Bridge, we wish to re-engage with those that have been long lost from intergalactic communication: not just human beings, but many other planets as well. Many worlds were shut down and isolated when the main lines of communication were destroyed.

The disruption in communication was because of a particular being's greed and the hubris of his people. They wanted total control over the elegant web of energy and light that joins the stars. This web provides corridors between stellar systems that can be used for fast, safe transport, although these corridors are not wormholes: in your metaphor, wormholes are about as dangerous as using the Niagara Falls to cross the street!

However, the ones that wanted to control these routes first put in tolls and restrictions, electromagnetic controls, and then finally tried to pull the power from the web lines directly. This "broke" the web, causing a slow cascade that disconnected planets wholesale.

Yes, several efforts were made to stop this from happening, but the ones who engineered it isolated themselves and were quite covert in their actions. The web is repairing itself, slowly. Mental communications travel from star to star with little interference now. However, so many worlds suffered from the break! And they are still suffering, Earth among them: the destructive cascade reached Earth 8,000 years ago.

D'Barni: I became an Ambassador to the Galactic Federation in part because of my work with you, Francesca. But I want to work with The Lodestone Bridge because I am fascinated with the delightful differences in human cultures, and how individual human beings relate to those cultures, whether by fitting themselves to the cultures, or fitting the cultures to themselves.

As noted above, I am also delighted and fascinated with your stage plays, television, and other media. I enjoyed watching "Singing in the Rain" with Francesca and learning about the early days of the "talkies," the new (at that time) movies with sound, and I was there near Francesca telepathically with Etienne, that beloved Frenchman from your past life that connected with you through Elaine, who wanted to see Gene Kelly dance.

The people on our planet are nearly as physical as human beings, so I am interested in that part of you too: how do you manage taking care of your physical, mental, emotion, psychic and spiritual bodies.

And for me, The Lodestone Bridge represents a refreshed and engaging connection to human creativity. You human beings have invented some very fine textiles, flower arrangements, and celebrations, all of which are important to our people, as you will see below.

Francesca: Who might be interested in working with The Lodestone Bridge?

D'Barni: (Laughs.) Anyone who accepts the idea that other intelligences are real and that they might want to communicate. People who are willing to trust wisely and not depend upon others blindly would find working with us very valuable. We Lodestone Bridge members are working through it and with you because we know we are human in our ways: fallible, subject to limitations and confusion, loving at times, and less than loving at other times. We are here to speak and to listen, to listen and to speak. We are here to renew old friendships and create new ones.

D'yet: I do enjoy other creative minds. Human beings need to work towards a level of psychic or etheric perception so that who and what we and others are can be real to them. We can and must be changed by each other. It is a fine paradox, is it not? The challenge of the work of The Lodestone Bridge is to remain ourselves through change and to discover what does not change but rather grows. I am certain joy helps, or at least enjoyment. So, those who join the Bridge, human or otherwise, might be prepared for joy...

I am a projective empath: I can translate my feelings into etheric or "psychic" messages. So, I can be called upon to create catharsis, inspiration, calmness, pleasure, or insight. My skill is to re-create a set of images and experiences and weave them together in a beautiful form. I find that beauty heals; so does my audience. For me, healing is primarily easing strain. Healing should take nothing away from challenges or courage, or the exhilaration of using both challenge and courage.

But as resting renews you, so also I intend for my poetry to renew. I was trained in my empathy; it is second nature to me now. D'Barni was trained in his abilities by circumstance; they are also second nature to him now.

Francesca: Please tell me a little about yourselves.

D'yet: Thank you for interviewing us together: we miss each other's company when we must be apart!

Our planet has no moon: if it were not for the fact that we have little water our world's life might have been washed away long ago. I've seen some moons on other planets: they're delightful! Our planet is an earthlike world, but very dry: it is quite some distance from Earth. Our home star is very like yours, but its color is a little redder, and the star is bigger: the colors its light creates would seem more saturated to you. Our sun would look more orange, and our sky greener. Our night sky is very dark and most of our water is in the air.

We are mainly vegetarians and must spend a good deal of time eating. We're diurnal, though we are not out in the middle of the day if we can help it. My brother and I are living on a planet around the star Spica now, which is much more temperate than home ever was. Rather than green, though, the Spican foliage is red and purplish, though its sky is blue very like your Earth's. We are here because my brother is an Ambassador with the Galactic Federation now.

As an empathic poet, I take feelings and re-create experiences through my telepathic projections so that others can share my emotions. My brother D'Barni has supported my work a great deal, helping arrange the times and places of my presentations with great care.

D'Barni: I enjoy my new area of work as an Ambassador for the Galactic Federation very much. With all those years of arrangements for my brother's concerts, and managing all the details of the cultural differences, I have had enough practice for any ambassadorial duties! When I was helping my brother to travel for his poetry presentations, I also worked as an herbalist, a respected position for me, similar to a nurse practitioner in your world. Since we moved to Spica, I have been too busy for most of my herbs, although I often have engaging discussions with other healers.

I very much used to like my flower shows, because most shows featured plants that would not grow well in my original area. Because of our jumbled terrain and shallow seas, our planet has complex weather and this leads to some exciting variations in the vegetation. Most of our food is eaten raw, which is why our jaw muscles are so strong.

We do prefer tender vegetation and do some preparation with our food to loosen the sugars or make the proteins more available. We eat eight times a day, not including snacks. Food can express friendship, be a form of bonding, status, or welcome. Everyone knows how to prepare at least several types of meals, though some have specialties.

In our home world, acting in the sense of presenting ideas in stories with costumes to an audience, is a very deep thing in our culture, so there are a great many plays, actors, and performances of many kinds. So, we are particularly interested in the plays, actors, and movies, and the depth and range of human emotions and presentations on Earth. We also think your concert symphonies are marvelous!

On our planet, we are full of holidays! We have days to celebrate and notice nearly everything: the changes and growth in us, our families, our communities, or our league's successes and growth. The leagues are like what you call brotherhoods. The leagues accept members from everywhere and so are not political. We have stage plays about holidays; we have whole groups of holidays all at once together.

D'yet's favorite holiday is what you might translate as the Male Investiture. This is where a young man formally breaks away from his family and takes up his responsibilities. A male may go through that more than once but of course, the first one is the most significant. My favorite holiday was the Flower Dancing. On this holiday in the spring, hundreds and hundreds of flowers are grown, chosen, and presented. There are sweet things to eat and lovely tunnels made up of living plants and flowers that our children, and many adults, run through laughing. With our new contacts with human beings, we may watch and then have our version of the Rose Parade!

D'yet: We eat with our hands out of bowls of various sizes. Families generally eat together for several of the meals. For banquets, there can be quite a protocol as to the size, color, and shape of the personal bowls and the presentation of the food. We have very few taboos about eating; I would guess it is because we have to do so much of it!

Even our stage plays give the actors time to eat something. Some plays try to work in a banquet every time, no matter how unlikely the reasons are! The one taboo we have is to eat unclothed because we have a nudity taboo as you do. Some may think it strange, because of our fur, but clothing has its status.

Many of us like to go climbing on our world, whether it is mountains, trees, or rooftops because climbing on roofs is a pleasant way to meet your neighbors. We tell each other stories, dancing by ourselves if we like, but usually in great circles. As mentioned, we also have theater festivals, where empaths create emotions for others to feel.

Sometimes the play is completely spontaneous, using suggestions from the audience: this is my favorite pastime as I get a lot of pleasure from feeling others' emotions and am fascinated to see the ways emotions change from the mind's surface to its depths! I also enjoy seeing how people affect each other emotionally, with the contrasts and harmonies.

Francesca: What about your families?

D'yet: In our culture, a pair of brothers will marry a pair of sisters, not necessarily twins, though that does happen too. Rarely there are three and three, or one and one; usually, a family unit is four parents. It is usually the sisters who choose whom they will marry because they have the greater cost of childbirth. Generally, the men feel privileged to be chosen by the wife and sister-wife. For courtship, the men give the women gifts of water, cloth, and woven flowers, symbolizing life, shelter, and beautiful sustenance. And of course, there is an extensive feast to celebrate after the marriage.

Children are very much loved. We have as few as two and as many as eight children. The children are healthier if the sisters or brothers care for each other and the intended parents treat each other lovingly as well. Same-sex siblings usually form close bonds that last through life.

If someone is the only girl or boy in the family, there are many different chances to find new siblings. There are many tales of "found" siblings loving each other more dearly than their original family members. And yes, sometimes the marriage works very well, and sometimes not as well. If married sisters and brothers do not get along together, then other arrangements can be devised.

I was a singleton: I had no brother until D'Barni was offered to my family, and so he is particularly special to me. When we have time, my brother and I both massage each other and comb each other's fur. This is accepted as a family gesture and helps us to know that we are friends. We will do the same with our wife and her sister and with our children, should we marry. But for me, the best pleasure is to know that someone who is with you loves you.

D'Barni: In our case, the quartet who birthed D'yet was friends with and attached to the quartet who birthed me, but there are nearly twelve years between his birth and mine, as my parents were "out of town," as you say, doing geological work. The family was close emotionally, but work often took them apart. Originally I was named Dey Too, as it was understood from the beginning that I would be there to help D'yet in his poetry. Before I became his "roadie," I didn't imagine the help I would offer him was going to be so practical!

Even though there are some differences in temperature and atmosphere, our people might visit your world physically someday. Spica, where we are now, is further away from Earth than even our world is. But because of the vibrant minds on Spica, it is easier to communicate with us there. To perceive your world, we go into reverie with the imagination that is the very key of being. We get to Earth in our minds because our minds have the freedom to reach into what is.

Our planet is a member of the Federation in good standing and we are known as good empaths and communicators. As for me, I was introduced to Francesca on a Star Cruiser. This was when the Federation was looking for telepathic and empathic "matches" of our people and human beings. Alas for me, she had already chosen to work with another being at that time: this was the delightful being known to her as "Samovar." It was not until she remembered me as someone alien who could work with the

Bridge that I got to connect with her telepathically again. Indeed, she gave me my present name (see above).

Francesca: What have you learned from us that has helped you?

D'yet: Several things not to do. Not to assume that the ostensible, conscious reason is what is driving other beings or the issues between them. Never forget fear's impact but at the same time, never let it drive you.

D'Barni: In some of our dealings with the other worlds, brother, you know we haven't lived up to these lessons very well.

D'yet: [Dryly.] That is one of the ways we discerned the value of the lessons. We have also learned the value of joy, of enjoyment, of friendship. Once they feel secure, human beings are good friends. You human beings can be so generous with your caring! D'Barni, you know how long friendship can last.

D'Barni: Years. For lifetimes, all over time and space. That is why I am a member of the Bridge. We both feel we can offer human beings several things of value.

D'yet: Such as a comedy act with a weird sense of humor, you mean? (Laughs) Well, just considering our own lives, we have learned to adapt to change and to reflect people to themselves, so that they can perceive their impact upon others. I have several "sagas," of long emotion-and-tone poems, that I would dearly like to share because they could show human beings what it is like in some of the other parts of the galaxy.

D'Barni: There is tremendous value in our empathic poetry: maybe we can offer a few ideas as inspiration? We could certainly offer you some stories. Your whole world is enchanted by stories, the told and the shown; the real and the unreal. In your creative arts, there is much strength and magic, and it would be good to draw that forth even more.

D'yet: Not draw it forth, because it is already there: rather, re-acquaint you with the value of creativity, so that it becomes more of a priority. We could offer support to the ones who have been taught that creativity, or a creative career, is too hard to pursue because creativity itself is too often unsupported in your world.

D'Barni: And although I doubt it is necessary, I can offer someone a way to appreciate being immersed in clean water such as a hot tub… As a desert being, I find the experience exquisitely luxurious and would love to share it.

D'yet: That and the fact that Earth may be another market for my poetry, should I live so long! (Laughs.) Truly, the Bridge offers me a place to learn and a place to love. I know that several human people are interested in seeing how we extraterrestrials work our part of the Shift from one Age to another; human beings may want to count us among the signs and portents of that Shift. Indeed, my brother and I are taking advantage of the opportunity the Bridge represents because we want to know and to be known, as all beings do.

D'Barni: I communicate within the Lodestone Bridge because Francesca is an ambassador herself and I feel the deep resonance between us, creating a friendship that oversteps the bounds of time and space. As to why we and the other members of the Bridge are communicating now, the answer is simple: opportunity. In ten thousand people, .001% of them are only one person: in eight billion, that same percentage is eighty million. If .001% represents those human beings who are also star beings and who remember it, then you see the potential.

D'yet: Our people do not know yours well yet. But we are aware of your creativity and similarity to us and are enchanted. We two have already had the chance to perceive several of your stage plays, including the wonderful musical "Cats." We feel privileged! In some ways, our cultures have a kind of "convergent evolution," but in other ways, your methods have excited us a great deal.

Francesca: How do you relate to us human beings?

D'Barni: Generally, our people are still a little cautious. I know the terrible risks of evoking fear in a fear-based culture or planet. As far as I can perceive, there is no danger greater than fear, unless it is that which intentionally invokes fear because fear can be masked and pretend to be many other things. In many ways, our planetary races are similar: I relate to those similarities while frankly enjoying the differences. I have learned how much love means to human beings, in respect caring, and regard.

In my work as an ambassador, and even before, when I was D'yet's "roadie," I knew how much these things meant to us. But I am coming to understand how much they mean to the galaxy and the universe. Respect, caring, and regard are constants. They are the treasures that all races seek and value. All suffer terribly without them.

D'yet: I have learned some human poetry, and have written a few poems in the human form, though as they are personal, I do not wish to share them here. I have been fascinated with the cadences of human speech. Verbal speech is rare in the galaxy, did you know that? Human beings have something priceless in their diverse spoken languages.

Watching human beings, I have learned how brightly honesty, patience, and many other virtues shine in the face of that which is dishonest, impatient, abusive, shallow, or empty. And, that there are even times when the jewels of kindness, integrity, or loyalty are masked by the hectic glitter of the false things that surround them.

Francesca: Do your people have sciences?

D'Barni: We have more than herbal healing in our world. We understand engineering because of all those stages, stage props, and special effects! Those who practice medicine here do it most frequently as a sideline, along with some other discipline.

Some of these other disciplines are impossible for me to describe. Some I can describe: Costumer, Engineer, or our equivalent of your Concierge, Farmer, or Ecologist. Oddly enough to you, all of these would be deemed a part of medicine. If I had not had my brother's concerts, I might also have become what you would call a doctor or I might have simply become another actor.

As an herbalist, I once pursued one interaction of plant chemicals through several stages, temperatures, and other conditions. I found out several useful things and am still known for some of them, which pleases me. Herbal healing began as the science of dyes for our clothes and evolved into methods of treating the body's imbalances. We are less skillful than some at repairing wounds, but we are very good at counteracting poisons. There is so much in our world that is poisonous, plants and animals both!

We also understand how our empathy works with our brains, minds, and psychic selves fairly well. We do not have your scientific method; our usual question is a lot closer to, "What if?" Considering how strong the craft of acting is in our culture, "What if?" carries a great weight indeed.

Only recently have we been asking "What if we had more water in our desert world?" Careful, empirical tests have been made, and we are weighing the benefits. We do not want to change things in ways that would create harm, so we give it time. But it seems such a good idea to have a hot tub for the cold desert nights...

D'yet: We have many myths, some from other beings that involve people we have met in the galaxy, though some have felt themselves to be completely unrecognizable in our versions of them! I have been deeply interested in the myths, teaching stories, and icons of the cultures I have known. The contrast between what is believed to be true or untrue, real or unreal, from world to world, intrigues me.

In your world, some special people make numinous presences real: your numens, for instance, or your archangels. I am fascinated by the cultural social and personal implications of the myths that form cultures. For us, the Presence of the All is like air. The Presence is lived in, enjoyed, remarked upon, accepted as a gift, and utilized for life. And when we think of it, it is given the meaning it is due.

D'Barni: Thank you so much for allowing us to present our planet's culture and for allowing us to become a part of this tremendously hopeful experiment of The Lodestone Bridge!

D'yet: I thank you also, and wish you all sweet feelings.

D'yet's Poem, 7/3/98

Presented At Galactic Federation Council Meeting

"The Human Earth"

In the dark, the wide dark, the stars shine so keenly. Each brilliant one shines; each with a world of life around it… but this one is alone.

The darkness can no longer be bridged! Every brilliant star, stark against the black brilliance of the silence within the darkness, is poised, waiting. All places are touched by starlight, but this star, separated, cannot be touched: it is alone.

Who can bridge their distance? Who can bind it again into the folds of love? The thinnest threads are those that can withstand the light-shock of love. And serve as the beginning…. which tips the universe into wholeness again.

These small threads are set aside; forgotten; left in an unimportant place, a disregarded corner where the threat awaits.

And with it, pushed aside as being of no importance, is also the secret: a gem, a treasure of the finest brilliance, of the clearest form, waits as alone as the stars have become.

Many have attempted to shatter this gem: to break it, discard it, to rip away its meaning from it, and laugh at its promise, and its strength: the gem is tossed aside, as being of no value.

Yet this gem has held its secret, whole in partnered brilliance, alone in neglected loss, knowing from the substance of its fire that love alone has the strength to bridge the impossible darkness between the stars: this gem is precious.

For love, alone, can gain strength from sorrow; can step aside from neglect and shine again; can retain its value, though it is forgotten, besmirched, and given in to danger.

Love alone can speak the hundred thousand tongues of those who are held by the stars.

It was meant to join the stars; it *will* join the stars. However long it was alone, this love remained: the pure gem of love remained. It did not shatter; it did not break: it endured with only its nature to sustain itself… for its nature was hope.

Cast aside as worthless, it kept its meaning whole and became of surpassing brilliance, surpassing value, of worth beyond measure… For the brilliance of this love, triumphant, overcame the gap of separation that the mad darkness thought fitting to put between the galaxies, so that even the fear becomes, in time, a star of unsurpassed brilliance.

D'yet, Poet laureate

VRRTVV VXX

Personal note: Vrrtvv Vxx, and the Rangers, is a "policeman" (a true "peace officer") of the Galactic Federation. Vrrtvv Vxx's physical form is quite intimidating. But you might not find a kinder father and more caring husband anywhere, on any planet.

Vrrtvv Vxx was Artonn's partner in the Galactic Federation Rangers. Artonn, you may recall, was Doris's main ET contact: his people from Vega had a reputation in this galaxy as somewhat dangerous, unpredictable beings, and by serving as a Ranger Artonn was trying to change that prejudice.

However, people on Earth are seen as even more dangerous and unpredictable, and if you consider things from an ET's point of view, especially an ET that has a strange form, such as Vrrtvv Vxx, Toh Ka Sei, Ka Ch Sei Ka, or even Thoyantir, you can easily imagine they would be seen as dangerous monsters by a paranoid society.

That bright spot on his chest is a sensitive patch that can "read" another person's emotions and physical state, especially when his people meet heart to heart. He can move very fast on those caterpillar feet of his, and since he is about six feet from chest to head, he is nearly 20 feet long. At present, he is teaching new Rangers how to work with frightened beings that might find themselves suddenly through one of the Stargates and overwhelmed by the crowds.

When I got to know VrrTvv Vxx's wife, Vexrra, I was astonished that she had a name with vowels in it... Sometimes in our house's quiet backyard, I communicate mentally to Vrrtvv Vxx and the others. I even came to know Vrrtvv Vxx's family: they had four children that I would read stories to, like the Russian fable "The Little Humpbacked Horse." I spent several hours with Uuatcha, their elder daughter, once: Vexrra helped us both keep the connection. But I lost touch with this ET family when my brain became less able than before.

Francesca: What would you like to say to the humans who want to work with the Lodestone Bridge?

Vrrtvv Vxx: I became a member of The Lodestone Bridge partly as one of the representatives of the Rangers, and partly to show an alien example of love and family. To the human adventurers within the Bridge, I can primarily offer a sense of strength. Although the situation concerning communications with Earth is still touchy, I have acted as a psychic protector for some human beings already.

There is still too much apprehension on your planet, the kind of anxiety based on illusions and lies rather than reality, driving you to the rashest acts: when you are afraid you cannot think. I can steady someone by my presence and I certainly hope that my very existence as a Ranger suggests that things are kept in balance intentionally within the greater galaxy.

Earth is a very special case, as you know, both in others' perceptions within the galaxy and in your world. I firmly believe the Earth adage, "Handsome is as handsome does." No matter how strange the form, what matters is the intention and the *vioxteytszah*, the living integrity and principles of the being or beings involved. If the form is beautiful, but the being does not adhere to tenets of love, compassion, and peace, then that being is to be avoided, or at the very least, treated with great caution.

Contact with Earth is limited, by mutual agreement because Earth is unique in its physicality. Each form, and the very substances of that form's structure, has its own "tone," its resonant pitch. Earth's pitch is one of the most complex in the universe because to be a being manifested on Earth is to be realized in nearly all the waves of the electro-physical spectrum.

If you were to get an analysis of Earth's physicality, Earth's "spectrum" would spike at almost every place along the reading. Sirians would have a whole "end" of the line empty, as would Altarians, because they are essentially etheric, but Earth has it all: all of the electro-magnetic-photonic spectra you are used to, plus the mental, emotional, physical, and psychic spectrums, and others I cannot describe. So several races can visit you, and have, but they will seem less than "real" to you because they do not have the same full "tone" of manifestation as you on Earth do.

The ones we hope can work with The Lodestone Bridge are human beings of courage who hold to their integrity, who are willing to learn from what they encounter, and who enjoy discovery, mystery, and the unexpected. I look for and ask to work with human beings who are willing to love where it matters because they know what love is, and know how to respect others because respect can almost be greater than love.

Francesca: What does working with The Lodestone Bridge mean to you?

Vrrtvv Vxx: For me, being a part of the Lodestone Bridge means connection and friendship. It means a chance to show who I am, as I know myself, and to discern my nature as I interact with others unknown to me. And now that I am semi-retired, I can enjoy waxing philosophical, and hope to have some listeners! (Laughs) But the main thing the Bridge offers me is an expansion of my sense of reality. And if it is done with respect and consideration, that cannot be anything but beneficial.

I have been a member of The Lodestone Bridge since the beginning, and it has been more than simply learning what I can from you, or sharing what I have. I also intend to help create a link between Earth and the other worlds of the galaxy. Earth has been cut off from the stars for far too long. There are even a few who feel that human beings have become viciously insane as a result of this separation from the other galactic races.

I trust that love matters to you all and that it will find its way through everything. I believe that if your humanity is insane, it is from loss and longing. If it is vicious, it is because of its pain. If the pain can be eased, genuinely eased, and not simply masked or buried, then I feel the viciousness will drop away as though it never was.

I most sincerely hope that the original intention of creating an open bridge, upon which many can walk in both directions, is not forgotten. I believe this connection can create a fundamental basis of respect between beings, the respect that understands the other accepts the other for what he/she/it is, and acts accordingly.

I also want to keep the lines of communication clear. Most of us in the galaxy are telepaths, so this helps when we try to understand you and work with you. But even amongst the best telepaths and other perceptive beings, differences in worldview can lead to misunderstanding. We need to return to the common truths: integrity, honesty, and love.

I also believe that the Whole knows Its Self, and is always seeking to know that Self even more fully.

Francesca: What is it like to work with human beings?

Vrrtvv Vxx: On your planet, you have many skills we consider sciences here: interior decorating in the sense of creating a place; wisdom in codifying and transmitting experience, and music. My people also study what you might call the psychic arts: psychic phenomena have principles that have been analyzed, understood with training, are predictable, and can be reproduced.

However, human beings are so unpredictable and paranoid that the higher-level galactic civilizations are determined not to come to Earth until you human beings have stopped all the wars, murders, trafficking, and child abuse. They have no desire to come here and get slaughtered by someone so fear-based that he cannot imagine that someone different is not automatically an enemy!

Many in the galaxy fear you because when we see what you fear, and what you do because of fear, several are appalled at the very idea of contact. However, I have seen a great deal of what the galaxy can offer and feel confident enough to try a genuine connection with Earth emotionally and psychically, and perhaps physically too, someday.

The challenge, as always, is to find what works under the different conditions of culture, circumstance, and so on. The sciences of the general galaxy are culturally-coded methods of perceiving what exists, to make informed choices towards the goal of promoting the life of the whole. In my relationship with the essence of life, I trust to love fundamentally.

I have learned how important rituals of protocol are to you. If someone has something important to say, the importance or value is not automatically accepted: you must be informed of the importance, and lately through social media. You must become used to an idea for a while, no matter how good or wise it is, and only then can you accept it. But the habituation and the acceptance must both be done properly, unless you run away in terror, or fight with ferocity.

I have also learned some of the things you do for the love you need. Sometimes wise, sometimes foolish, you appear to have made it a virtue to live with as little love as possible. And, when a tiny bit of love is offered, you can cling to it in fear that it will be torn away, and warp yourselves around that need accordingly. I feel you pay too high a price, but then, you do value what is expensive, even if the expense is your human sense of self.

Francesca: Tell me a little more about yourself.

Vrrtvv Vxx: Although I am not from Spica's world, I live there, to be near the Galactic Federation Council. I am a Ranger, a combination of undercover agent, detective, and police enforcer. I have been stationed on Spica for many years. When my partner, a being of much worth, was killed, I became semi-retired, and have since been teaching, working most directly with the Galactic Federation's offices.

I am married and have a family. My wife is Vexrra, a woman of great competence and administrative abilities. Our eldest son, B'rett'che'che, is away from home now, as is our eldest daughter, Uuatcha. She is a translator, working in the Federation offices, and is doing very well, for this is work she truly enjoys. Our younger son is named Brrr. Our baby was born unexpectedly about twenty-one years ago, your time, and she has decided her gender and chosen a final name, Chnn'l Tua; she wants to be a teacher for 3rd-stage children, your equivalent of Junior High students.

Our children are born as embryonic infants and stay with both parents from three days to three weeks. Then, they create a new skin around themselves, which becomes a soft eggshell. With much ceremony, the new egg-shrouds are brought to caves, with as many as a hundred other children. Nurses will stoke the eggs, exuding a clear liquid from their forearms, which is rich in nutrients. As they do this, the child chirps a call, so they know it is developing well.

The children hatch all at once, even though some of them are younger by as much as three months. Free from their soft shells, they scurry around, peeping. The parents are informed of the commotion and go down to see their children, who usually find their parents again immediately. When the children come home, they are usually female, and to you, they would look somewhat like millipedes.

As they grow, they shed their exoskeletons and change form about four times. At the second change, or perhaps the third, they choose which sex they will become, quite deliberately. We generally have our closest, family-like ties with those who were born with us in the cave. These, though unrelated to us physically, can be as close as blood siblings. I am a part of a hatching group of twenty-three.

In some ways, we are very different from human beings, but in other ways, we are very like you, almost as much alike as you and Ka Cha Sei Ka's people. We enjoy gathering friends and sharing food. We serve your equivalents of teas and juices, protein shakes, and puddings! Because my family lives on Spica with me, we have had some unusual beings in our house, with some unusual needs and pleasures. My wife Vexrra has only objected to hosting the beings that imbibed electricity directly; she was distressed by the smell of ozone.

We also eat various fish-like creatures. There are no mammalians on my planet. But the fish-like creatures do have some of their skeletons inside, like your mammals, and are considered an oddity in a world where most everything has a carapace. I have mandibles under my beak, which have sharp slicing plates on the inside, followed by layers of grinders of a substance very like your teeth. These teeth are the hardest things in my whole body, harder even than the densest parts of my exoskeleton.

As a Ranger, working with people from many other planets, I have learned to eat a great many foods not native to my world. Some meals are very artistically arranged: the artistry itself is considered edible. Were I at home, my diet would consist mainly of a bread-like substance, cooked and flavored in various ways, and a type of stew of meat and vegetables. When refined, that stew can serve as your tea or fruit juices.

Before she went on to become a translator, our elder daughter Uuatcha kept some beautiful off-world shimmer-flies for a while. They have long, flowing tails, very gossamer, with many colors, that they use to confuse their predators. They will also use these shining tails as a signal to larger animals so they will come over to the shimmer-fly clusters. The shimmer-flies land on the other animal's back and can eat the parasites, dead skin, and so on, for their nourishment.

In my world, we have trained a species of snake-like creature to play with us. They wrap their bodies around us as we move. On a practical level, this helps to keep our exoskeleton sections in good order. They are also a great deal of fun. The snakes' unity with us evolved, but I think they began as our shimmer-flies or like your own "cleaning fish:" a truly symbiotic relationship.

Francesca: Tell me a little about what it means to be a Ranger of the Galactic Federation:

Vrrtvv Vxx: You can call the Rangers peace officers: we are simultaneously under the jurisdiction of the Galactic Federation, the Galactic Council, and the beings of the Galactic Center Council. This is not as difficult as it sounds, though the politics can get intricate occasionally. We work in pairs, for physical backup, and partners are usually from different planets, because we find the additive skills of those dissimilarities quite valuable, as two beings of different abilities can solve the same problem in different ways. We know that the view of any one being is not enough to discern the true nature of a situation.

We study psychology. We know that there is a deep difference between distress that leads to growth, which we must allow, and what kind of distress that leads to senseless and abusive pain, and we work to discern that difference as clearly as we can. Physical, mental, and perceptive competence has saved our lives many times because we do go into danger at times. Some misunderstandings can escalate because of unexpected or volatile combinations of minds and energies. Some beings are dangerous by their very nature, but there are far fewer beings that intend active violence than some human beings seem to think, what with your stories of invaders from other planets.

Some of the Rangers, such as Shambeytas, the Head of the Corps, can see into what you would call the psychic or the etheric realms of information quite well, and she is often conversing with beings I cannot perceive without training. For some of these beings, we would not use physical compounds for first aid, but emotions or ideas. All realities are as real as all other realities; the challenge is in their interaction. Because I am nearly as physical as a human being, I am of such a nature that your Earthly compounds would be of real use to me.

As a Ranger, I do know much about first aid, but my confidence in it is limited to the beings I have worked on personally. As a teacher in the training center, I share what I have learned, especially some of my mistakes. We Rangers are aware of what a body needs to be healthy and so I know my wife and I at least will both have a long life.

The essence of medicine, as I understand it, is to stop what is not wanted and to promote what is in best balance. Ideally, this is in all realms of the self, and that demands many different methods. One of the intricacies of healing is the degree of physicality of the beings involved. Even though you perceive the galaxy and the rest of the universe in terms of your physics, there is much that is not physical, yet is as real.

Francesca: How do you enjoy your life?

Vrrtvv Vxx: When I am not on Spica, I go to my home, which is further out on the galactic Rim than Earth. For fun, I like a form of sport similar to "bungee jumping:" it uses a kind of catapult, which flings my body forward. When I hit the ground I must roll into a ball. I do it for the simple pleasure of the launch, the roll, the landing; I have only cracked my carapace once, not too badly, when I was learning.

I also entertain myself with a kind of body-song. It is a little like Ka Cha Sei Ka's music, but it is much noisier because the curved plates on my back are even tougher than hers. Sometimes I use a stick and become a drum! The rhythms I tap out then are based on my verbal language, and upon natural sounds. I enjoy the entertainment of other worlds, as well.

I find beautiful places entertaining, especially if there is a little danger with the beauty. That danger and beauty are often found together fascinates me. No wonder, I suppose, I am attracted to being a Ranger, and even to you unpredictable human beings.

Indeed, my best pleasure in life is to succeed in my work as a Ranger. When I was in the field, my work played me against beings that were agile, able, and fully determined in their actions, and sometimes those actions did not consider the consequences to others. Now that I am teaching, I love to succeed as a teacher by being a little more agile, able, and determined than my students! I enjoy teaching them how to outfox, outface, and, at times, outrun, beings who are dangerous.

I have studied the laws and mores of hundreds of planets. Through these laws, I see that there are dependable ways of determining an individual's true relationship to the effects he creates, and to perceive how that being's actions affect others. My most successful encounters are when those beings that oppose what is gentle become gentled themselves, or when those who create fear cease to project that fear. Through the language of my actions, I show the harm that has been done is not in accord with the most authentic self of the one who has done that harm.

SHAMBEYTAS

Personal Note: The Galactic Federation Council, on Spica, is another Star Council I am familiar with. Unlike the wide open, "come as you are" Sirian Council, the Federation Council works with galactic issues. It is there that I worked with Shambeytas and Toh Ka Schei: Shambeytas is the head of the Galactic Rangers; Toh Ka Schei is her "secretary;" they are both of the same species. She is wise, astute, and has a good way of working with the Rangers.

Francesca: What does The Lodestone Bridge mean to you?

Shambeytas: The Lodestone Bridge offers me an opportunity to reconnect with those on Earth who are from other stars so we of the Federation can truly see what is going on with your planet and your people.

I feel that Humanity should describe its truth, instead of those who can only view it from a distance. The Bridge promises to be a way of safe communication and I will be watching its development with great interest. I also want to be fully engaged in my task as the Spican Representative, so that I can offer Spica's particular energy to those who ask.

For me, this is more than opportunity: I was instructed to speak to human beings through the Bridge by those beings in the Federation who perceive more clearly than most. To follow an analogy, if I am the head chef of the Rangers, these more skilled beings are both the first-class professors of the cooking school, as well as the librarians with all the best cookbooks. To us, if it is clear that another being is wise, with experience and grace, it is inefficient at best and plainly stupid at worst to ignore what the wise one has to say!

I may not even know the "why" of being asked to communicate with Earth after so many of your years where Earth was kept sequestered. But as volatile as your present situation on Earth is, several things should be respected. For instance, too many people on Earth feel insecure about their relationships with Reality or the very nature of Reality itself. At such times, the information received through contemplative reflection is an invaluable aid. The Lodestone Bridge can offer this.

Francesca: Shambeytas, what have you learned from us?

Shambeytas: I have learned that some of you are "natural" Rangers, for you are beings of integrity and principles that do not abandon love even when it is difficult; nor do you abandon courage, even when it causes you some pain. Watching your world and how you interact with each other, I have learned a great deal about emotional pain. I have learned something about how things such as the sense of joy are lost and how some things are found, like a fresh sense of purpose.

I have learned how much kindness matters in your world and something of what happens when that kindness is abused. I have learned about the fear that possesses and drives you, though that is not something I wish to study in depth. I do not wish to experience that kind of fear as fully as human beings have!

Still, I have learned how powerful Love is, which takes lifetimes worth of learning. I am most glad for this opportunity!

Francesca: Who would you like to work with you?

Shambeytas: Anyone interested in finding effective and love-based ways to rejoin Earth to the civilizations and cultures of the greater galaxy should be working with us. Those who react only from fear or that wish to promote only fear and its consequences of pain, hatred, bigotry, or viciousness need not apply. The most important thing about the work of the Federation and its Rangers is that love, respect, understanding, kindness, and joyous communication may unite Earth and other beings that love.

I became a part of The Lodestone Bridge, which you and Thoyantir evolved because I wanted to learn from your different cultures. I enjoy our contacts: I find human minds to be agile and compelling. Many of you reading this collection of interviews are transplanted star beings, as you very likely already know.

Some of you stellar expatriates are already within my jurisdiction, as you have been and are now part of the Federation and Galactic Councils. I care for those who are doing demanding work under difficult circumstances, as so many human beings are.

Earth-to-Federation contacts are closely monitored. So of course I was aware of you, Francesca, as a contact and channel on Earth from early on, and I am especially aware of the connections with you as a human being and with us as galactic citizens made within the Bridge itself.

The important thing is to remove the damage fear has created, both in human beings and in the other worlds. We cannot hope to do this comprehensively. But we can love each other one at a time, respect one another one at a time, understand all as best we can, and strive to be kind. It is my wish that your Human relationships with the Galaxy at large will become based on love, joy, and mutual comprehension.

Indeed, I regret that I cannot offer much to any of you, even telepathically, because there are so many demands on my energy and time. However, as a representative of those beings who have integrity, compassion, and courage, who dedicate their actions towards honoring Life, I hope I can offer evidence that such things are valued in other worlds. I do offer my profound admiration towards your Humanity as a whole because human beings have evidenced unconditional love in places where any love seems absent.

The science of being a human being is demanding on all levels: certainly being human is very demanding emotionally. Sey

Seyarayk's people live their science in their bodies, as it were, as they constantly deal quite directly with physics. But for human beings, in some ways it is even more involved.

Still, the main core of all spiritualities I know about comes to this: to discern and then to decide how you relate to Other than yourself and how you relate to yourself. Relating, of course, demands communication: there are numerous forms of that!

You also need to know your intentions and desires. Some have studied the cultural implications at great length; I have simply learned enough to at least avoid offense.

Francesca: Tell me a little about yourself.

Shambeytas: I am middle-aged and have at least another 160 years left in me, so there will be continuity in the administration. I am being more careful now, delegating more and more to other able beings that I have trained. I rarely go out in the field anymore: most of the Rangers know I am very busy with taking care of the lines of communication, command, support, and information.

I was brought to Spica when young because, quite frankly, I was getting into so much mischief that my parents had to find a way of applying my deep intelligence and desire to be of use. In other words, yes, I was a "holy terror." But the first time I saw the great doors of the Ranger Enclave, I felt at home.

You have drawn me accurately, by the way: I do not have the complex color patterns Toh Ka Schei has, and, yes, I did lose my right leg in an accident in space: I was trapped, and they could not reach me in time. I was swimming in and out of unconsciousness when they had to amputate my leg, so thankfully I do not remember much.

However, because the information I was carrying was very time-sensitive, I had to demand to speak with someone even as they took me into care, although this was a strain. But now, when I come in and talk to those Rangers who have been injured, I feel I can understand their situation better. In the Galactic Federation, we who serve others are supported well, if only because we can then be of better service.

You can read Toh Ka Schei's account, which follows this one, for general information about our species. What Toh Ka Schei did not mention is that we tend to be matrilineal, in terms of who was born to which family. I was the third child, first-family daughter, of two particularly intelligent parents.

My mother was a seventh granddaughter of direct lineage to one of the most accomplished Ambassadors to the Federation of our race, so I had something to aspire to if I chose. I am the only child through my mother with that father. He is a truly accomplished concierge, as you might call him. His talent and delight is to create accommodations for visitors. The two siblings after me and the two before were of two other fathers. For us, as with Thoyantir's people, this is normal: it mixes up the genes beautifully.

I communicate with you by telepathic and empathic resonance: thoughts and emotions together. Although I might be able to manage on your planet in terms of atmosphere, gravity, and so on, I have neither the wish nor the privilege to do so at this time. Give me a hundred Earth years and then I may be able to come.

The Galactic Federation would probably be rather anxious if I were to go, though. They take very good care of me here in Spica. I have a garden and pavilion out behind my office that is fully shielded and yet open to the sky, the stars, and the airs of the night. It is a large place, perhaps ten thousand square feet, though it is quite private.

The lost leg does not trouble me too much. Even after my accident, I can still climb a fair amount, sometimes scaling the outer walls of some of the Rangers' living areas for fun. I also have a floating chair to use most of the time.

Francesca: Please tell me about the Rangers.

Shambeytas: Some of the Rangers, such as Vrrtvv Vxx, describe themselves in human terms as "peace officers," or, "cops." We do not focus nearly as much as Earth people do on Rules, Regulations, and Laws. The Federation, comprised of so many different planets, must necessarily be more diverse and everyone must be more comfortable with diversity. But we are not so foolish as to imagine that diversity can comprehend itself automatically.

We have seen much evidence of the cost of confusion, misapprehension, misunderstandings, and so on. Too many lives have been strained, altered, wrecked, or even lost because of "two rights making a wrong." Untangling such confusion is the Rangers' main task, but there are times when such work can be very dangerous.

Needless to say, being a Galactic Ranger is not a common occupation. There is much physical training, cultural intensives, and sheer practice in telepathy that a Ranger must accomplish. Rangers must be beings of ability and integrity, courage and principles and they must not fear self-honesty.

As the present head of the Rangers, I am privileged to encounter a great many different systems of science, belief, and perception. Most of the lectures I attend are mentally demanding, needing discernment, memory, comprehension, and a good imagination to follow the details. Some sciences, particularly healing, are physically demanding as well, as it is with Thoyantir when he is healing someone: he is one of those few who have learned how to transfer his physical energy into a patient. Some of the Mantis types do this also.

Francesca: What kinds of things do you like to eat?

Shambeytas: I am very fond of a particular dish from my planet, which Toh ka Schei and some others know how to make. Imagine, if you will, a bamboo-shaped tube of light, crispy cooked sweet dough, stuffed full with a green pudding-like mixture of leaves and flowers, drizzled with a light, caramel-like sauce: it's good! Toh ka Schei and I are mostly vegetarians, but we do eat some bug protein.

I generally eat things that can be held in one hand while I am working with the other, so I can nibble through bowls of nuts or drink sap-and-bark. (Tastier than it sounds, since the sap tastes like maple syrup and the bark tastes like cinnamon, with crunchy bug-bits like raisins.) Honestly, a great deal of the logistical support within the Federation has to do with food!

However, I believe that you would find many of our medicine and healing methods to be quite advanced and remarkable. I believe this is because we have come to some different assumptions about the way living systems work than you have. Certainly, if a healer of Thoyantir's caliber were to offer her or his services, we would gladly take advantage, as we do have quite an extensive hospital here.

Francesca: What do you like to do for fun?

Shambeytas: While I do have times of rest that I take at my discretion, I have not enjoyed a family holiday for some time. Perhaps I should look into that if only to give you more cultural information. Yet as Spica is one of the main administrative areas of the Federation and a great many different beings pass through here, it is quite fascinating at the Federation offices: it is like your New York, with visiting artists, musicians, actors, and the like.

I have listened to D'yet several times and not just because of our mutual association with the Lodestone Bridge. Toh ka Schei usually makes notes of such cultural events for me; she knows what I like and, of course, as one of my secretaries she also knows my schedule. How these offerings are presented varies a great deal, of course.

Most performers and presenters prefer "live" productions, where there is as little technology in the way as possible. Most of our recording technology is very unobtrusive anyway. A being such as D'yet can certainly hold an audience without any electronic enhancements.

TOH KA SCHEI

Personal note: I had never seen To Ka Schei's people before, and she had to show me how to draw her picture, one color at a time: "This yellow here, and then this brown, and then this darker brown," and so on. I have always been impressed by her optimism and sheer positive energy. I do know she would truly love some of the forests of Earth.

Francesca: Why are you working with The Lodestone Bridge now?

Toh Ka Schei: Working with human beings, even peripherally, is fascinating. Most human beings are somewhat poor at balancing work and rest. Some of you are complaining about time going faster. Working for the Bridge, I might be able to share my perceptions, and this might allow you to awaken an expanded sense of time or an expanded sense of self.

I love that The Lodestone Bridge offers a chance to exchange cultures in an honorable way. The sharing that is possible, and the learning from that sharing, is very special. I know some are very cautious about this! While I agree that caution should be engaged, I am still looking forward to sharing.

This work with the Bridge is more than just the interest of a few powerful people making this communication happen between human beings and the greater galaxy: this is the proper time. If it does not work just now, there may be other opportunities. But this time is heavy with promise and I want to help to make that promise hold. You see, I am a mammalian a little like yourselves, so you are like very distant cousins.

My work on Spica with the Federation has increased my telepathic abilities a great deal, and I like to use my abilities. Now, you know that many human beings have incarnated into Earth from the galactic community; several who are now human were Sirians, for instance, and there are Altarians who are now human, to say nothing of the Vegans, Pleiadians, and Arcturians: there are many of those!

Communicating with human beings is foremost an opportunity to help things change between the worlds. I am a Telepathic Communicator: I know firsthand how blockages create difficulties, even though the blocks seem like a good idea at the time, such as our earlier decision to keep Earth sealed away from nearly all forms of contact. This was selfish: we wanted to protect ourselves. I am a rebel: I want to see the old ways set aside when they are no longer useful, even if a few cherished notions must be put aside.

I come into the telepathic fields of Earth by sliding through the networked linkages created by minds that are used to sharing each other's thoughts. I have already learned a great deal from working with The Lodestone Bridge, even though my work has had to be sporadic.

I know some of the other non-Earthly members of the Bridge and have felt privileged to meet D'yet and D'Barni, Mir Tarr, and Sssssss Ssit. In my work with the Galactic Federation Council, I have met Ka Cha Sei Ka, Thoyantir, and Vrrtvv Vxx before. I have learned finer telepathic control, especially from Mir Tarr and Thoyantir.

I've learned how to work with human emotions from Mir Tarr, Sssssss Ssit, D'yet and D'Barni, Vrrtvv Vxx, and his wife Vexrra. From the challenge that the Bridge represents, I have learned a good deal about patience: not only for and about Earth, but for other planets also.

The Galactic Federation has been very interested in the "lost" worlds that have been cut off from contact for so long, and in some cases far too long. Some of their cultures have become quite divergent from anything they were before. In that respect, human beings have retained more continuity. You have new ways of putting your cultures together, but you haven't stopped being human.

Francesca: Who would you like to work with in The Lodestone Bridge?

Toh Ka Schei: In the galactic community, I would recommend the Bridge to anyone who can suspend their disbeliefs and prejudices long enough to hear what is being said by Humanity, although occasionally I think this would disqualify 80% of the beings I know about. Regarding your people, I would not add much to what has already been said by the other ET members. It would help if you have an automatic assumption that all beings are created equal, no matter what they've done with that equality since.

Many of you have already had direct contact with alien beings. If this happened when young, some of the fear-reaction has already been eased. I know that human beings do not trust easily, though it would help you and us if you could give us the benefit of the doubt. I know that Earth and humanity have both been interfered with, and this is being worked on. But most of us act from love.

You may meet my people someday, perhaps many years hence. Indeed, you may decide to visit us. My people do not travel in space with ships; we have not had that interest. Still, I am confident that you will see us, as our world is much like yours, though perhaps it will seem a virgin place to you because we prefer to adapt to it rather than adapt it to us.

I think I will be happy to see your Earth. I am fascinated by contrasts: intensity and laxity, awareness and inattention, clarity and obscurity. When properly applied, contrasts create mingling at the edges of their domains, highly creative areas that are greater than the sum of their parts. I love to mix opposites and see what happens with the results.

Francesca: Please, tell me a little more about yourself.

Toh Ka Schei: I have been working with Shambeytas for several decades now, and we are getting skilled at working together. She is no direct relation of mine, but we come from allied families. We do not need to be of allied families to work together but at the same time it is not quite a coincidence if we do, as many families in my world are related by now.

In our world, our people live in the great trees and tend to move around a lot. I was curious about The Lodestone Bridge because I knew it would be interesting to work with human beings. I like the way your thoughts arrange themselves: you can be very persistent like I am. You are artistic, and I find much of your art captivating.

Doing the job I do for the Federation, I am quite organized and can do my work efficiently and well. Were I able to talk with a human member of the Bridge clearly and at length, I could tell something of the day-to-day processes of the business here, the elegant arrangements of beings, tasks, and time. Also, I can help to show how to be a secretary without bureaucracy.

As I suggested above, in my home world I live in the forest, running along the tree branches to visit friends, learning how everyone is doing. What you might call gossip we call our government! We learn who needs help and then who can give help, going from area to area, from community to community, meeting and sharing.

Our society is very non-technological. We do have comforts; ways to shelter us, keep us warm or cool, give us light, give us food and fresh water. But you might wonder what would be entertaining about weaving pieces of bark together, or why is it less entertaining to carry it from place to place, but more entertaining to leave it up on a tree? Why would plucking a taut vine amuse us, especially if we hang various things on the vine, which toss and turn when someone plucks it? But these things do engage and amuse us enough.

We have very strong family bonds, but we are not stuffy about it. Children may receive more support and training from older cousins, aunts, or grandfathers than from parents, at times. We do have two sexes. The male almost always initiates the family by creating a home. The females wander through the forest in groups, examining the homes being offered.

Some females wander for years, joining group after group until they find who meets their needs. The males wander mostly to find good building sites, learning what crafts they need. Once a pair is joined, they remain bonded until the first child is about fifteen and thus fully grown. At that time, the couple usually draws apart, though there are exceptions.

When they are old enough, the children must choose whether to seek a new family in a neighboring area or not, if they feel they need one. This separation is seen as normal and natural, and the children are prepared for it. I have four grown children, two of one family and two of another.

In between my jobs of work, I have been wandering for the last five years. With my duties in the Federation, it suits me better to not commit to creating a new family now. I have not decided to settle down again yet.

We have roving holiday revelers. Like itinerant performers and traders, they move from place to place and bring stories, dances, songs, and beautiful things. They are anticipated, from community to community, and there is much romance associated with them.

We also have a family calendar. It may seem cumbersome to you, but "The Day Grandmother is Three Years Past Her Sabbatical Year" could relate to "The First Day the Second Grandson was Able to Climb Alone" very directly. This "calculating" calendar is quite flexible and can be used freely, or quite meticulously, as we prefer. Any excuse for a party!

Francesca: Surely you must fall out of your trees now and then. (Toh Ka Schei laughs.) How do you work with healing and medicine?

Toh Ka Schei: To us, healing is like a shared dream. There are "dreamers," shamans, who stay in one general area to work directly with a person or persons regularly. Many of us also arrange their travels to find the dreamers, too. We have learned how to persist with healing work until the benefit brings real results. Still, I have seen some "fads" of healing: ideas that have gone around my world three or four times, fads such as eating only red bark, or weaving and then unweaving something you have made fourteen times to release your mind from an illness.

As you might imagine, because we are roamers, illnesses can be brought by those who travel to us. However, we bring the remedies with us or bring them to new places as soon as we know what will work. This is considered common courtesy now, though I am told it used to be sheer self-preservation a long time ago. Because we have been so careful of other visitors from other worlds, we have had few new diseases, even though our race is nearly as physically manifested as your human race.

I tolerate the buildings here on Spica because I must, and so I would probably not like your cities either. Your redwood forests, Sequoias, and national parks would be very good to see. And I would like to see your oceans and lakes, especially the Great Lakes that Francesca remembers from her childhood.

Our food is seeds, fruits, roots, bark, tree saps, new leaves and branches, some of the insects in the trees, and what small animals we can catch or breed: think of a very small rabbit. Because of the other beings we have met, we have changed some of our ways, but not many. We eat as we go, grabbing here, finding there.

We rarely put everyone in the same place at one time to eat a specific meal, since transporting the food through the trees would be difficult. Frankly, we would not be able to gather everyone together long enough in the first place: everyone would want to wander off. I am unusual because I am not as restless as most. This helps with long Council meetings!

We take our living and our health from our trees. We use extracts of herbs and combinations of metals and minerals; sometimes we change our diets for healing purposes. I remember subsisting on nothing but sharp-laces, the main tubular structure inside of a specific leaf, for almost three months, a good 47 days longer than I had ever imagined I could. It was good advice, though, because the imbalance in my internal organs righted itself.

Francesca: How do you manage to eat well on Spica when you work with Shambeytas?

Toh Ka Schei: Sometimes that is troublesome, but you do understand that I am not there on Spica continually: I take frequent breaks to rush back home, though it's true I've developed a taste for some of the Spican plants, even though they have strange colors: purples, blue-greens and even black. I have to cook some of the leaves or they would be poisonous to me, but there are nutritionists here who do their best to take care of me. Shambeytas is even more settled a personality than I: she has gotten a little pudgy from sitting still in one place for so long. But she finds her work fascinating.

In comparison to some, our science is very haphazard, but that is because of our language: it is not as practical as many languages are and is instead full of referents to areas and particularly significant relationships between aspects, people, and circumstances. Because we are tree-dwellers our minds are a curious combination of topographical and dimensional: we consider the line (a path on the ground) only a small part of what is so.

To us, the fact that the blue of a certain leaf is the same as the blue in a certain animal's wing means a lot. Our science is also embedded in our stories. One of the "fads" of our science had to do with evolving different ways to layer several meanings into one story. It was seen as a method of condensing information.

On my planet my people are more creatures of the dawn and evening twilight than of either day or night, so we sleep when we will. I have told you of our "dreamers," our shamans or healers: they study dreaming with great intensity and integrity. I think our storytelling creates some of the same benefits as human dreams in sleep. One storyteller may begin a healing story and have it taken up by another or by the listeners, leading to another and another teller, so the story may last a long time.

There is conscious intention with this storytelling and other aspects I find difficult to describe. We dream in the sense of having aspirations. It was because of such a dream that I followed Shambeytas to Spica: I met her on our planet one of the times she came home for a while. I had only intended to stay working with her for half a year or so but it has been over thirty of your years on Earth now, and there does not seem to be an end in sight yet: we two get along so well.

Francesca: How to you relate to your spirituality?

Toh Ka Schei: Spirituality is very individualistic for us. Some of us conceive of a holy Order, of grand, spherical, or multi-dimensional structures or patterns that relate every living thing to every other thing. Others imagine that the universe is nothing but cycles that repeat, endlessly: differing in details, but nothing else.

For these, what is alive is made for the cycles' perception of themselves and not for any meaning of the living. For still others, it is the other way around: living things make cycles because they are pleased to do so. For me, every moment quivers with life, and knowing this is how I feel my sense of peace.

It has been most interesting to work with other races! However, considering that some beings think of Shambeytas and me to be as cute as some of your pets, it is hard for me to warm up to everyone. We don't have pets, though I know you human beings and many other races do.

However, though we are aware of the other beings in the forest, and take careful note of them, we cannot imagine owning them. Some of them can become hunting and gathering companions, assuming our food sources do not conflict, but this is something that happens in the moment, and we do not demand that it continue indefinitely.

Our children may designate a beetle, worm, crawler, or whatever as something they care about. They watch over it, to learn about it, but this usually only lasts a season. We do not have the life-long companionship with another animal species as you do. Maybe, if we had domesticated somebody, would we have gone the route of your sciences and technology? Instead, we have worked very hard on creating our relatedness with each other, which is certainly a different way to amuse ourselves, I suppose.

I find living a pleasure. I also do weaving for pleasure, rather like my colleague D'Barni used to in his world. Not to make clothes, because we need none. I weave plant matter together to form different artistic patterns and textures.

SSSSSSS SSIT

Personal note: When I first did Sssssss Ssit's portrait, I drew her with a cat's head, wearing an enigmatic expression, although I knew full well she looked nothing like that: the sense of feline mystery is so strong in her personality. She and I both enjoy the fact that, so dissimilar in form, we do nevertheless come to a natural meeting of minds. And it was she who insisted that her transliterated first name be spelled with seven S's, and the second name with two.

Francesca: How did you decide to work with The Lodestone Bridge?

Sssssss Ssit: I responded to the call for The Lodestone Bridge because I am interested in creating contact. It excites me that a structure is being created now with The Lodestone Bridge in the love and minds of many to enable deeper connections. To be a member of this new method of association interests me even more.

The Lodestone Bridge offers me a chance to extend myself and to be part of the underlying order of things. To me, working with human beings means to have an engaging adventure, and the wonder of experiencing alien minds. This way, I can see differences and similarities, deriving understanding from both.

The Bridge also offers me some old friendships. Vrrtvv Vxx knew me a long time ago when we were both Sirians. I hope to know D'Barni in the future; I already feel the touch of his life on mine. And there are others. The work of The Lodestone Bridge is to discover common aspirations and common areas of expression and feeling.

We can also enjoy shared experiences when they can be mutually perceived. From the members of the Bridge, I have learned again how large joy is: as large as my planet's sky and all other skies put together. I have learned the enchantment of different ways and the artistry of each being. I am delighted!

It is easiest for me to engage with you if you sense me as a mothering being: one who is steady, nurturing, competent, and loving. By devaluing the women of your planet, you have cut yourselves off from those qualities quite unwisely. I fancy that if you perceive that feminine quality in a being as alien as I, then you might understand how basic that quality is.

I can offer serenity and the kind of peace based on inner strength so that the peace can withstand upsetting forces. I do not work with distress directly, because a great deal of it is "invisible" to me. Intense emotions are too huge for me to perceive, so I must come in after they are spent and catch the roots of the feelings before they rise or fall again. In this, I must be a bit ingenious, and work to have a deep understanding about when to become perceptible to you.

I have the time to do this work now; I have the interest. The mental call I responded to was a call of the living minds, seeking to know themselves and to reach through love. I am ready. You are ready. The fact that human minds and mine can work together is rare and wonderful, even in such a diverse galaxy.

Francesca: Who might be interested in working with The Lodestone Bridge?

Sssssss Ssit: Those who are called to it because they feel at home with it; there are even those who recognize it. This idea has been tried before, though of course not quite in this new way. Those who would enjoy working with the Bridge are those who love the reflections of themselves in the truth of others and those who are eager to reflect others in their truth.

It would be foolish for anyone to join this that did not have the time to treat it with respect. It would be wise for the sighted, perceptive, and adventurous to come; perhaps artists also. Those who are not empty of their selves and who are stuffed full of narcissism instead.

That the work retains my interest in loving engagement is the most important part of the work for me: that a whole can be created from disparate parts, negating none of them and yet meaning more than all of them together.

Francesca: Please, tell me a little about yourself.

Sssssss Ssit: Though we do not have families, as you understand them, I think you would consider me a motherly being. I am unusual in my world because I can communicate with other beings on other worlds, as though I spoke several "languages."

My species is changeable: our forms are gelatinous and fluid so that we can deal with the buffeting winds in the heavy clouds we ride. When I first discovered that there were "solid" beings whose forms only changed over lifetimes, I was at first unbelieving and then curious.

That we do not see the stars does not mean we do not sense them, though it takes training to perceive the other worlds. However, because our perception is etheric (psychic) and mental, we can travel unerringly once we discern another world's energy-signature.

I relate primarily to your emotions because I can understand many of them. When contemplating physical contact I perceive that our physical forms would not agree with each other, nor would our worlds' atmospheres, and of course there are other difficulties. Thus I can only understand you at a distance, though that much nourishes me

Your people and mine are very alike in our emotions, though of course there is the matter of degree of intensity. I am not as skilled as Mir Tarr, though I pride myself that I can perceive what human beings desire, even if they do not know it themselves. New openings surround us: the changes in the Sirian Council, the changes in the Galactic Center Council. I feel that human beings, and others like you, will be heard at last.

Francesca: What are the changes in the Galactic Center Council?

Sssssss Ssit: If I told you that some new perceptions of the valences of sodium started the change you would not understand, correct? Or perhaps you would think me ridiculous. But the change in the Council has been as profound as a sudden change in sodium's structure would be. If the fundamental perception of some original element has changed, the element itself must change, and so must everything that this element has touched. That is what has been going on: there is a deep, systemic change in the way reality is being perceived, so there is a change in reality.

Francesca: Tell me more about your world.

Sssssss Ssit: Our physical forms are so different it is unlikely that you would visit me, though some kind of technological interface could be devised. My planet is larger than Earth: there would be some interesting challenges with the gravity. And because our atmosphere is so thick you would probably have to use another kind of light to see with such as "lasers" made out of radio waves; that might be useful.

But although my star is comparatively close to yours, about 37 light-years, we don't see you coming to visit for some of your centuries yet. To travel mentally, I enter something very close to your dream state, or your meditative state, casting my mind into the vast potentials of Being. We have always known that this travel is effective and you can find us with your thoughts, too!

You would consider our world a warm gas giant, somewhat smaller than your Neptune; it is in an orbit comparatively similar to your Earth's, though a little further out. Its color is white, blue, gray, and occasionally orange. We are very lucky in that the winds are not very fast: we have a solid core of nickel-iron-carbon-basalt that has heat inside, so there are areas of upwelling as there are in your world.

Such upwelling creates whole groups of volcanoes, like the Deccan Traps in India. These not only provide heat but also nutrients for the other creatures that live around us. Most of these are in the middle-to-lower levels; there are plant-like rafts of pollinating algae that range in the higher levels; they are what give the planet's clouds their orange tinge.

Our atmosphere carries food, and our skins ingest what comes to us. There are areas of hunger, empty places in the clouds like your deserts. Since our feeding is constant, these empty clouds can be dangerous places. It does not take too much time without food to make us starve. We eat what is available: plant particles, tiny organisms, seeds and spores of all kinds.

We have also learned to farm those "plants" and animals that freely leave parts of themselves in the air so we can ingest them. After seeding, some plants disintegrate, so that the particles can be absorbed. This is similar to your spawning salmon, which give richness through both their lives and their deaths. As we see it, life is a light that flows through forms, changing forms. Where form is, death is the shadow of the light of life.

Our families are unusual by the standards of many other worlds. We are both male and female and at times do not even need others to procreate. We give and receive through the skin, not through generative organs. Every act of lovemaking creates children. The child's first form is the seed held in our bodies until we put them in various protected places. But few of the seeds are fertile enough to grow into babyhood.

Very young babies are small: bell-shaped, they move by pulsing, very like your sea jellies. Only a few of these survive and it is the same for the next form, the more globular form that clings to stones in the depths of the clouds and other solid places. Once these clinging ones mature, they look like a miniature adult, but a child this size does not have language [telepathy].

A child becomes an adult after two more changes. Some children choose to stay miniature for many years. Others take the next form and create a shell. From this shell blooms forth a young adult, with a light, feathery shape. This "chrysanthemum" has hundreds of delicate, crystalline "petals" of arms and legs and other sensing appendages. Of the perhaps hundreds of seeds created by a loving pair, only three or four survive to the chrysanthemum stage.

Children die from accidents, predation, failure to thrive, stagnation of form, and by choice. This choice to slip free of a body is recognized and accepted as easy and natural. We do not grieve for the children who do not grow up. To us, family is a tide, a current of life, that flows freely into form and back out again. Those who live do so lovingly; those who die are easily let free. Forms always change: the love always continues.

Francesca: How do your people enjoy themselves?

Sssssss Ssit: For pleasure and to keep connected, we "sing." Our bodies vibrate when we are near each other, creating waves in our thick atmosphere. It can be as interesting to create interference patterns with different sequences, as it is to harmonize with another so perfectly that we seem to be one being. We do not exactly have concerts or choruses, though two or three singing together does draw a crowd and many will join in.

We carry songs of vibration, one from another. We are amused when the song has been communicated exactly and also when the song is confused because it has been traded from one to the other over long distances. There are rumors that there have been songs that were so altered they changed back into their original forms, though I do not believe this: the universe never repeats its creativity.

I also like to feel the "colors" of the air: we feel the differences in temperature, density, movement, and so on, as I believe you see colors. An evening wind can be glorious! And I love the feeling of simply being. The vibrant stillness of being alive is quite a treasure.

We also send scents to each other, creating condensed air as we move from one area to another. On your more solid planet, this would be rather like herding fog! But to see how far we can go and how much is left of the original scent-message is enjoyable.

We also do acrobatics: we use the varying thickness of our atmosphere to give us just that very last bit of support so that we lean outward, climb up on one another, or tangle each other into intricate shapes, as you might with synchronized swimming. It is challenging, and that is the fun!

In the sense that we have specifically bred and altered certain plant/animal species for beauty, harmonious vibrations, or a sense of companionship, you might say we have pets as you do. Often these "pets" are veils of differing thicknesses that move like diaphanous scarves in the wind. They shift between the cloud layers like thoughts in a mind.

Sometimes they recognize us enough to circle us, humming. But we do not restrain them, because they are more beautiful when they are free to move with as much grace as the clouds themselves.

Every time of wakefulness has rest within it. Every time has celebrations and solemn moments. As the cells in our bodies are constantly fed, we refresh ourselves continually with new energy and delight. We do find that some moments are particularly special. We might gather several special moments all into a rush of joy. But every passage of time renews us.

Francesca: What are some of your sciences, such as healing?

Sssssss Ssit: I have been trying to understand your concept of medicine: it seems to be a calculated imposition of effects upon causes, miring your world deep in undisciplined chaos. With your allopathic disciplines, you seem to look at the result, the illness, and work your changes from there, instead of understanding the interior causes. We are in that sense more holistic and naturopathic.

You see, for my kind, order, and chaos, are two aspects of that same thing: chaos has order within it and must do so. For you, breathing in must be followed by breathing out, or else you will be damaged. If medicine is a method of discerning the relative effects of order and the chaos within a living system, then that is what our perceptive ones already do. These perceptive healers use singing or presence to ease us, giving us a feeling of beauty or peace. I suppose that is what you might call our medicine.

Each individual creates its healing until perhaps that one truly cannot heal itself. Then, the family is called, to give that individual the needed love. If there is no relief, our elders or our wise ones join. If it isn't enough, we ask if that one is ready to pull away from that form. If the individual is ready to move on we simply give time and space for the process.

Our forms are long-lived, and injured limbs can be dropped at will. Sometimes we choose to grow the limbs back. But sometimes we decide that that part of our lives has come to a close and the dropped limb is not re-grown.

Is your "science" the analysis of phenomena, as perceived within the function of the phenomena itself? For me, that seems as perceptible as measuring the weight and density of the clouds of our atmosphere using the clouds of our atmosphere to do so!

Measuring things is another human concept. It means comparison against a standard, yes? That seems delightfully artificial, to me. I can enjoy the idea of contrast through juxtaposition. Yet to compare an object to a standard that is imagined to be outside of that object, you must choose your limits, the things you notice, so carefully!

I suppose, in contrast, that you might call my people vastly empirical. When we have a desire, we learn what allows us to fulfill that desire and what leads away from it. We can ask for the results of others' experiences, though. If that is your science, perhaps I understand it. However, measuring the unknown with the known seems to lead to confusion automatically.

We do have a form of metaphysics. That is where our minds know they have reached the end of their ability to perceive. If you do not want to merely speculate, this encounter with the outer edge demands that the mind grow beyond its known self. We have discovered several things. When our minds first grew large enough to perceive other worlds, we found them to be full of meaning. Our next apotheosis was when we integrated the differences of other worlds into our experience.

I feel my integrity most when I have been able to understand other worlds on their terms as well as my own. We realize that we are a small world, yet the universe is great enough to hold us all. Uniqueness is its infinity.

SEY SEYARAEK

Sey Seyaraek was a surprise member of the Bridge because she was so alien. But again, congruent minds communicate well. It is she who says that there are no black holes in the center of the galaxy. I imagine she would know since she works there frequently, but I have no explanation for the phenomena observed by astronomers. In any event, most of her people are dedicated and work with great integrity. She is a glider, and can expand her shape, though it is easier not to change too much.

Working with Sey Seyaraek is quite interesting, although she is often busy. She is very much like a conscious, sentient field of energy that is linked to very diffuse matter: she uses her "feathers" to catch the solar wind to give her a boost in moving between planets. She works with stars and star systems, keeping things in balance. She says that her people were responsible for giving Earth its present moon, as there used to be a much smaller one before that didn't regulate the Earth's orbit and its seasons enough. Her people also placed Jupiter where it is now to stabilize things after the planet between Mars and Jupiter was destroyed.

Her people travel throughout the galaxy: when they are finished working in a specific area, they drop their forms and move instantaneously to the next project. She chose the form I drew for her quite deliberately, even though she and her people can look like rods, or spheres of many colors, depending upon the work they have to do. But she has a human face because, again, there is much about her that is human: she feels things deeply.

Her people are not afraid of death: they are so aware of their constant conscious state that the worst that could happen, such as one of the beings getting blown apart by a supernova's blast, would only destroy that particular body at that time.

Francesca: What drew you to work with The Lodestone Bridge?

Sey Seyaraek: My work with the Bridge is to foster communication between its members. For that, I am a translator. I am used to diverse communication styles and am fascinated by the challenges The Lodestone Bridge affords. It is in my nature to assist others, for when I do help another I feel I assist another part of myself.

The dedication and love that the Bridge represents inspires me. Where I am between the stars, my work can be so timeless that it is good to experience urgency now and then. The Lodestone Bridge has also benefited me personally: some years ago through a bad combination of circumstances, one of my friends was killed by an accident while he was working. Francesca and one of her human friends gave a ritual of passing for him, honoring his life and its end. I was quite touched and struck by the depth of caring in that ritual.

I remember myself in other lives on other worlds. I communicate almost entirely through the thoughts in my mind. Other than the primitive and basic ones you are already familiar with, my emotions would be nearly too alien for you to comprehend. You were able to touch my grief when my friend died; I was glad of that. You can also perceive some of my enthusiasm and interest.

I will relate to each of the members of the Bridge in different ways. I find Sirian and Altarian minds most comprehensible, though I tease Toh Ka Schei that I have yet to understand her... (Laughs.) I admire the Rangers and the strong empaths in the Galactic Federation.

Some human beings are more than I expected, which proves that my expectations were inadequate. In the very beginning, I was not sure why I felt called to join this experiment. But now that I have had time to think about it I realize that I was drawn to the Bridge by what has drawn us all together: caring. Caring has significance to it, and it matters. And its significance adds to our own.

Since my work takes me on long journeys I confess do not know your human members of the Bridge well enough to give specific suggestions as to which type of people could work with me. But I feel that the beings that will benefit the most already know themselves well enough so that they are not afraid of the unknown.

Also, the best minds in the Galaxy are willing to learn from what the Bridge can do. Working with the human participants of the Bridge, I can help more systemic energy flow towards and within a person. Also, because my people have such divergent forms and yet still work together effectively, I can reflect a spirit of tolerance for differences, which may reduce friction.

I could also step in with the right thing needed at the right time, such as an inspiration, a memory, a different point of view, or a new perception, though doing so would demand quite a close connection between me and that Bridge member. I could also help give an Earth-human a greater sense of what Space means.

I love the beings that remember themselves, as well as those who are attracted to beauty no matter the strangeness of the form, and those who have silence inside themselves, so they can listen, and be content with stillness.

Human beings present another way of being and perceiving: a different sense of time and different forms of wisdom. But the love is the same and the ideas of consideration and appreciation are the same. We can both be similar to each other, finding closeness in friendship and acting grander to each other, inspiring each other to reach further than we have imagined. This Bridge also offers me a chance to speak.

I hope for something different in the galaxy to come of this Lodestone Bridge. In the crowded Galactic Center, I feel the stellar waves like the currents of an ocean and also feel the echoes of those currents as they bring back the tempo and resonance of worlds far away. In those wave-shapes, I sense great change. I wish to be a part of that, to enable that change, to help its formation. The coming change is a lightening of the way energy expresses itself.

I am also looking forward to re-establishing the communication lines between the stars by repairing the galaxy's inner network more fully. Because of the recent work done already on this repair, many beings are not only reaching into new areas of joy and healing, living beings are turning away from the very concept of pain in several worlds. If a lesson is learned once harshly, it is foolish to continue to teach that lesson harshly. I am a gentle being, so I welcome these attitudes of release and comfort.

Francesca: What is the most important thing about this work with the Bridge?

Sey Seyaraek: The fact that it is being done. Communicating with you needs a few extra steps since being with you physically will probably be impossible. I would find your star and its planets much, much too cold and still. I am used to the light, magnetism, radiation, and vibrations of the stars. My atoms are no different than yours, but different forces hold my molecules together.

On Earth, I might be perceived as a color and a scent! With my people, I speak in a kind of quantum resonance. Not in waves, but in instantaneous changes in electron spin. Sometimes I must ask some of the others here to help render my thoughts into something you can follow. But that is how I can be with you.

You already know that there is an extensive library in the Galactic Center near where I spend a lot of my time. It was built using stellar energies and radiations as power, creating its force-fields from static fluxes. My people do not work in the library, though some of our knowledge was used in its field-potential "technology."

The library is accessible by any good psychic from Earth or any other planet. It has information specifically tuned to each planet and each being. [Its "card catalog" conforms itself to the perceptions and methods of communication of the person or being that is searching it.]

Francesca: Tell me a little about yourself.

Sey Seyaraek: I work in the Galactic Center, which is full of stellar winds, magnetic fields, gravity, and many free photons. The "feathers" on my gliding surfaces catch the stellar winds, so I can travel nearly at the speed of the photons themselves if that is necessary. Or, I can use the light's energy and EM energy to simply expand my size. I have stretched myself over as many as four whole planetary orbits, though that was quite a challenge. I can also go faster than light: it requires a massive shift of my form, but this way my travel between stars is instantaneous.

I work as an energy transformer, damping the waves of stellar radiations, especially following novas and supernovas, though my people and I can also enhance the effects as the need arises. I can redirect solar flares if needed. There have been several instances when we deflected a solar flare away from Earth.

We have different forms depending upon which energy we work with: we take jointed, spherical, conical, or tubular forms, as well as gliders like I am. Some of us are very nearly physical. We can either be opaque to magnetism and affected by it or become transparent to it at will. I have the form as it has been drawn above, but there are those with long, multi-limbed forms like Earth's stick insects and some have other, rounded shapes, like huge gas balloons. Some of those spherical shapes are semi-solid, though others are filled with energy.

When one of us changes from this opacity to transparency, there is an outburst of light, and the different colors are beautiful. It is the laughter of light; it is magnetic joy. Our lives are pleasurable because we create freely. I am also honored to be what you might call a nurse. This means that I see how to add efficiency, accuracy, and success to others' work. I step in where I am needed and act at the right time. There are many satisfying things, but I find this most satisfying!

Although I am drawn with a mouth, I do not ingest other objects in that way. That form in the drawing was chosen to convey my friendliness as much as anything else. We absorb the stellar energies directly, being aware of the mixtures and proportions. Because my physical form is re-created every time I move to another star system, I do not need to "eat:" I can refresh myself using the star's energy directly.

Francesca: Can you tell me more about your planet and your people?

Sssssss Ssit: For my people, our similarities of forms create families, not circumstances of birth. Birth is not the creation of a new thing, but pulling a new form over a self that is already ancient. Our forms are created from the tremendous energy that surrounds us: we slide into the new forms quite easily. We can be very intimate with each other in our creation. As a glider, I presently have six who are very close to me.

Were I to choose another form, there would be others whom I could draw to me and evolve into a family. There are four beings that I have assisted in their creation of form: in your terms, I have four children. Three of them have forms different than mine, although my latest co-creation has my form. They are all special to me. My youngest promises she will be a lot like me when she grows up, only more so.

When we tire, we rest, and allow light to re-form us. Here among the stars, there are huge tides and rushes of light, gravity, magnetism, and radiation: we draw our life-force from those. I fly through those energies when I want to rest and enjoy myself. We gain nourishment from friendship and companionship. What you call Brownian motion, the constant, quantum-level shivering of particles, nourishes us. Because we are so diffuse, it takes effort and energy to retain our boundaries.

Francesca: How do you enjoy yourselves?

Sssssss Ssit: My people work with all of these energies, shifting and balancing, smoothing out the ripples and interference patterns, to stabilize the flows. We ride the shifts of power that result from the energy in stars. My work is my pleasure. How else would it be?

In our spinning, diving, and weaving through the thunder of the star-breaths, we take challenges and make joy out of them. I enjoy watching the others of my kind work. True, our work is so strange and our forms so diverse there are times when few understand my people. But humanity's flexibility of mind delights me when I sense it, even though that flexibility is not used consistently.

For enjoyment, my people and I can create prominences, auroras, or pulsing fields of magnetic flux that are very beautiful. We also tell stories. Our stories are re-creations of energy, like a pantomime or silent movie involving energy. Energy itself entertains us and is constantly fascinating.

There are times when the stellar energy shifts and new workers come forward. It would be foolish of us to depend on a set calendar because the ways the stellar forces interact are so unpredictable. Nevertheless, there are "seasons" of light and life created by the grand movement of the galactic turning. Stars change positions; the types of light change and we take time to work with that. We celebrate the way our lives change and take time to honor things that are personally significant to us.

Francesca: Is there anything else you would like to share?

Sssssss Ssit: We understand ourselves as best we can and seek to live from that understanding. We deal constantly with chaos' turbulent unpredictability and so are deeply aware of its effect upon us. We are enchanted by beauty. We derive much benefit from aligning ourselves with the joyous patterns of order within chaos, and the chaos within order.

But is beauty chaos or order? Is work either order, or both, or something else? Or joy? Is it laughter? We cannot escape paying attention. Being aware and alert is our spiritual discipline. In this, our science and our spirituality have no division between them.

However, medicine is a concept I find much difficulty with. I know that I have called myself a nurse, which is a term from your medical traditions. I wanted to use a concept that seemed most in accord with my actions of helping to promote what was already whole.

What is healing for you human beings? We are wise with balancing energies; is that what you mean? If we have any illness, it is an illness of the soul or emotions. Sometimes the only "cure" is time; sometimes the cure is solitude. Since the ritual at my friend's death, I have been investigating the wellness and ease that ritual can create, for his consciousness was shattered, and is still coming back to wholeness.

Certainly, physical illness is hardly known in my people. Those who have strength enough to ride the currents of the star-streams, live. Those who lose their strength, rest, change form, or simply drop their forms entirely to become another type of being.

We do not fear chaos: it is turbulence and mystery. But we do respect it and always remember its nature. We are aware of its effects and how to counter those that cost us too heavily. It would take too long to explain how this is done. If I were to tell you it was like mixing a color with a sound with the meaning inside a memory, it would give you the beginnings of an idea… or perhaps just leave you confused.

We *are* our science. Our lives depend on our command of what you call science: physics, chemistry, measurement, and relationships. But we give no thought to it, no more than you do to your breathing. We do not consider science a separate concept from our lives. Have we understood how things work? Yes, we must. Have we learned that there is always more to learn? Of course, because that is the way what is living encounters life. Have we learned how to learn? That, we are still learning!

You have mentioned dreaming. I believe I understand what you mean by that: is it to wander in parts of your minds of which you are not usually aware? And so create new combinations of thought or image? In that sense, we do dream and find much peace in it. We spend these times discerning the natures of flux and flow, using what is outside of us to help us create what is within.

We touch other minds: that is dreaming while awake. We learn what is true about ourselves; that is being awake within the action of dreaming. When we are enchanted by wonder, then are we living a dream?

CHETRUN TOHYYAN, EHNKRAHN

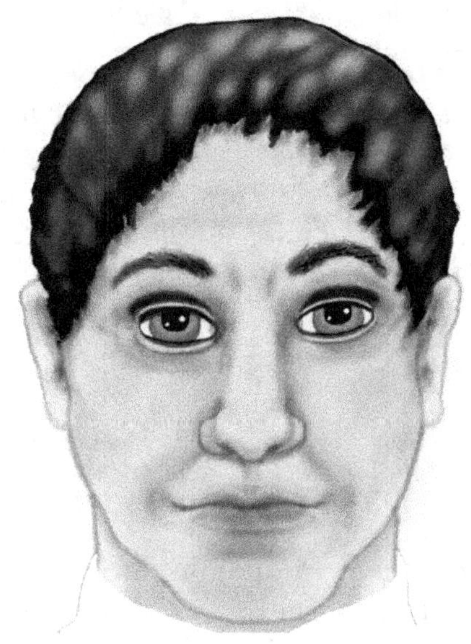

Chetrun Tohyyan is a Representative of the Galactic Federation Council and the Galactic Center Council and has asked to become part of the Lodestone Bridge quite recently. Unlike many members of The Lodestone Bridge, he looks very human, with dark hair that is so fine and dense it almost looks like fur; large, expressive eyes the color of dark amber, and lightly brown skin. His hands are large and expressive, and he has an efficient, focused energy.

He is fairly tall, about 6'6", and he takes time out to move his body by dancing, doing gymnastics (a combination of the balance beam and anti-gravity hoops), and walking in the many parks in the city where he works on Spica. Originally from a very Earth-like world, he lived on one of the more ancient worlds near the Galactic Center for many years before he came to Spica, but he still goes to his home planet when he is working with the Galactic Center Council. His people live for thousands of years if they choose, though this can demand that they renew their bodies in healing chambers.

Chetrun has been working in the Galactic Center Council for 350 years, and most of that time has been spent studying Earth. "EhnKrahn" is his title: its closest meaning is a combination of Administrator and Commissioner: that is, he has been given a fair amount of latitude to arrange things, help groups to work together, receive visitors to the Galactic Center and the Federation Councils; check on the needs of those visitors and see that they are fulfilled.

He also oversees the personnel in both those Councils. He knows who is working on specific projects: their worlds; the details of their family lives as pertain to their work; their specific skills and training; the work they prefer and do best. He also has the authority to realign someone with the expectations of the Galactic society, if needed: if someone is creating distress or disturbances, he can act to get that person help for their problem, healing for their distress, or ask them to leave.

Francesca: What do you wish to accomplish, working with The Lodestone Bridge?

Chetrun: A great deal, I hope! But the main reason why I asked to work with you, besides giving you and other aligned beings the opportunity of visiting the Galactic Center Council, is sharing and communication. Earth has been kept "out of the loop" for far too long, and I do understand that a great many stellar expatriates feel more than a little abandoned.

I also want to see if I can begin to arrange something in the way of reparation for Humanity: to help redress the whole issue of ET interference with so many aspects of your human experience. This will not, and cannot, be an immediate thing, but understand that the human beings who work with extraterrestrials in The Lodestone Bridge, as well as others in other groups, will show those assessing the situation how you can work with ET's, and each other.

Yes: Humanity's future selves agreed to the uplift process, but as you allude to in your Afterword below your process has been consistently interfered with by more than one race. There have been too many times when human beings have been "conned," that is, taken advantage of by deceptive and disingenuous extraterrestrials, where human beings have been offered something that is presented as for their benefit, but that truly is beyond their understanding instead, and that has had hidden cultural consequences.

For instance: not all of the crashed alien ships on your world were accidents! But to grab the technology, without the least idea of its consequences of possessing that technology, much less insisting on weaponizing it, is as foolish as creating artificial intelligence when you have not come into your own full intelligence.

As long as those who interfere are promoting climates of fear and distrust, anxiety and helplessness, as well as pushing lies regarding your worth with such skill that those lies circulate for so long that you feel you are the dregs of the universe, you cannot know who you truly are: you cannot reach into the courage of your spiritual beings.

So, the more people that choose to experience alien beings, alien cultures, and the different forms of spiritual heart-connection that are possible, then the more human beings will be able to understand their own natures within the context of the whole, the more your will become a part of that whole. When you feel surer about your inner value, I believe, you will be less likely live in a paranoid state of mind, which drives you to protect yourself from whatever causes your fears, whatever the cost.

You are in several respects an adolescent race, and adolescents look at maturity as an end to their carefree ways: they see only the downsides of responsibility, accountability, grace, and generosity. They cannot understand how dear maturity, centeredness, graciousness, tenderness, creativity, love, joy, and peace can be or, if they do have an idea, they resist what they think will cost them too much.

Most adolescent races cannot understand that they can retain their childlike wonder even after 1,000 years of living. Nor can they understand that peace is truly the greatest thing anyone can have. They cannot yet conceive of the breadth and depth of inner wealth that peace creates.

And too many believe in scarcity: that if someone else has something, you don't; that if someone else believes a certain way, it takes away from your belief; that unless you have many millions espousing your belief system, that your belief's worth is lessened, and so on.

So, I will hope to be working with those who already understand the values of wonder, tolerance, kindness, sweetness, grace, and inner strength. I know that a fair number of the people who choose to work with you and The Lodestone Bridge will automatically be Starseeds, and that they will remember the joys and richness of living in a mature and civilized society.

Yes: when you as an adolescent race choose to grow up, you must give up old habits, old expectations, and sometimes this loss seems too great to bear. But I can help with the reassurance some may need: you do not lose yourself by gaining something new!

Francesca: Please, tell me a little about yourself.

Chetrun: Thank you: I would be honored. You have already found out I am often unexpectedly busy in addition to working a great deal of the time in my daily expressions of caring! Thus, I do not offer myself as a specific guide to the members of The Lodestone Bridge: that is, I will very likely be unable to work one-on-one with the human Citizen Ambassadors. However, if someone wishes to be confirmed as a Citizen Ambassador, or gain access to the Galactic Center Council, to explore, learn, and receive instruction from the many skilled and wise beings that are there, I can provide those opportunities willingly.

I am married, and I love my wife Reysha very much. She is also part of the Liaison Services between the Federation and the Galactic Center councils: we make a point of meeting together as often as possible and sometimes, as she puts it, "Especially when it's *impossible!*" She has a fine sense of humor, an infectious smile, blue eyes, and medium brown hair.

As part of the Liaison Services, she may be called upon to diffuse an argument between two or more Ambassadors or other planetary representatives, but generally, she helps gather the various support people, like cooks, hotel owners, translators, technical support, and childcare if needed, so that those who come to the council in physical bodies, instead of their etheric forms, are cared for. We have a daughter, who works quite ably as a teacher, and a son, who is still in training as a starship engineer. He is also training to become a pilot, which needs a great deal of mental discipline.

We do take vacations as a family, even though they might be only three-day excursions. We do not need to go far: there are extensive parks, campgrounds, open spaces, museums, libraries, and what you would call luxury hotels here, although we do not use money to get permission to stay there. Because Spica is a blue-white binary star, its light is too strong for us to be out in the middle of the day: we usually do most of our exploring in the evenings.

Francesca: Can you tell me more about where you work for the Galactic Federation?

Chetrun: As has been mentioned, the foliage here on the planet where the Galactic Federation makes its headquarters tends to create darker colors, reds, and purples; some of the plants have striking yellow, blue, or orange flowers, many of which look very like orchids. It does rain here a lot but if we don't care to use our force fields, we do have umbrellas. The air is mildly humid, and often there are ground fogs that can get quite dense at times.

Although it cannot compare to what is on Arcturus, we do have a large star-gate here. This is where the main training centers and hostels are for the Rangers; to practice her skills at communication, my daughter used to "hang out" in some of the hostel's common rooms.

Yes, the majority of races in the galaxy are telepathic, but, if you do not mind a technical analogy, the various minds work at different baud rates, so training is needed. Even on your Earth, some languages are spoken rapidly, such as Spanish or Hindi, and of course, there are regional variants and "accents" of thought. It can get quite complex and fascinating!

D'yet has presented his poetry here a few times; I went to see him perform when D'Barni was still his "roadie," and, although I missed D'Barni's investiture as an ambassador, I have worked with him in that capacity. He is too modest to say, but he has been quite effective as a Federation representative. He puts others at ease with his kind and delightfully positive attitude.

Shambeytas, Toh Ka Schei, Vrrtvv Vxx, D'yet and D'Barni, and Thoyantir have all met with me here and, when the idea for The Lodestone Bridge had crystallized, Reysha arranged a banquet in one of our larger halls, since Vrrtvv Vxx and Vexrra do take up room…

The other thing that I and my wife do is to check up on the various Representatives that are working on Earth and other planets that are being uplifted, to make sure that they have what they need when they need it. This is not something we do as part of our regular duties, but rather is like someone on Earth volunteering to help a food kitchen or another charitable organization: it is a sometimes thing, but we always enjoy it when we do it.

It is good to have a reminder now and then of how difficult, but also how satisfying, the uplift work can be. You might call this spiritual work, in the sense that we do pull in the Divine Presence, the Living Wisdom of the Source, to help us with this effort: we always wish to act in service to the Divine Right Order, as the human phrase goes.

For you do understand that part of the uplift is to emplace a sense of the Divine, a sense of your human souls and your angels, your deepest and most humanitarian aspirations. I know from you, Francesca, that one of the tests for intelligence in animals is whether the animal can recognize itself in a mirror. If it can, then it has reached a certain level of intelligence.

For more developed beings, the mirror test asks, "Can you recognize yourself in another person, and can you do unto him as you would have it be done unto you, and can you *not* do unto him what you would *not* have done unto you?" That is the beginning of spiritual intelligence!

Francesca: You look very human: can you tell me about that?

Chetrun: My wife, family, and I look, and am, very human because my ancestors were human: the planet where we were born is one of the "large Earths" that have already been discovered by your orbiting telescopes: it has about a third more mass than your planet, and also has a G-type star, although the star is a little larger so we are on a planet a bit further away from its star than your Earth. We do have seasons, as there is an axial tilt, but our sky would look slightly greener to you. We do have trees, oceans, rivers, and ice sheets, plus tectonic plate movements and thus volcanoes.

The ET representative, Valiant Thor, has a similar genetic history, but he and his people prefer to live in the Home ships rather than on or inside a planet, although he has lived in Venus. The scientist Pacadee, who was mentioned earlier in this book, is more of a pure Pleiadian type, although she, also, was moved to another world, much further out, to an arm of the Milky Way that is near the Large Magellanic Cloud, your satellite galaxy.

Pacadee's people have gone to several planets as scientists and advisors, as they have particularly good telepathy. She has worked with the Shein/krugn representative, the wolf-like being who called himself "Samovar." He is presently working with the Galactic Federation again, after his adventures on Earth.

However, there are two major differences between your planet and ours: first, there are fewer of us, only three and a half billion instead of your eight billion, for we do keep care that our population does not increase, and second, we all know that our Humanity came from a mixture of Pleiadean, Earth-human, and *Ourbon* people, who were from another Earth-like planet. We also know that we were graced with the gift of our world, Tohlb, so that we might live in it as custodians and guardians. This is because we came to the planet civilized, and remain so.

Francesca: Can you describe your home planet?

Chetrun: There are four major continents in our world, and two of them have been left entirely wild, as there are two intelligent animals, one a lizard-type, the other a mammalian bat, rather like the flying foxes you might find in Australia, Madagascar, and India. I have spent quite a few years studying these "foxes:" they have a stripe-and-blotch pattern in pale cream, medium brown, and black and, unlike your bats they do not hang upside down. This means that they have strong legs that seem absurdly small, but that have a powerful grip.

These mammals catch insects, small mammals, and birds, and eat a particular type of fruit that has high-protein seeds. They have a complex social arrangement similar to your lemurs, with ranks, hierarchies through the matrilineal line, and they already have tool-making, and some of them recognize themselves in a mirror, which as you know is one of the most important signs of sentience. I have great hope for their eventual development!

The other developing species, the lizards, are fewer, but they have the same camouflaging abilities as your chameleons and octopuses, and several of our scientists have discerned the clear beginnings of language in that group. These lizards are more warm-blooded, although they do enjoy spending long hours in the sun, with their camouflage shifting to the colors of the stone they are lying on as the sunlight shifts to shade.

Some of my people have discussed the possibility of uplifting them more quickly by changing their DNA, but this is still under discussion, and the consequences of such an action must be considered responsibly. Would it be ideal, for instance, to have two fully sentient races on one world, or three? Since we were brought to that planet before the two other species' rising intelligence, should we simply leave?

Our world has two moons, a larger one and a smaller one that is perhaps a 6th of the size of the larger moon, which has become tidally locked with its larger sister. We have a string of islands, similar to your Hawaiian chain: there is one island that is an almost-perfect teardrop shape with a slight curl on the narrow point.

There is another range of mountains similar to the mountains in Southern California where the tectonic plates have caused the two ranges to collide into each other at nearly right angles: where they meet is a particularly high mountain that some call "the Spire."

Although our world did have periods of glaciations, we don't have anything as stunning as your American Great Lakes. But we do have three lakes in ancient calderas, like your American Crater Lake. There is one long island chain similar to your Indonesia, where the land is particularly active: we do not settle there.

Several of our scientists have put in motion-sensing "camera-spots," photosensitive, "intelligent" gelatinous patches fixed onto tree trunks, rocks, or even old *ch'vrr* nests. *Ch'vrrs* are large, feathered flyers with long, swan-like necks and reptilian heads, with teeth: they hunt fish. They build large nests from layered branches that are added to each year. This is how we have kept track of the development of the "bats" and the lizards.

In our tropical regions, we have many different flowers and plants, trees, and vines. One vine has broad, fleshy leaves that open when the two moons are aligned with the sun, that is, when the moons are dark; the leaf will open up into a large, light-blue flower, with its stamens full of pollen and a wonderful scent.

Several different animals gather around this flower, from a caterpillar-like worm with beautifully-patterned "fur," a small flying lizard that is almost as agile as your hummingbirds and as beautiful, and *ehnchey yee*, which are small mammals much like your mice or a pygmy marmoset: they climb trees and have beautiful fur.

As you can see, our ecology is almost as diverse as your planet's: indeed, there are a few creatures here that came from Earth, as well as several that came from the 12 worlds within the Pleiadian Consortium.

Francesca: Can you say anything else about your culture?

Chetrun: We are a joyous people: we sing and dance, often quite spontaneously, and love the craft of storytelling. Even though our storytelling is similar to yours, we are nearly all of us literate, and since we have many gifts from the worlds that helped make us, we are in that sense very wealthy.

Our children are taught more than one skill in life, since we may live as many as 3,000 years, should we choose: we can spend a lot of time in mental training, which has allowed me to be of service to the Galaxy.

For relaxation, when I don't want to walk or do my gymnastics, I have a keyed wind instrument that is similar to an oboe and a clarinet, although of course it isn't made out of that beautiful black African wood that you have on Earth. I have been careful not to make this a skill: it's something I do for fun.

I have been to Earth several times, and I love to see the Sequoias in California because they are not only beautiful, but I have seen some of them take root for the first time. On the few occasions I have come to your world, I did not come in a starship, but rather through astral projection. I can tailor my etheric body so that I can be seen by clairvoyants if needed; I have been mistaken for an angel at least once.

My purpose at that time was studying a few Earth populations and their greater ecologies; I was in the Basque region of Europe, for instance, when that area was first being settled, and also in the Four Corners area, working with Ka Cha Sei Ka's people, the "ant-people" of the Hopi tradition. But although I have not been to your planet for several centuries, I am looking forward to the challenge and opportunity of working with the Citizen Ambassadors through The Lodestone Bridge.

Francesca: Is there anything that we need to know about working with you?

Chetrun: Be honest and in your integrity foremost; remember that everything is alive in the sense that it has been crafted from Consciousness; try to be patient with me because even though I am very busy I will always get back to answer a sincere request.

I am not liable to give personal advice: to do so would limit your natural human development. At present, I believe I can commit to being a guide to the Federation and Galactic Council, and that might be considered enough when added to my important office as one who discerns the suitability of the Citizen Ambassador candidates.

The Citizen Ambassadors will give a gift to the galaxy: a better understanding of what it is to be an Earth human. In return, if you see what you feel is an improper action on the part of a specific ET or group of ET's, you can inform me or your main ET contacts, whether they are from your original home worlds or one of the ET members of The Lodestone Bridge.

As I said above, some things need redress, such as some of the abductions, and some of the hybridizations. Granted, those who have experienced abductions and missing pregnancies have, on the whole, agreed to the process, but this is an important issue that must be addressed in greater depth at another time.

Suffice it to say that links of communication and friendship that we hope our work creates will do much to change the emotional points of entry through which some of the negative extraterrestrials are approaching human beings. For we do intend to give Humanity its well-deserved gifts once human beings choose to advance in their natural development and recognizance, so that they will choose peace over war, generosity over greed, and friendship over fear.

Chapter Thirteen

The Citizen Ambassadors

Chetrun has said that he would be the person to vet the applicants for Citizen Ambassadorship. Candace Stuart-Findlay and I have already finished The Lodestone Bridge website, **etswithfrancesca.com** where I can offer the ET Postcards from Home, personal connections with any of The Lodestone Bridge members with those who are interested in working that way, and a chance to become a Citizen Ambassador to the galaxy from Earth.

A Citizen Ambassador is someone who agrees to connect with specific ET beings telepathically and to share positive, creative, and joyous aspects of human life with those extraterrestrials, at the Citizen Ambassador's discretion. Thus, if you go to a concert, you can share it by opening up the link and allowing the ET to enjoy the experience with you.

If you take a walk, watch a movie, read something that delights you, or you are in a fascinating seminar: all of these things could be shared, because this way you can present a different view of human beings to the galaxy.

Unfortunately, many of the civilized ET beings find us Earth beings still too rigid and unpredictable, too quick to mask our fear with violence, and too unsure of ourselves. This is changing: many children being born in these times remember who they are: they are the children who have conversations with their deceased relatives; tell you the elves and fairies in the backyard are sick to death of the rusting garbage in the backyard; the children who look up at the stars they remember as their home. These children do not understand any need for war, hatred, cruelty, viciousness, or greed.

These children and the many adults who chose to be born before them to open the way, already know what it means to live in a civil society, where beauty is more important than status, where compassion is always the first response. These new inhabitants of Earth already know that there is far more to life and human experience than the adage, "Life is hard and then you die." They already live in a larger world, and many are being reminded of this through their experiences.

All of these people have earned the right to change the world from within, person by person, action by action, point by point, embracing the light of love, and the love of light.

Afterword

"This Wasn't My Idea. Was It?"

I feel remarkably privileged. Just the sense of their friendship is dear to me, regardless of the delightful experiences we've had together in our meetings and travels. I have been anxious about what they have done, sometimes, but my familiarity with them helped me accept them. I believe this familiarity pleased these other-worldly beings.

We human beings project our fear onto them all too often. Since they are telepathic, I would imagine this would be hard for them to bear for it must seem like an assault at times. Granted, their very sensitivity would enable them to understand why, even though the fear would make their experiences with us more difficult.

But the upliftment I feel in their "presence," the profound and positive effects the hypnotic sessions gave me, and the fascination, delight, and camaraderie of the ET members of The Lodestone Bridge, are undeniable. This feeling of friendship has a quality of shared trust that has been among my greatest joys and has encouraged me to maintain an open-ended view of what is possible.

After many of the "space people" hypnotic sessions, particularly those retelling the physical "abduction" when I was thirteen, I felt energized and alive, with a kind of positive buoyancy that frequently lasted well into the following week. I do know that the work with this "space people" material has given me a much stronger sense of myself, which is certainly what I wanted out of the therapy sessions in the first place. I just didn't realize that the route to that end would lead us into such fascinating channels!

During the sessions, Dr. Field was particularly careful (with a few small lapses) to give me no leading questions. The material just rolled out of my mind like a movie film. So if, as it has been challenged by some (regarding similar experiences), I was recounting what he wanted to hear, then this quite likely involved telepathy of some kind, a phenomenon also worthy of study! (The doctor and I never discussed the content of the "abduction" sessions, just their emotional effects on my perceptions of me.)

Now that I have been with these beings for a while and worked within my Akashic Records, I remember some other things: I and many people alive on Earth now helped to create Earth's healing, joy, prosperity, beauty, and peace!

I also remember being part of the extraterrestrial teams that created the human form. I was with the task force that decided which animals to uplift into sentience and civilization, and to become aware of Divinity. I remember arguing with the others that the lowland chimps were too violent, too dominating, and vicious, to be a good source of DNA. I felt that we really should put more of the bonobo genes and perhaps even lemur genes into the DNA of these proto-humans. The idea of creating a male-dominated, brutish, and dangerous animal with full intelligence appalled me.

But I and others like me were argued down by those who felt that if there were too many bonobo influences then human beings would just pleasure each other so much that they would never change, perhaps not even if we were to force more planetary changes, as another group had done with the meteor that killed the dinosaurs. This extra work was deemed too "expensive," too demanding, to be worth the trouble.

So, what was created was a world where we human beings would go into the deepest darkness we could, with lies, cruelties, viciousness, inhumanity, war, and several rounds of utter destruction, so that we could prove that we were strong enough, after all, to choose the Light at last. Our experiences have given us strength, and there may be a time in the future when we can act for the betterment of others who are traveling similar paths to ours, and know when to step in to stop the worst from happening.

The Sumerian story, uncovered by Zecharia Sitchin, of Enlil and Enki, the bother "gods," creating human beings for two different reasons, applies here. Enlil, who hated these jumped-up animals, used them as slaves to mine gold; Enki, who appreciated the potentials and possibilities within human beings, was our Prometheus: he wanted to bring light to us, and not leave us in darkness.

In some ways, this story is a myth, but I feel that Enlil's contempt for us and prejudice against us has resulted in several heavy cultural artifacts: race prejudice, for one, where the shining, white-skinned human beings are automatically assumed to be better than the dark-skinned, dark-eyed ones… but *why*? Was it Enlil's poorly controlled feelings that washed into our nascent human souls, imprinting and shaping them with his powerful telempathy?

And slavery: No other mammals have it, to the best of my knowledge. Yes, ants "farm" aphids, but it is mutually beneficial, as are other symbiotic arrangements in this world. But no wolf runs down a deer to drag it back to the den and have it do all the things that the wolf doesn't want to do! No rabbit chains the nearby ferrets and uses them to become its army!

Even though the lowland chimps might have a Mafia-like social arrangement, they do not catch other monkeys and enslave them, using them to gather fruit or watch their babies. No: Enlil and other beings like him were the source of the very *idea* of slavery. And, because it was an alien concept that was imprinted upon us at the very beginning of our humanity, we have been struggling to offload this download for uncounted centuries.

There are also some aspects of religion that I still find disquieting: the idea that an intermediary is needed between the human being and God; that only a few are "saved" and the rest are thrown away. Was this from Enlil's self-serving practicality that not only wanted to make us slaves, but adoring slaves who thought themselves to be so much less than the gods that they were helpless without those gods? Misogyny may or may not be a truly human thing, but it could also have been a reflection of this man's prejudice.

I believe that there are many different beings in the galaxy, and I do know that some wish to compete with us, others to use us and others wish to help us create ourselves into the best we can be. I still remember what Thoyantir said about "those who wish to do harm…"

I doubt I've made this all up. Yes, as noted in the text, I have read a variety of UFO books, most notably The Andreasson Affair, The Interrupted Journey, and Whitley Strieber's Communion, to name the main ones, and more lately Making Contact and The New Human. I realize that my accounts echo those of Mr. Strieber's and others in some places, such as Mr. Strieber's account of the small black aliens changing color. Some of these similarities could be altered memories from my reading.

If the tale you've just read is correct, then Thoyantir, Cythromaa, The Lodestone Bridge members, and I agreed to work together before I was born. But even though my contact with them may appear easy and "human," I would hesitate to ascribe only "human" motives to their actions. Their reasons may be as alien as their forms: either inexplicable out of context, or even out of reach of our understanding entirely.

I do believe the ET's have influenced me. I've found a lot about this planet Earth difficult to understand. There are so many things that bewilder me fundamentally about how we run things here. Why do people want power over others? Or fame? Or want to use dishonesty for callous gain? Wealth I can understand. It makes life easier in this presently money-based economy and gets a lot of things done. But why aren't the people who can work more compassionately with money given most of it, instead of almost none of it?

I believe that their message *is* in their method of contact. Through their "will-o-the-wisp" comings and goings, their telepathic communications, and their refusal to be physically pinned down, I feel they are trying to tell us something about the nature of our universe. I believe they are trying to tell us something about ourselves.

How do we view reality, and with what "real" effects? Where does our fear of the unknown come from… or our acceptance of that same unknown? How "real" are our inner minds? Which paradigms of reality still make sense in "abnormal" experiences?

Whether or not we create our realities, we certainly see them through the colors of our expectations. And if we forget that our pictures of reality are not reality, and demand that "reality" conform to our pictures, then we have a "reality" that discounts, denies, or dismisses more and more. More of our and others' experience is ignored, so that what we perceive remains within the expectations we've chosen. And that can be a tragedy.

Now that we have been discovering other planets, perhaps we should begin to think a little differently about our value as human beings. Rather than make a Cargo Cult of Enlil's prejudices, let's reach forward with Enki's aspirations and confidence in us, so that we may embrace our gift of spirituality and step forward with wisdom, compassion, insight, and peace.

APPENDIX

Finding Your Core Tone

From Nikola Tesla through Francesca Thoman:

"Although similar to spiritual centering, finding your Core Tone does not contract your awareness to a single point: rather, it is the ability to be aware of your multi-dimensional perspective. To uncover your Core Tone, focus on the heart chakra. As the pituitary has been called the "master gland" of the physical endocrine system, the heart chakra affects the other chakras in much the same way.

"If you are practiced in sensing the chakras' subtle energies, you may simply focus on the heart chakra as though searching for a known voice in the hubbub of a crowd. Simply ask yourself to "hear" the silent tone of your inner Self, the singular tone that is only your own. When you hear its silent note, you feel a gentle, welcoming elation and a sense of peace.

"This Core Tone is so complex and refined a sound that the physical body cannot perceive it directly. 'Hearing' this silent sound is much like feeling emotionally touched by someone's kindness, remembering a quiet, secret joy you once had, some special news, or a gift from a much beloved friend.

"If you have not had much practice with subtle energies, the second method is to sit somewhere peaceful. Fold your hands over your heart and breathe gently for five to ten breaths. These intentional breaths are sufficient to engage the silent, super-refined Core Tone. You will gradually have a sense of: 'It's all right now,' or, 'I remember more of who I am now.' You will very likely feel, 'Things are going right for me at last,' or, 'I have something I can work with.'

"You may find yourself suddenly breathing deeply or yawning: this inward breath aligns your subtle bodies beautifully. Just touching your Core Tone in the day or within your spiritual practices can in itself have very good effects, helping to regulate and harmonize your 4-D and M-D relationships.

"This is one meditation you can do any time you have a moment."

New Material Concerning Working with Your Core Tone:

"The Zero Dimension, as I have said before, is in every place, in no one place, and it causes you to be the center of your universe. In this same way, your Core Tone is the resonant echo of the Divine Tone and as such, can be as infinite. When you can plumb the depths of your Core Tone, you can open up into previously unimaginable vistas: you can see and hear your true nature.

"And your Core Tone is utterly unique: not only to your present personality, but all of the tones within all of your other manifested personalities: past, present, future, potential, and even those beyond imagination, are unique and at the same time profoundly harmonic and resonant. This is why when you uncover a past life in hypnosis or through the help of a gifted psychic, you know that you know it was *you* who stood there watching that particular spectacle of that time, whether it was the Rape of Nanking or the establishment of the first Women's College.

"You can use your Core Tone to find and see, experience, uncover, and understand the other manifestations of you throughout Time and Space; you can send healing to those lives, and learn wisdom from them. This process might seem as inaudible, invisible, and as effective, as Love. You know you cannot prove your love for anyone or anything without action, but the Love in your Core Tone is centered in Timelessness and Spacelessness, and so reveals more than could ever be imagined...

"If, when you consider the 8 billion people on this planet alone, much less the untold quadrillions of beings on other planets and existences, you wonder how your Core Tone might be utterly unique, think of the number for Pi: it is a real number which repeats infinitely. It has been calculated by computers to be over one trillion digits, and there is no end in sight.

"In this way, you can see how the Dimension of Identity works with the Torsion Field of Numeration to create your core Tone: one tiny fragment of difference, one slight change of pitch, and your tone is guaranteed unique. And, as you might expect, there will be people whose Core Tones resonate with yours automatically and those Tones that become dissonant instantly.

"Human beings are used to finding thirds, fifths, and octaves harmonious, but of course, the harmonies between Core Tones are much more complex and layered. As I have mentioned before, the Mandelbrot and Juliette sets of fractals describe the universe beautifully: any one area within the fractal may be focused upon, whether into smaller and smaller, or larger and larger, areas of view, and the level of complexity remains the same… and these fractal sets are created from very simple numeric operations!

"Now: can you imagine a sound, and sounds upon sounds, that resonates in several ways at once because it is so complex that it can match in fifths, thirds, and octaves at more than one point, in more than one way, all at the same time? For that is how you, and other beings, work! More parts resonate positively than disharmoniously. This is why totalitarian societies must depend upon creating fear, force, propaganda, lies, and coercion to make the people of their country focus on disharmony consistently enough to create the negative results desired.

"This Core Tone allows, amongst other things, you to find friends in the world and throughout the galaxy, in all realms and all expressions of being! For friendship is a Galactic constant, much as love, courage, compassion, and peace are: it is possible in all beings.

"How might the Core Tone work with the enfolded Dimension of Primordial Chaos? As this Dimension is the source for all potentials, it includes *impossible* potentials: infinities of infinities, resonance created by tiny differences, as tiny differences that create dissonance. The Dimension of Primordial Chaos includes unexpected combinations and can affect the nature of numbers as well. You see: the universe could be created with nothing less.

"Your Core Tone is perhaps not as much as a door into that infinite potential of all possibilities, but it certainly is a window.

The more time you spend working with and within your Core Tome, the more likely you will see different solutions to old problems, refreshing your perceptions and point of view. The Core Tone also perceives the essential nature of all of the three Main Dimensions: within the dimension of Identity, the Zero dimension, and the Dimension of Primordial Chaos, is the infinitely created, and creative, Divine Love.

"Love does not lie, but it does present itself according to your human needs. Comfort for the bereaved and betrayed; Presence for the lonely and lost; Truth for those who have lost their inner compass and gyroscope; Renewal for those who have been battered and brought down.

"The Core Tone's window to the Divine Love allows that love in so that it might heal, help, teach, and encourage. It shows you what you are; it shows what matters to you; it shows what is beautiful to you; it shows where you have given gifts to yourself. Your Core Tone can reveal the love and healing in even the most dreadful and disruptive disorder or the most rigid and unforgiving ordered restrictions.

"Your Core Tone can be your window to what is best in you; it can show you the way to create that best. In truth, it is a superlative gift!"

ABOUT THE AUTHOR

A conscious clairaudient channel for 30 years, Francesca Thoman has had the honor of channeling Nikola Tesla's intelligent, compassionate, and shining spirit since 1995.

Pursing a spiritual life since 1968, she has channeled wisdom from other discarnates, extra-terrestrials, and elves.

Living in the San Francisco Bay Area with her husband, a computer engineer, Francesca is an award-winning author and also a Certified Akashic Record Consultant.

https://etswithfrancesca.com/